M

Oxford School Shakespeare

Antony

Edited by

Roma Gill, OBE
M.A. *Cantab.*, B. Litt.

Oxford University Press

Oxford University Press, Great Clarendon Street, Oxford OX2 6DP

Oxford New York
Athens Auckland Bangkok Bogota Bombay
Buenos Aires Calcutta Cape Town Dar es Salaam Delhi
Florence Hong Kong Istanbul Karachi
Kuala Lumpur Madras Madrid Melbourne
Mexico City Nairobi Paris Singapore
Taipei Tokyo Toronto

and associated companies in
Berlin Ibadan

Oxford is a trade mark of Oxford University Press

© Oxford University Press 1997

ISBN 0 19 831964 9 (Schools edition)
ISBN 0 19 832000 0 (Trade edition)

Illustrations by Victor G Ambrus

Cover photograph by Donald Cooper shows Judi Dench as Cleopatra and
Anthony Hopkins as Antony in the National Theatre's 1987 production of
Antony and Cleopatra.

For Sandra

Oxford School Shakespeare
edited by Roma Gill

A Midsummer Night's Dream	The Taming of the Shrew
Romeo and Juliet	Othello
As You Like It	Hamlet
Macbeth	King Lear
Julius Caesar	Henry V
The Merchant of Venice	The Winter's Tale
Henry IV Part I	Antony and Cleopatra
Twelfth Night	

Typeset by Herb Bowes Graphics, Oxford
Printed in Great Britain at the University Press, Cambridge

Contents

Star Quality

Not many people have it, and it's not something you can easily put your finger on. But we can all recognize it when we see it—that indefinable *something* that lifts mere talent into absolute stardom in some particular sphere: stage, screen, or radio; sport; politics; even royalty. Think about it—who has it, who had it? Simply being good at the job isn't enough—not even being *very* good. Take just one (fairly safe) example: there have been a great many English monarchs, but which of these stands out in the national memory like Elizabeth I—the Virgin Queen, Good Queen Bess?

We *need* stars like these: whether we applaud or deplore individual actions, they have a magnetism that is irresistible. Their performances, their achievements, their lifestyles compel our attention, and their influence lifts us above the routine of our own daily lives and humdrum surroundings.

Star quality was what Antony and Cleopatra had—almost to excess. Both were legends in their own lifetimes, even before they met each other. Antony, when he was not leading armies and conquering his enemies, cultivated in his public image 'a manner of phrase in his speech called "Asiatic", which carried the best grace and estimation at that time, and was much like to his manners and life'. Plutarch, his biographer, made note of this—though he was not impressed by it and commented that 'it was full of ostentation, foolish bravery, and vain ambition'! But this flamboyant exhibitionism met its match in Cleopatra. On their first evening together her entertainment showed a style that literally dazzled Antony:

> amongst all other things, he most wondered at the infinite number of lights and torches hanged on the top of the house, giving light in every place, so artificially set and ordered by devices, some round, some square, that it was the rarest thing to behold that eye could discern or that ever books could mention.[1]

---

[1] 'The Life of Marcus Antonius' in *Parallel Lives of the Greeks and Romans*, translated by Sir Thomas North (1579, 3rd edition 1603).

Together, they were without parallel for living in the grand manner—*and they knew it!* 'For they made an order between them which they called "*Amimetobion*" (as much to say, "no life comparable and matchable with it"), one feasting each other by turns.' Plutarch's disapproval is evident, but it cannot overmaster his admiration and even affection for the stars of his 'Life'. Shakespeare also seems to have been star-struck, responding to Antony's 'Asiatic' speech by creating a style for his play which is without parallel in his own work (and has never been attempted by any other dramatist). The poet Coleridge said that it was wonderfully daring—'*feliciter audax*'. Star quality!

Events in history

During the first century BC, the balance of power in Rome and its ever-expanding empire was in the hands of three men—Gnaeus Pompey (Pompey the Great), Marcus Crassus, and Julius Caesar. These, the Latin 'tres viri', formed the 'First Triumvirate', which was an agreement to work together with each other for their mutual benefit. But in 53 BC Crassus was killed whilst fighting against the Parthians. Neither Pompey nor Caesar could agree to share power with the other, and so civil war broke out. At the battle of Pharsalus, Caesar defeated Pompey; shortly afterwards he conquered Pompey's two sons, Sextus and Gnaeus.

Caesar now appeared to have absolute power, but his autocratic rule was resented by the republican faction and soon Marcus Brutus and Caius Cassius headed a conspiracy to assassinate him. The assassination led to a fresh outbreak of civil war, in which Octavius Caesar (Julius Caesar's greatnephew and adoptive son) and Marcus Antonius (Mark Antony) contended with each other for domination. Antony was defeated at Mutina (Modena), and retreated across the Alps to form an alliance with Aemilius Lepidus. A temporary reconciliation with Caesar brought about the formation of a 'Second Triumvirate', legally appointed by act of tribunal and united in opposition to the republican conspirators responsible for the death of Julius Caesar. At the battle of Philippi, Brutus and Cassius were defeated; both committed suicide.

In *Julius Caesar*, Shakespeare presented the events leading up to, and resulting from, the assassination of Caesar. This play ends in 42 BC when Antony and Octavius stand victorious at Philippi. The action of *Antony and Cleopatra* begins a year or two later, and ends with the suicides of its two protagonists in 30 BC.

Under the 'Second Triumvirate', the Roman empire was divided between three dictators: Caesar was in command of the European provinces; Lepidus governed North Africa; and Mark Antony ruled Rome's Asian territories. Whilst he was gathering money for fresh campaigns, Antony encountered the rich and powerful Egyptian queen, Cleopatra (who had previously formed an alliance with Julius Caesar). Antony surrendered himself to her enchantment and, abandoning his wife Fulvia, took up residence in

Alexandria with Cleopatra. At that time Alexandria was the greatest cultural and commercial centre of the eastern Mediterranean, affording a lifestyle of unsurpassed luxury, elegance, and sensual excitement.

Meanwhile, in Rome there were renewed hostilities between the factions of Octavius Caesar and Mark Antony, stirred up by Fulvia and Lucius, the wife and the brother of Antony. Further afield the Triumvirate's power was weakening: the eastern provinces were threatened by Parthian forces, and Sextus Pompey (son of Pompey the Great) was seeking to gain control of the Mediterranean. As Antony dallied in Egypt, Caesar and Lepidus struggled to maintain their supremacy.

With the death of Fulvia, and the increasing menace of Sextus Pompey, Antony was at last recalled to Rome and (under pressure of events) to reconciliation with Octavius. Their peace treaty, agreed at Brundusium, was ratified by the marriage of Antony with Caesar's sister, Octavia, and together the three triumvirs addressed themselves to confront Pompey. A summit conference at Misenum achieved a temporary truce and Antony was able to leave Rome and live for a year or two with Octavia in Greece.

Eventually, however, he separated from Octavia (whom he later divorced) and returned to Egypt and Cleopatra. Instead of enlarging the Roman empire, he freely gave away the kingdoms he had conquered in a spectacular ceremony, the 'Donations', held in the marketplace of Alexandria—and the incensed Romans prepared for retaliation. At the battle of Actium Antony fled from the fighting, and Caesar pursued him to Alexandria. The defeated Antony committed suicide, and soon afterwards Cleopatra followed his example.

Chronology

BC

60   First Triumvirate.

53   Death of Crassus.

48   Battle of Pharsalus: Pompey the Great defeated by Julius Caesar.

48–7   Cleopatra in Rome with Julius Caesar; birth of Caesarion, reputed to be the son of Julius Caesar and Cleopatra.

44   Assassination of Julius Caesar.

43   Civil war; Antony defeated by Octavius Caesar at Mutina; alliance between Antony and Lepidus; reconciliation with Octavius; Second Triumvirate.

42   Battle of Philippi: defeat of Brutus and Cassius by Antony and Octavius.

41   Cydnus: meeting of Antony and Cleopatra. Civil war in Italy; the wife and brother of Antony rise against Octavius.

40   Death of Fulvia. Treaty of Brundusium; marriage between Antony and Octavia.

39   Misenum: summit meeting between Triumvirs and Sextus Pompey.

37   Antony leaves Rome with Octavia, then returns to Cleopatra.

34   'Donations of Alexandria'.

32   Antony divorces Octavia.

31   Battle of Actium.

30   Battle of Alexandria. Suicides of Antony and Cleopatra.

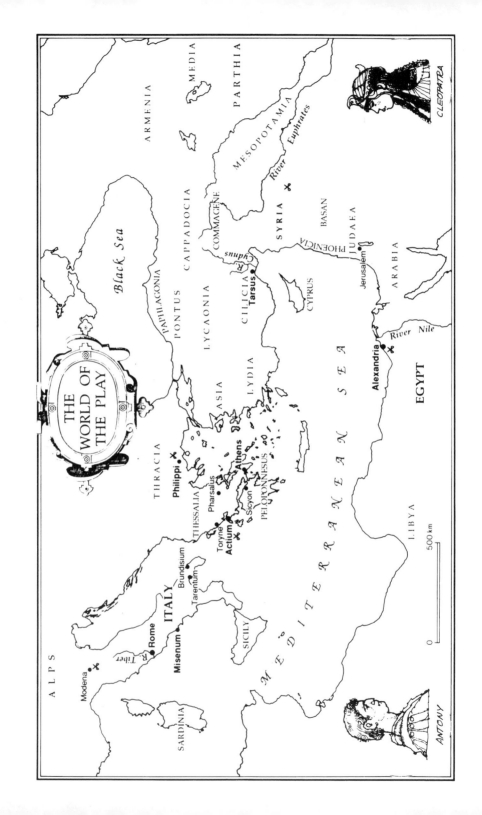

THE
WORLD OF
THE PLAY

ALPS

SARDINIA

ITALY

Modena

Rome
Misenum

R. Tiber

Brundisium

Tarentum

SICILY

MEDITERRANEAN SEA

LIBYA

0   500 km

Black Sea

THRACIA

THESSALIA

Pharsalus

Toryne
Actium

Sicyon

Athens

PELOPONNESUS

Philippi

PAPHLAGONIA

PONTUS

LYCAONIA

ASIA

LYDIA

CAPPADOCIA

CILICIA
Tarsus

R. Cydnus

CYPRUS

ARMENIA

MEDIA

PARTHIA

MESOPOTAMIA

River Euphrates

COMMAGENE

SYRIA

BASAN

PHOENICIA

JUDAEA

Jerusalem

ARABIA

River Nile

Alexandria

EGYPT

CLEOPATRA

ANTONY

Leading Characters in the Play

Although there are thirty-four named speaking parts in *Antony and Cleopatra*, few are fully developed as characters. Outstanding and easily the most complex is Mark Antony, who veers between the extremes of restraint and self-indulgence. Both qualities are together present in his nature: separately, each is embodied in the persons of Octavius Caesar and Cleopatra.

Mark Antony Aged 42 at the opening of the play, Antony has already enjoyed a brilliant military career which has led to his becoming one of the Roman triumvirs. He holds special command over Asia Minor, and it is here that he has encountered Cleopatra. Antony encourages the traditional belief that his family was descended from the mythical superman, Hercules.

Octavius Caesar According to Plutarch, 'It was predestined that the government of all the world should fall into Octavius Caesar's hands'. Octavius had been adopted and named as heir by his great-uncle, Julius Caesar, and he shares the government of the Roman empire with the other two triumvirs. At the beginning of the play he is only 23—which allows Antony and Cleopatra to refer to him with contempt as 'the boy Caesar' and 'the scarce-bearded Caesar'.

Cleopatra The queen of Egypt, she was born and married (twice) into the Ptolemaic dynasty. Before meeting Mark Antony, she had been mistress of Gnaeus Pompey (son of Pompey the Great) and Julius Caesar. Plutarch commented that 'Caesar and Pompey knew her when she was but a young thing, and knew not then what the world meant: but now she went to Antonius at the age when a woman's beauty is at the prime, and she also of best judgement'. When the play opens she is 29 years old, but Shakespeare seems to visualize her as being much older and 'wrinkled deep in time'.

Two important figures in the first part of the play are:

Lepidus The third member of the triumvirate. He is an older man (about 50 at the start of the play) who had taken the side of Antony after the murder of Julius Caesar.

Pompey A son of Pompey the Great. Outlawed from Rome when his father was defeated by Julius Caesar, Pompey took possession of Sicily. Now, aged about 27, he is raiding the coast of Italy and plundering its villages.

An observer throughout most of the play, a critical commentator, and a wondrous necessary guide for the feelings of the audience is:

Domitius Enobarbus This experienced soldier is a subordinate officer but a loyal friend to Antony. Shakespeare created his character out of two names mentioned by Plutarch: 'Domitius Aenobarbus' had fought alongside Antony in Parthia and later married one of his daughters; but it was another 'Domitius' who deserted Antony. It is possible that the name 'Aenobarbus'—meaning 'the red-bearded one'—was chosen to associate the deserter with Judas Iscariot, the traitor (traditionally portrayed with red hair and beard) who betrayed Jesus and who later committed suicide.

Synopsis of the action

Antony and Cleopatra: commentary

Act I

Scene I   'Nay, but . . . ' The play opens in the middle of an argument, compelling immediate attention. Philo's anger explodes on to the stage. Admiration is lost in racial and sexual disgust as Philo prepares the audience for the entry of the play's main characters.

Philo and Demetrius are Roman soldiers, and they represent the values of their particular western world—values which will be demonstrated later in the play, and that are summed up in the Latin words *virtus* and *pietas. Virtus* encompasses masculine (especially military) excellence, fortitude, discipline, and self-restraint; *pietas* insists on unswerving loyalty to family and to state. But the procession that now occupies the stage presents an alternative lifestyle. Here, leisured opulence and self-indulgence, made manifest in the waving fans and sexual indeterminacy of Cleopatra's eunuchs, offer both an affront and a challenge to the Roman values. An unusually detailed stage direction for this procession was printed in the first edition of the play, and almost certainly indicates the dramatist's own supplementing of the words of his text.

Antony appears to have succumbed entirely to the seduction of this lifestyle. He declares his love and dismisses Rome with equally grand gestures—but Cleopatra seems more detached. She is completely in command of the situation—and is unconvinced by Antony's theatricalities. She taunts Antony, and delights in needling him: his conduct in shrugging off Rome has empowered 'the scarce-bearded Caesar' and 'shrill-tongued Fulvia' to call him to order and to summon him to their presence. Heedless of her derision, Antony continues in his self-delusion: the known universe cannot contain his emotion; without his support 'the rang'd empire' of the Roman world will collapse; and the emissaries from Caesar must be made to wait on his pleasure. At his command the little procession departs, leaving those who have observed the demonstration—Philo, Demetrius, and the audience—with a mixture of impressions.

Unlike the opening scenes of many plays, this one gives little
guidance to the audience about the play's characters and the future
direction of its action. We can sense that a crisis is impending; that
there is an east/west conflict which could well be global in
implication; and we have seen that Philo's initial promise has been
fulfilled—though Demetrius can hardly believe his eyes! But where
do *we* stand? Can we begin to take sides, either with the
disapproving Philo or with the 'strumpet's fool'? Are these epithets
appropriate—or is it possible that this could 'be love indeed'?

Scene 2   In the theatre there is no time even to articulate such questions
because the pace of *Antony and Cleopatra* is unusually fast. The
action cuts quickly between sequences and locations, and the
characters respond immediately to each other; there are few long
speeches and very little soul-searching soliloquy.

A relaxed prose allows Cleopatra's servants, watched by the
silent Roman officers, to tease Alexas and giggle over the
predictions of the Soothsayer—who, as the play will show, is no
mere gypsy fortune-teller. Enobarbus calls them to order at the
appearance of Cleopatra, who first demands to see Antony and
then refuses to speak with him when he approaches. But Antony is
not aware of the queen's wiles; he has more serious business on his
mind.

Tension rises as messengers from Rome, with news of fresh
conflicts, follow one after another on to the stage and drive Antony
to an outburst of self-recrimination whose climax is a declared
decision to return to his Roman duties. He confides his resolution
to Enobarbus, who makes light of the situation but, in so doing,
raises more doubts for the audience.

Once again the scene ends with questions. How sincere is
Antony's grief for Fulvia—and can it 'be love indeed' that Antony
feels for 'this enchanting queen' whom he wishes he had never
seen? And what of Cleopatra, who 'hath such a celerity in dying'
and whom Antony knows to be 'cunning past man's thought'?

Scene 3   Cleopatra is alarmed at the thought of losing Antony and reveals to
Charmian her strategy for holding him—thereby preparing the
audience to watch her devices later in the scene. The threat, she
suspects, comes from Antony's wife, 'the married woman', and she
now associates herself with Fulvia as yet another woman betrayed
by Antony's false charm.

The news from Rome means nothing to Cleopatra, although
Antony is now seriously worried: there is civil unrest in Italy and

Roman dissidents are flocking to ally themselves with Sextus Pompey whose naval activities are terrorizing the coastal regions. And Antony's wife has died. But Cleopatra can turn even the news of Fulvia's death to her own advantage in taunting Antony: 'I see, In Fulvia's death how mine receiv'd shall be'. When Antony begins to show anger at her accusations of play-acting with emotions, Cleopatra retaliates with scorn: 'Look, prithee, Charmian, How this Herculean Roman does become The carriage of his chafe'. Her adjective is well-chosen, and Antony is stung: he had always encouraged the belief that his family was descended from Hercules, and (according to Plutarch) he wore his beard, tunic, and sword in the manner of the legendary hero.

Although she tries once again to detain him, Cleopatra must eventually concede victory to Antony's Roman 'honour'. Antony can only offer her the 'metaphysical' comfort of knowing that even when the two of them are parted they are still one in spirit. The notion was popular among poets of Shakespeare's time—but the play's audience must wonder about its validity.

Scene 4   After the extreme mood swings and strong feelings of the first three scenes, all set in the easy-going atmosphere of Alexandria, the action moves to the cold formality of Rome. A tight-lipped Caesar is reading the latest news report from Egypt and retailing its contents with disgust to Lepidus. The more tolerant Lepidus is inclined to be generous and make excuses for Antony, but he is gradually silenced as Caesar's invective heaps up the store of Antony's failings with an increasing passion which is further fuelled by interruptions from two messengers. These messengers, unlike those who came to Antony in Alexandria (Scene 1), are given immediate hearing. Their bulletins bring news of more terrorist aggression from supporters of the pirate Pompey, whose numbers are daily being augmented. The Roman empire, never very stable, is now seriously under threat and urgently needs solidarity between its leaders. Caesar's anger is understandable—but the audience knows that help is at hand: Antony is coming to Rome!

The usually dispassionate Caesar has given way to his emotions in this scene, presenting Lepidus (and the audience) with two portraits of the man he calls his 'great competitor' (= colleague): Antony as he is now, idle in Alexandria, 'the abstract of all faults'—and the Antony that Caesar can remember, the epitome of Roman *virtus*. The details, in both portraits, are graphic and immediate. The images in the first are coarse and violent ('to tumble on the bed', 'reel the streets', 'stand the buffet'); they diminish their subject, associating him with the 'knaves that smells of sweat', and they reveal Caesar's fastidious, nose-wrinkling contempt as he looks down on Antony.

But in the second portrait Caesar is looking up to a god-like figure on the highest Alps, one who has subdued not only his enemies but even his own body, overcoming (although he had been 'daintily brought up') any natural revulsion at the 'gilded puddle' and the 'strange flesh Which some did die to look on'. This man has earned Caesar's admiration (despite his having been 'beaten from Modena' by Caesar's own forces) and he has been regarded by Caesar with awe and wonder. Now admiration has turned to disillusion and bitter disappointment: Caesar has lost not only a 'competitor' but an idol.

In the efficient last lines of the scene Caesar assumes command of the situation and Lepidus, respectfully, acknowledges his right to do so.

Scene 5   Now it is Cleopatra's turn to give *her* picture of Antony. She is bored and lonely without him in Alexandria, and Mardian, her eunuch, is powerless to amuse her. When he refers to 'What Venus did with Mars' she bursts into an ecstasy of longing—perhaps recalling what *she* did with *Antony*! In this reverie, dreaming of Antony as a knight of chivalry, remembering the lovers of her youth and rejoicing in her mature sexuality, Cleopatra is interrupted by Alexas. He gives an account of Antony's words and gestures which extends Cleopatra's own image of him and encourages her to indulge her fancies still further.

This little scene does nothing to advance the action but, sandwiched between scenes of political manoeuvring and emotional austerity, it is helpful to fix in our minds the alternative lifestyle enjoyed in Egypt. Cleopatra will not appear on the stage for some time now (in *Act 2*, Scene 5) but we can be sure that, however she is called in Rome, she is a powerful force to be reckoned with in Alexandria.

Act 2

Scene 1   The characters who now appear on the stage, 'in warlike manner', are already well known to us by reputation: 'the condemn'd Pompey, Rich in his father's honour' (*1*, 3, 50) and his associates, Menecrates and Menas, the 'famous pirates' (*1*, 4, 49). They exult in their own strengths, and they *think* they know their enemies' weaknesses. But there have been serious miscalculations—as the audience is well aware—and their discomfiture comes quickly. Only Pompey understands the gravity of the new situation, and he spells it out for his colleagues: the individual triumvirs have plenty of reasons for fighting amongst themselves, but an outside threat may well re-unite the triumvirate again.

     We are now prepared in advance for the coming meeting (*Act 2*, Scene 6) between Pompey and the three Roman triumvirs.

Scene 2   Antony has made excellent progress from Egypt, and here Lepidus is trying to smooth the way for a peaceful reconciliation with Caesar. Enobarbus refuses to urge Antony to any compromises. The two mighty leaders enter at the same time—but from different sides of the stage. Both are apparently deep in conversation and pretend to be unaware of the other's presence until Lepidus, like some wise old schoolmaster attempting to pacify two headstrong youngsters, draws them together with his soothing words.

     Antony is quick to respond, and Caesar reacts with the courtesy of a host: the trumpets are sounded to welcome the guest, who is invited to take a seat. But Antony will not sit whilst Caesar stands—this would put Caesar in the dominant position. Physical positioning, spatial relationships, are of vital importance at summit conferences, most interviews, and all stage performances!

     Once the opponents are seated, their verbal fencing begins—and both are on the defensive. Antony knows that he is in the wrong, but Caesar is afraid to antagonize so powerful an ally whose support at this time is so much needed. Eventually Antony manages to slide out of the tricky situation with a few apologies and minimal damage to his self-respect. Caesar, persuaded by Lepidus and Maecenas, agrees to be satisfied with this. But Enobarbus speaks to the heart of the matter when he points out that their quarrel need be only postponed—they can continue at a more suitable time, 'when you have nothing else to do'. His flippancy annoys Antony, but Caesar is willing to take up his meaning and wish for a more permanent solution to their differences. Agrippa has a suggestion, which is 'a studied, not a present thought', and he proposes it in suitably measured tones with subtly balanced word-play: 'knit'\'knot'; 'worse . . . best'; 'little . . . great'; 'Truths . . . tales'.

Caesar and Antony listen intently, but neither is eager to speak without first knowing the other's reaction. Agrippa's proposition has Caesar's backing, and Antony accedes in words that seem to echo the solemnity of the Christian marriage ceremony: 'May I never, To this good purpose that so fairly shows, Dream of impediment'. It is an 'act of grace', sealed by the shaking of hands and ratified with the 'amen' spoken by Lepidus. The triumvirs turn their attentions to the cause that first brought them together, but before any action is started Antony will 'dispatch' the 'business' of his marriage to Octavia, to whose 'view' Caesar now invites them. The language is coldly efficient—and the onlookers (as well as the actors) must interpret the emotions for themselves.

The triumvirs leave the stage and Enobarbus, Agrippa, and Maecenas are left behind to renew their old friendship. The two Romans are longing to hear the truth about Antony's Egyptian exploits, and Enobarbus does not disappoint them. He describes Cleopatra's first meeting with Antony, 'upon the river of Cydnus'.

The passage is a masterpiece of poetic narrative. Enobarbus begins with the approach of the barge as it would appear to the waiting crowds: the assonance of 'burnish'd' and 'Burn'd', together with the position of the verb, create the impression from afar before the explanation—'the poop was beaten gold'. As it draws nearer, the vessel's perfumed sails strike the eyes and the nostrils; the ears detect the harmony of the flutes, and the pulses feel the rhythm of the oars. The elements of fire, air and water all conspire to titillate the senses and raise them to even further heights in order to conceive the human beings involved in this pageant—if indeed they are human! Enobarbus makes no attempt to describe Cleopatra—'her own person . . . beggar'd all description', but he waxes lyrical in the description of her attendants. The gentle caesura pauses seem to enact the to-and-fro movements of the waving fans

                            whose wind did seem
    To glow the delicate cheeks which they did cool,
    And what they undid did.

Enobarbus halts in mid-line to give greater dramatic effect to his arresting paradox, and Agrippa completes the line by bursting out in admiration: 'O, rare for Antony'. His interruption gives breathing space to Enobarbus—and to the audience, who might otherwise be satiated with the luxury of the report.

Enobarbus resumes with an account of Cleopatra's 'gentlewomen', and their artistic handling of the barge's ropes—its 'silken tackle'. The sights, sounds, and scents of this spectacle compelled universal attention—so that Antony, who had been expecting an audience for his appearance in majesty, could only whistle to himself to conceal his embarrassment. Enobarbus breaks the line again, and Agrippa's exclamation voices the general applause for Cleopatra, who has evidently won the first round in this contest of personalities. The next move, we hear, was Antony's: he invited Cleopatra to supper—and Cleopatra responded with a counter-invitation. Courtesy obliged Antony to accept, and his sexual susceptibility ensured his complete surrender.

In this passage Shakespeare has followed Plutarch very closely (see 'Plutarch', p. 144), using every resource of poetry to transmute the materials provided by the historian into something rich and strange, still more splendid than the original—just as Cleopatra excelled the imaginative picture of the goddess Venus, which itself surpassed the natural beauty of any woman.

Encomium now becomes gossip. Agrippa can tell how Julius Caesar's military strength capitulated to Cleopatra's sexual power when he was made to 'lay his sword to bed'; and Enobarbus himself is clearly enchanted—though not, like his master, wholly bewitched—by Cleopatra. Maecenas rather naïvely assumes that the spell can be broken now that Antony 'must leave her utterly', and Enobarbus tries to put him straight with a decisive 'Never! He will not'. He even attempts to describe Cleopatra's ineffable fascination and, although Maecenas is unconvinced, the audience must respect his judgement.

This vivid reminder of Cleopatra is enough to negate everything that has been achieved by the political negotiations, which had otherwise seemed to promise a long-term solution to the problems of the triumvirate.

Scene 3   Whilst Enobarbus has been speaking, time has elapsed—long enough for Antony to have been married to Octavia. But the first words we hear him speak refer to future probable separation, and his question to the Soothsayer (after Octavia has left the stage with her brother) perhaps voices his own longing: 'You do wish yourself in Egypt?'. The Soothsayer does not hesitate with his solemn warning: he understands Antony's luck and can predict the triumph of Caesar. Antony is forced to take heed. Military matters—most immediately, the Parthian campaign—demand attention, but his mind is resolute:

> I will to Egypt;
> And though I make this marriage for my peace,
> I'th' East my pleasure lies.

Scene 4 There is no time to lose: preparations for war are well in hand and the battle with Pompey is imminent—

Scene 5 —but the action of the play moves to Egypt, where the bored and lonely Cleopatra tries to amuse herself with recollections of Antony. She recalls two particular incidents—both, significantly, moments when Antony was completely in her power. In the fishing episode he had been publicly (see 'Plutarch', p. 144) outwitted and embarrassed; in the more intimate bedroom scene he had been first incapacitated with drink, then stripped of his manhood when Cleopatra 'put [her] tires and mantles on him, whilst [She] wore his sword Philippan'. Cross-dressing like this, which might have been fun for Cleopatra (and even for today's audiences/readers), was something altogether more dubious in the eyes of the Romans—and of Shakespeare's contemporaries. The 'sword Philippan' was the weapon used at the battle of Philippi, when the rebels, Brutus and Cassius, were finally defeated by Antony and Octavius: Cleopatra's wearing of it would seem to symbolize not only the dominance of the female over the male, but the subjection of a world power to the will of a woman.

The reverie ends when Cleopatra receives the messenger from Rome. Her desire for Antony expresses itself through the sexuality of her language—'fruitful', 'barren' and, forcefully positioned, 'Ram'. She longs to hear—yet fears to know. Her promises and threats, following each other with bewildering speed, anticipate his answers. The messenger is evasive—understandably so: the audience already knows his message! The poor man makes a feeble attempt to be flippant with Cleopatra—

> **Messenger**
> He's bound unto Octavia.
> **Cleopatra**
>   For what good turn?
> **Messenger**
> For the best turn i'th' bed.

—then drops his bombshell: 'Madam, he's married to Octavia'. The explosion is instantaneous. Cleopatra's wrath is as extreme as her delights had been, and the messenger must run for his life. Repenting the lack of 'nobility' in her conduct, Cleopatra calls him back for further questioning until his repeated asseverations convince her that Antony's betrayal is a fact, and her misery is complete. But the messenger's information is only partial: the audience may remember the last words they heard Antony speak— 'though I make this marriage for my peace, I'th' East my pleasure lies'.

Scene 6   The expected battle has not taken place: the opponents on both sides are honouring the decision to 'talk before [they] fight'. Pompey claims to be both an avenger and a freedom-fighter. He wants revenge for the death of his father, defeated by Julius Caesar at the battle of Pharsalus, just as Octavius and Antony had themselves fought to avenge the death of Julius Caesar, assassinated by Brutus and Cassius; and at the same time Pompey allies himself with the republican cause of Caesar's assassins, 'courtiers of beauteous freedom', in opposing the threat of dictatorship and tyranny. He blusters with confusion in his anger, but Octavius and Antony are unmoved—and Pompey retreats into a personal attack on Antony, which Lepidus easily deflects as irrelevant. Pompey knows he is outnumbered: the triumvirs speak as one man, and Pompey accepts the terms of their offered peace treaty.

With the threat of war—temporarily—averted, thoughts turn to friendship and feasting. Although he still tries to provoke Antony on the subject of Cleopatra, Pompey takes a hint from Enobarbus with good humour (as Caesar had done in *Act 2, Scene 2*) and leads the triumvirs aboard his galley. Enobarbus is left to make the acquaintance of Menas. They are known to each other by reputation only, but they have much in common. Both are critical of their respective leaders, and neither has any great hopes for the success of the new political settlement. One crisis has been averted—but the warfare is merely postponed.

Once again we are assured of Antony's feelings about 'his Egyptian dish': 'Antony will use his affection where it lies. He married but his occasion here'.

Scene 7   For the present, all is revelry among the captains of the nations— but their servants, preparing the banqueting-room for after-dinner drinks, are unimpressed. The guests have dined well, and as they enter now they are being entertained by Antony with his traveller's tales of Egypt. Lepidus is already very drunk, and Antony plays on his credulity for the amusement of Caesar and Pompey.

Menas draws Pompey aside from the general hilarity with a temptation—'Wilt thou be lord of the whole world?'—and a proposal. Although he rejects it, Pompey's reaction shows how thin is the veneer of harmony that unites the leaders. Menas is disappointed in his commander, and Enobarbus seems to offer sympathy—or a drink, at least.

The fun grows faster and more furious, each of the characters demonstrating the truth of the proverb *'in vino veritas'*—under the influence of drink the real person is revealed. Lepidus, who 'bears the third part of the world', is helplessly drunk; Antony needs no encouragement to enjoy himself; but Caesar, although he joins in reluctantly, is disdainful of the 'wild disguise' that imperils the dignity of all concerned. His words eventually break up the party, but the drinking will continue for a time—like the temporary cease-fire.

Act 3

Scene 1 The action cuts sharply to Syria, where the fighting still continues in this extreme outpost of the Roman empire. The contrast with the celebrations in the last scene, focused through two bodies, could hardly be greater: Lepidus, dead drunk, was carried from the barge—and now Pacorus, dead indeed, is carried on to the stage. The Romans are still requiring vengeance for the defeat of Marcus Crassus, a member of the first triumvirate, who had been captured by the army of Pacorus, son of King Orodes, and cruelly put to death by the king in 53 BC (see 'Events in history', p. vii). Ventidius has successfully carried out the duty he was charged with in *Act 2*, Scene 3, and an admiring subordinate, Silius, urges his captain to make even greater efforts and win still more praise from Antony. But the wise Ventidius knows that there are limits to achievement! He will tactfully notify Antony what has been accomplished 'in *his* name . . . with *his* banners and *his* well-paid ranks'.

This scene is sometimes omitted from stage productions, although it serves several useful purposes—offering still further criticism of the leadership ('Caesar and Antony have ever won More in their officer than person'); giving more information (that Antony 'purposeth to Athens'); and making a break—which is logically as well as theatrically necessary—between the heightened excitement of the festivities and the 'morning after' depression of the coming separation scene.

Scene 2   Back to Rome where, after the celebration, life must go on: Enobarbus and Agrippa prepare the audience for the entrance of the world leaders, exchanging cheerfully derisive comments about all of them—and especially Lepidus. They stand aside to watch the emotional parting of Caesar and his sister, but their critical observations undermine whatever delicate pathos is engendered by the tears that Octavia sheds and the few words that she speaks. Caesar and Antony both appear to be moved, but their real feelings are always open to suspicion.

Scene 3   Another swift transition takes us back, in *time* as well as place, to Alexandria. Cleopatra is still as she was when we left her in *Act 2*, Scene 5, recovering from the shock of Antony's marriage. She has further questions to put to the messenger from Rome—the same man who ran away from the violence of her initial anger. He has now regained enough composure to provide answers which both satisfy Cleopatra's curiosity and reassure her that there can be no competition from Octavia.

This extended episode (from *Act 2*, Scene 5 to the present *Act 3*, Scene 3) demonstrates still more aspects of Cleopatra's emotional volatility, and leaves us with a final impression of her complete sexual confidence.

Scene 4   Yet another change of scene takes us across to Athens—we learned in *3, 1, 36* that this was Antony's intended direction. He is now in residence with Octavia, and already there are signs of a rift with Caesar. In this scene Shakespeare makes two alterations to his source material. Antony accuses Caesar of having 'made his will, and read it To public ear'—the will presumably containing bequests to the Roman citizens comparable to those in the will of Julius Caesar (which Antony read aloud in *Julius Caesar, 3, 2, 241–52*). But according to Plutarch it was *Antony's* will, in which he had found 'certain places worthy of reproach', that Caesar read to the assembled Senate in order to arouse their hostility against Antony. It is a minor detail, but the change of wills serves to increase Caesar's aggressiveness and to diminish Antony's culpability in this renewal of hostilities.

The second alteration concerns Octavia who, so far in the play, has had very little to say for herself. She enters now whilst we can still remember Cleopatra's dismissal of her as a creature 'Dull of tongue and dwarfish', and the ingratiating concurrence of the Roman messenger that Octavia is 'a body rather than a life'. Octavia is a very unhappy woman, torn between two conflicting loyalties, but she is not without spirit. Having been used as a political tool to make peace between her brother and Mark Antony, she now takes it upon herself to be actively instrumental in furthering that peace. In Plutarch's account she spoke twice to her brother after her return to Rome, but Shakespeare—using the historian's words—has created this additional scene for Octavia, thereby developing his dramatic character and also avoiding Plutarch's repetition.

Antony willingly agrees that Octavia should return to her brother and to Rome. He presents himself as a loving husband and as the injured party in the broken agreement: desirous of peace, he is nevertheless prepared to go to war for the sake of his honour— 'If I lose mine honour, I lose myself'. The fine-sounding words cannot conceal the truth of the situation: when Octavia leaves Antony, the breach will be irreparable.

Scene 5   There is no obvious location for this scene other than 'Antony's house', where he can be found 'walking in the garden' (line 16). This could be in Athens, where Octavia parted from Antony, or else in Alexandria, where Antony is next to be found. In the theatre it needs no particular setting, either in place or time.

The little scene is deceptively simple. The easy conversation between Eros and Enobarbus imparts a great deal of information to the audience whilst allowing time for Octavia to travel from Athens to Rome—and simultaneously moving the play's action forward across three or four years. At the beginning of Scene 4 we learned that the peace treaty had already been broken and that Caesar was fighting with Pompey; now we are told something of the outcome of that fighting. Caesar has been successful not only in conquering Pompey but in discrediting and discarding Lepidus, his ally in the conflict. And Pompey has been murdered.

For this scene Shakespeare took his facts from *The Life of Octavius* by Simon Goulart (which was appended to the 1603 edition of North's translation of Plutarch's *Lives*), but he distorts the facts so as to blacken Caesar and to show Antony's conduct in a better light than it deserved.

Goulart describes how Lepidus betrayed Octavius Caesar in their joint struggle against Pompey, but was himself betrayed by his own soldiers when they deserted to Caesar. Caesar then deprived Lepidus of his position as triumvir, but allowed him to live in Italy as a private individual. The defeated Pompey was pursued and killed by one of Antony's lieutenants. Shakespeare's play, however, makes no mention of the treachery of Lepidus. According to Eros, the ungrateful Caesar, 'having made use of him in the wars', denounced and sentenced Lepidus with no further evidence beyond his own accusation; Antony's response has been to deplore the folly of Lepidus, and regret the murder of Pompey.

A situation has now arisen which Enobarbus is quick to comprehend and interpret: with no third party to maintain a balance of power, it is inevitable that the two world leaders must contend with each other for absolute sovereignty. With apparent equanimity Enobarbus and Eros, two old friends, contemplate the doings of their superiors and point the audience towards the next action: Antony's navy is 'rigg'd For Italy and Caesar'.

Scene 6   Just as Antony had spoken out (in Scene 4) against Caesar's violation of the Roman treaty with Pompey, so now it is Caesar's opportunity to voice his complaints about Antony. The irate Caesar has learned of Antony's outrageous conduct in Alexandria where, with spectacular pageantry and god-like liberality, Antony has established Cleopatra as queen of Egypt and scattered the eastern kingdoms of the Roman empire amongst the sons she has borne to him. Now that Lepidus has been eliminated, Caesar and Antony are joint rulers of the empire—but neither partner is willing to share his conquests or yield to the wishes of the other. An impasse has been reached when suddenly Caesar's wrath is refuelled by the arrival, unannounced, of his sister.

Octavia's entry into Rome should have been accompanied with all the splendour of a state visit—which would reflect glory on Caesar himself as well as honouring Antony's wife. The trustful Octavia explains that this visit is at her personal request, but Caesar knows that she is ignorant of Antony's latest double dealing, treacherous to her as well as to Rome. He does not mince his words: Antony has 'given his empire Up to a whore'. The audience hears an impressive roll-call of named 'kings o'th'earth' who, as well as 'a more larger list of sceptres', are enlisted on Antony's side—so that we recognize at once the political dimensions of Antony's perfidy and, in Octavia's cry, the purely human hurt which he has caused. Forcefully expressed sympathy from Maecenas, referring to 'th'adulterous Antony', 'his abominations' and 'a trull', can offer confirmation but little comfort. Octavia must resign herself to the inevitable: 'let determin'd things to destiny Hold unbewail'd their way'.

But whilst Octavia must be patient, Caesar seems to be triumphantly expectant, conscious (according to Plutarch) of a prophecy 'that the government of all the world should fall into Octavius Caesar's hands'.

Scene 7   'But why, why, why?' The main action of the play is now about to begin, and the two world powers are preparing to fight each other for absolute sovereignty. But the preparations in Antony's camp are complicated by the presence of Cleopatra, who is found in the middle of an argument with an exasperated Enobarbus. The experienced soldier has advised Antony to send Cleopatra home to Egypt, but she is stubbornly determined to remain at the front. Caesar has already gained an advantage for himself by surprising Antony and challenging him to fight by sea, and now Cleopatra's taunts further provoke Antony's rash bravado into accepting the challenge, although it is evident to all that his strength is in the land forces.

Caesar and Antony appear almost to be fighting different battles. Antony, knowing his own skill as a swordsman, has countered Caesar's challenge by daring him to fight single-handed, or at least to fight on the time-honoured battlefield of Pharsalia—but Caesar reiterates his original offer. He will confront Antony with a fleet of ships designed for fighting and manned by professionals. Antony can oppose him only with heavy vessels crewed by untrained conscripts.

And every fresh bulletin brings new threats.

Scenes 8–10   The battle of Actium is fought—lost and won! Offshore—and off-stage—there is fierce fighting, which Shakespeare creates in the audience's imagination by quick movements, curt directives, and the noises of battle. All the resources of the theatre must be summoned in assistance. Shakespeare's own stage would provide cannon, drums and trumpets; the Victorians mounted small-scale naval battles in front of the audience; and modern productions have the advantage of film and slide projection as well as sound recordings.

Suddenly—it is all over!

Scene 10   In full view of the battle, Cleopatra panicked and fled from the action. She was followed by Antony. Words failing him, Enobarbus reports the unbearable catastrophe he has just witnessed and Scarus fills out the details, loading every syllable with hatred and contempt for the grotesque spectacle. Cleopatra becomes a nightmare creature, a composite of ribaldry and debauchery as well as 'the token'd pestilence' and 'leprosy'; at the same time she is a figure of farce, a maddened cow who runs to escape the flies that buzz around her tail. Antony, a 'noble ruin' in which 'Experience, manhood, honour' have been shamefully destroyed, is transformed into a flying duck, 'a doting mallard' taking wing to follow his mate.

    Enobarbus has sunk even more deeply into his sorrow when Canidius, only a little more controlled in his emotions, brings news of the flight from Actium. Decisions must be made, and the three characters show different reactions: the cautious Scarus will wait to know more; Canidius yields himself to Caesar; but Enobarbus, against his better judgement, remains true to Antony.

Scene 11   Shakespeare here conflates two episodes from Plutarch's narrative. When Antony fled from the fighting, he went alongside Cleopatra's galley and was hoisted into the vessel where he 'went and sat down alone in the prow of [the] ship, and said never a word, clapping his head between both his hands'. The confrontation with Cleopatra was at Taenarus, some little time afterwards.

    As he comes on to the stage (or ship), Antony's heavy tread makes the boards creak—and his self-disgust is quick to interpret this. All that remains of Antony is his bounty: even in the deepest depression he considers his friends, and makes provision for them. In silence, they leave him to his misery.

    Cleopatra has to be urged to approach, and at first Antony does not seem to notice or to recognize her. His reproach, when it comes, is spoken more in sorrow than in anger. Cleopatra is contrite, but her offered self-defence only shows how grossly she has underestimated Antony's love: 'Forgive my fearful sails! I little thought You would have follow'd'. Now Antony speaks from the bottom of his heart. His shame is profound, and he contrasts the heights of greatness from which he has fallen with the 'shifts of lowness' in which he must now 'dodge And palter' with Octavius Caesar, 'the young man' he despises. But Cleopatra's tears prove more than adequate compensation to him—just as other tears satisfied the injured lover in Shakespeare's Sonnet 34:

> Ah, but those tears are pearl which thy love sheds,
> And they are rich, and ransom all ill deeds

Although he is reconciled with Cleopatra, and can pretend a stoic fortitude, Antony is heavy-laden, 'full of lead', as he faces the future. Without friends or allies, he has sent a humble schoolmaster as his ambassador to Caesar.

Scene 12   Dolabella rightly interprets the significance of Antony's emissary, who speaks ingratiatingly as he presents his petition. Caesar's response is severe: he will hear nothing from Antony, but Cleopatra will be safe if only she will betray and even murder 'her all-disgraced friend'. Having promised safe-conduct to the schoolmaster, Caesar unfolds his plans to set Antony and Cleopatra against each other. His own ambassador will be followed by the silver-tongued Thidias, who can name his own price for his 'cunning'.

Scene 13   Enobarbus has some sympathy for Cleopatra but none for Antony: she is only a woman (he implies), and 'that great face of war', the armada of ships drawn up in battle array, could strike fear even into fighting men. But Antony's conduct has been inexcusable: his manhood as well as his 'captainship' has been called into question. Antony himself seems aware of this, reacting to Caesar's ambassador with yet another challenge to single combat—and Enobarbus recognizes yet another victory for Caesar in this show of bravado: 'Caesar, thou hast subdu'd His judgement too'.

At this point Enobarbus, until now a reliable—though cynical—commentator on procedures, begins to question his own involvement. His loyalty is being severely tested, but for the moment it holds firm whilst he listens with Cleopatra to the blandishments of Thidias.

Cleopatra gives every sign of acquiescence, even abasing herself before Caesar as 'a god [who] knows What is most right'. Her words are capable of double meanings—but Enobarbus does not wait to consider them. He rushes away to fetch Antony, who arrives to witness what he believes to be the final betrayal.

His rage is terrible to behold! Its first frenzy is spent on Thidias: 'whip him . . . Whip him . . . Whip him'. Antony seems to take a vicious delight in the ignominious and cruel punishment, but Enobarbus is unimpressed by this show of power, recognizing it as merely a sign of weakness. Unabated, the fury turns on Cleopatra.

Antony can find no abuse too strong as he castigates her past life and present actions, heaping up insults and hardly stopping to draw breath until the chastened Thidias is brought back on to the stage. Images of gross sensuality are used to emphasize the physical relationships of Cleopatra and her several lovers, whilst Antony's anger best expresses itself in language that reverberates with overtones of the Bible (see notes to text, lines 116–20, 131–3, 150–1).

It is surprising to find this last quality in such a pagan, Roman play. Perhaps Shakespeare, dealing with grand passions and their far-reaching consequences, could find expressive precedents only in the translations of the Old and New Testaments.

With the departure of Thidias Antony seems to collapse: his wrath is spent and the powerful language is silenced, leaving only bewilderment and hurt expressed in the simplest terms:

> To flatter Caesar would you mingle eyes
> With one that ties his points?

Cleopatra, who said earlier that she would 'stay his time' and wait until Antony's hysterical frenzy should subside, now delivers a passionate declaration of her loyalty. Her words equal Antony's in their grandiloquence and, like his, take images from the Bible (see notes, lines 164–72). Antony is convinced—'I am satisfied'—perhaps because Cleopatra is now speaking in his language! His resolution returns and, with Cleopatra joining in the pretence, he plans a further magnificent assault on Caesar. First there will be 'one other gaudy night' of celebration.

But to Enobarbus this is madness and desperation: it is only 'A diminution in our captain's brain [that] Restores his heart'. Enobarbus has seen enough. He must leave Antony.

Act 4

Scene 1   'Caesar sets down in Alexandria' (*3*, 13, 173). There are no more sudden changes of time and place. The play's action closes in on Alexandria, and the net tightens around Antony and Cleopatra (just as Vulcan's net once entrapped Mars and Venus—see *1*, 5, 19).

Caesar is contemptuous of Antony's challenge, recognizing the desperation behind its bravado. He expects to fight 'the last of many battles' on the next day, confident that his forces are more than adequate; meanwhile he will allow his soldiers a celebratory feast—he can afford it, and 'they have earn'd the waste'. The gesture impresses more by its economy than its generosity!

Scene 2   Antony too, undaunted by Caesar's response to the challenge, will feast his army of loyal comrades, his companions-in-arms. He speaks to them as individuals, promising lavish hospitality and moving them almost to tears. Enobarbus recognizes a familiar stratagem—which he himself can scarcely resist—but the audience cannot fail to note the contrast with Caesar's plans for a similar festivity.

Scene 3   Time is now passing very quickly: in Scenes 1 and 2 both Caesar and Antony promised a battle 'tomorrow', and already the guards are changing the night watch, perhaps at midnight. Shakespeare gives dramatic force to a detail narrated by Plutarch (see 'Plutarch', p. 145), introducing the dialogue of the Soldiers and creating suspense and wonder for an audience.

The First Soldier hands over his charge to the Second Soldier, who is joined by his Company. They take up their new positions, precisely placed '*in every corner of the stage*' by the Folio direction, and wait, uneasily. Nothing occurs—but noises are heard from underneath the stage.

The sound of oboes can be deep and mysterious—as Shakespeare knew when he used the same instruments for supernatural effect in *Macbeth* (4, 1, 106). The Soldiers try to interpret, but can only agree that the happening does not bode well for Antony—

Scene 4   —who is already awake (probably he has not slept), and arming for the fight. The *tomorrow* anticipated in the previous scenes is almost *today*. As he prepares for his military role, Antony assumes a chivalric *persona* using the language of medieval romance: Cleopatra is his 'squire' and also his 'dame', and he leaves her with a melodramatic farewell, offering 'a soldier's kiss' from 'a man of steel'.

For her part, Cleopatra is charmingly feminine, struggling with the unfamiliar pieces of armour, wanting praise for her efforts ('Is not this buckled well?'), and admiring her knight in his departure ('He goes forth gallantly'). But when Antony has left the stage we realize that she has not been deceived: had it been single combat, 'Then Antony—but now—'. The silences tell all.

Scene 5   Heading for the battlefield, Antony encounters one of his soldiers, the same man who had warned him against fighting by sea at Actium (*3*, *7*, *60*). He had been right: Antony admits his mistake then receives a heavy body-blow. Ever since the battle of Actium the audience, with Antony, have been hearing of fresh desertions, and now there is one more—Enobarbus!

Antony can hardly believe what he hears, but upon the Soldier's third reiteration of the news he reacts with characteristic generosity. The name 'Enobarbus' is on his lips as he quits the stage—

Scene 6   —and immediately the character, as though summoned, appears. But now he follows Caesar, who is anticipating not a single victory but the fulfilment of an age-old prophecy: 'The time of universal peace is near'. Such a time (comparable to that prophesied in Isaiah 2:4) had been spoken of by the poet Virgil—

> Ours is the crowning era foretold in prophecy:
> Born of Time, a great new cycle of centuries
> Begins. Justice returns to earth, the Golden Age
> Returns, and its first-born comes down from heaven above . . .
> ('Eclogue IV', translated by C. Day Lewis)

—and Plutarch is even more specific: 'It was predestined that the government of all the world should fall into Octavius Caesar's hands'.

Enobarbus listens as Caesar orders the positioning of his troops, with the deserters from Antony in the forefront of the fighting, and then—alone on the stage—meditates on the ignominy of desertion. His shame is made absolute when one of Caesar's soldiers tells him of Antony's generosity, adding his own observation: 'Your emperor Continues still a Jove'. Self-accused, Enobarbus convicts and condemns himself in lonely misery.

Scenes 7, 8   The sounds of battle, a quick skirmish, then suddenly—and contrary to all expectation—Caesar is in retreat, and Antony is victorious. Antony is the conquering hero now, using again the language of chivalrous romance, with his virility restored by the magic of 'this great fairy', Cleopatra. In triumph Antony shows his best nature, handing out lavish sympathy and praise, and promising joyous celebration to all his men. And once more we seem to be invited to recognize the rare quality of Antony's magnanimity in his relationships with his soldiers, and to contrast this with what we saw of Caesar's behaviour in a comparable situation (*Act 4*, Scene 1).

The winners depart, whilst the 'brazen din' of a loud fanfare on the trumpets applauds the close of the scene.

Scene 9   The quiet stage is now occupied by watchmen from Caesar's camp: they are exhausted after a day of fierce fighting, and apprehensive about the resumption of hostilities on (apparently) the following day. Like the guards who watched over Antony's army in Scene 3, these men are called upon to eavesdrop on a most solemn incident.

The desolate Enobarbus, vanquished at last by Antony's overwhelming generosity, surrenders all will to live. According to Plutarch he had been 'sick of an ague', but Shakespeare's audiences would recognize the physiological symptoms of melancholy, a potentially fatal condition affecting both mind and body. Whatever the explanation, the death of Enobarbus marks yet another turning-point in the play, and challenges the audience to make a fresh assessment of its leading character and their own reactions to him. Enobarbus, cynical but loyal, the epitome of reason, has always served as our guide through the bewildering maze of emotions—but now reason has been conquered by something even greater.

Scenes 10, 11, 12   The battle of Alexandria is conducted in three short, closely-linked scenes, and the audience (as at Actium—*Act 3*, Scenes 8, 9, 10) is able to view from both sides through the eyes of the leaders, Antony and Caesar.

In Antony's camp the news is ominous: Caesar is preparing for a sea-battle. But Antony himself is oblivious, still exultant after his earlier victory.

Caesar's comment illuminates his strategy, leaving little doubt about the outcome of the fighting.

Trumpets sound the call to battle, but at first nothing happens. Antony leaves the stage to Scarus (who now takes the place of Enobarbus as impartial commentator), but he is not away for long. On his return, Antony expends the first outburst of his fury in dismissing the remainder of his troops before acknowledging total defeat. His hopes are gone; his men have surrendered to his enemy; and, worst of all, he believes himself to have been betrayed by the woman who meant more than the whole world to him. There is no evidence, and not even the slightest suggestion, that Cleopatra had any responsibility for this second defeat—but Antony remembers Actium!

As soon as Cleopatra appears, Antony renews the verbal onslaught of his wrath with a threat which so terrifies her that she withdraws in silence. Antony, alone in his rage, reaches out to compare the enormity of his passion with the supernatural madness of Hercules, the classical hero whom he had always claimed as an ancestor. At last, when he has exhausted his hyperbole, the simplest words speak the uttermost of his grief: 'To the young Roman boy she hath sold me'.

Antony's final threat is the death of Cleopatra, but he had earlier predicted for her a fate worse than death—the disgrace of exhibition in Caesar's triumphal procession through the streets of Rome. The thought of this procession will never leave Cleopatra— or Antony himself—throughout the remainder of the play.

Scene 13   Images of madness, super-human in proportion, occur to Cleopatra's mind as she attempts to avert and evade the fury that has been unleashed. Haste and desperation increase in the repeated 'To th' monument'—at first suggestion, then agreement, finally imperative. Plutarch says that Cleopatra 'had long before made many sumptuous tombs and monumental, as well for excellency of workmanship, as for height and greatness of building'.

Scene 14   Antony, all passion spent, contemplates his situation: he has lost everything, and now he feels that even his own identity is dissolving, disintegrating like the insubstantial clouds at evening. He speaks with a sad, quiet dignity of his love for Cleopatra, 'Whose heart I thought I had, for she had mine', and of what he believes to have been her treachery to him. His anger flares up momentarily with the arrival of Mardian, but the eunuch brings news that silences it for ever.

What the audience hears, however, sounds like a cruel lie, made yet more hurtful because—in Mardian's narrative—almost believable.

Antony's response is instant: this is the end. Love and— misplaced—admiration raise him to romantic heights: he can compare with classical heroes, and recall poetic achievement—but he is soon cast down again. Once again he visualizes the triumphal procession, with himself as the humiliated prisoner of the victorious Caesar. This must never be, and Eros will not live to see it—but he cannot kill his master. Antony interprets his servant's

deed as an act of bravery and yet another reproach to his own lack
of valour. With assumed courage, and a highly dramatic gesture, he
throws himself on his own sword—and misses! He has even failed
to commit suicide.

Like Eros, the Guards refuse to put Antony out of his misery:
to touch him, even wounded as he is, seems a kind of sacrilege to
them—though Dercetus is willing to take advantage of the
situation, hoping to profit from his knowledge by informing Caesar
of Antony's end.

Now Antony can be brought no lower. Defeated by his enemy
and deserted by his followers, thinking himself betrayed by the
woman he loves, and deprived of the dignity of a heroic death
through his own clumsiness, he must writhe in the agony of his self-
inflicted wound and beg to be released from his pain. To
Diomedes, however, he is still the 'Most absolute lord'.

When he learns that his worst suspicions have been
unfounded—that Cleopatra is still alive, and that she has never
broken her faith with him—Antony speaks no reproach. He calls
upon his Guards as 'friends', asking for help from those whom he
had once commanded. He will be carried to Cleopatra in her
monument.

Scene 15   Huddled together high in the monument—i.e. on the balcony
above Shakespeare's stage (see 'Background', p. 165)—Cleopatra
and her maids wait in terror for their lives. Diomedes arrives at the
foot of the monument with the latest news, and directs them to
look to the other stage door, where the dying Antony is being
carried in. For the next few minutes all is confusion: Antony, who
is helpless and immobile, must be hoisted up the monument to
reach Cleopatra, who is too scared to come down to him. The three
women struggle with the heavy weight, and at last the lovers are
reunited—although even now they are slightly at odds! Antony is
trying to advise Cleopatra about her future safety, but Cleopatra
insists on speaking her own thoughts.

With fine words of stoic bravery Antony dies, and Cleopatra
attempts to articulate her sense of loss, which is at once unique to
her and common to 'the maid that milks'. To Charmian and Iras
she is 'Lady . . . Madam . . . Royal Egypt' but Cleopatra, rejecting
these titles, sees herself as 'No more but e'en a woman'. It is with
majesty and pride, however, that she announces her next decision.

Act 5

Scene 1   As the scene changes to Caesar's camp, the audience waits expectantly to hear Caesar's reaction to the death of Antony. Its political import appears to strike him first: 'The death of Antony Is not a single doom'. He is ashamed of his tears—but explains that Dercetus has brought 'tidings To wash the eyes of kings'. Agrippa and Maecenas express sincere but formal condolences, whilst Caesar draws aside, apparently to confront his own mixed emotions. He has fought to the end an enemy who was at the same time his 'brother' and 'mate in empire'.

Any further feelings must give way to more urgent business. What is to become of Cleopatra? Caesar sends reassuring messages—then confirms for the audience what Antony had suspected and what Cleopatra fears: he wants her living presence as his captive to be the crowning glory of his Roman triumph.

Having dispatched Proculeius to make his overtures to Cleopatra, Caesar continues to insist that he is not guilty—to deny any responsibility for this sad business.

Scene 2   Suicide now has a more positive aspect for Cleopatra: after the death of Antony she thought only of comforting her own loneliness, but now she sees it as a means of triumphing over Caesar and even over Fortune. No longer careful for security, Cleopatra allows Proculeius to have access to her in the monument (i.e. on the main stage), and she is easily surprised by Gallus and the Roman soldiers. Her dread of captive humiliation increases her defiance of Caesar, and the message she sends by Proculeius is simple and uncompromising: 'Say I would die'.

In the absence of Proculeius and the official military deputation, Cleopatra relaxes and, with the sympathetic and admiring Dolabella to listen to her, tries to articulate the magnitude of her loss. But she is describing the indescribable, and the plain-spoken Roman can only marvel at her words. Of course he has never seen such a man—neither has the audience! The Antony of the previous four acts has shown himself in many different guises, but not like this. Cleopatra's imagination is re-creating the Antony of her love, and it is this aspect of Antony that will remain dominant until the end of the play.

Critics have tried to compare passages in other works that describe wonderful beings—classical gods, angels, and men of super-human abilities—but although these use similar cosmic imagery, none of them can parallel Cleopatra's hyperbolic portrait of Antony[1]. This is metaphysical poetry in the truest sense and it is uniquely Shakespeare's.

Coming down to earth after her flight of fancy, Cleopatra meekly asks what is to be done with her, and Dolabella can only confirm her fears. Caesar arrives to find her in this most abject condition, and it seems at first that he does not recognize her, asking 'Which is the queen of Egypt?'. Some critics interpret this as the opening thrust in a duel of wits—but to me it seems more likely that Shakespeare is following Plutarch, who says that when Caesar came to the monument he found Cleopatra sick and 'laid upon a little low bed in poor estate'.

Cleopatra's submissive mood is not sustained for very long, however, and its sincerity is called into question when Seleucus reveals the truth about the inventory of her possessions. Her spirit returns, and she berates the steward with something of her former gusto. Caesar feels bound to restrain her, and she appeals to him as her equal in 'pomp' and social status. The episode reassures Caesar that Cleopatra, far from intending suicide, has plans for survival and may safely be left without a guard. He parts from her as a friend—but Cleopatra is not deceived: 'He words me, girls, he words me'.

Dolabella returns to the stage to disclose Caesar's plan of action, and Cleopatra elaborates on what is to come, so that Iras (and, more especially, the audience) is left in no doubt about the humiliation and ignominy that she would endure in Caesar's triumph. Shakespeare has never before shown such confidence in the power of his poetry (and of his actors): the lines speak with contempt of any actor who tries to 'boy [the] greatness' of Cleopatra—and this is exactly what the speaker of these lines (in Shakespeare's theatre) is doing!

When Charmian joins Iras on the stage, Cleopatra sends the two handmaids to prepare for her final performance, which is to be comparable with her first encounter with Mark Antony at Cydnus. Stage directions allow only Iras to go out, leaving Charmian to hear, or overhear, the conversation that follows—and which brings for everybody some light relief from an unexpected source.

---

[1] The representation of Jove described in an Italian volume translated as *The Fountain of Ancient Fiction* in 1599; the 'mighty angel' in the Book of Revelation which came down from heaven ' . . . and his face was as it were the Sun, and his feet as pillars of fire . . . and he set his right foot upon the sea and his left foot on the earth' (10:1–2); the portrait of the superman conqueror in Christopher Marlowe's *1 Tamburlaine*, (published in 1590, 2, 1, 7–30).

Only Cleopatra has remained on stage throughout this very long scene, in which Shakespeare conflates several episodes from Plutarch's narrative. Characters have left the stage at various times, and their places have been taken by others, each one striking a different note. Now a hitherto unknown 'rural fellow' brings comedy along with his figs. The fact that he is identified as 'Clown' in the Folio speech prefix indicates that the role was played by the company's comic actor—although his comedy has a serious point to it.

Cleopatra says little: her mind is resolved and the way is clear—the Clown has provided the means for her end. Like some great actress she assumes her new role: queen of Egypt, conqueror of Caesar, and wife of Antony. Charmian and Iras have set the stage for her—perhaps by removing the wretched couch on which she lay at the beginning of this scene and replacing it with the 'bed of gold' where Caesar (according to Plutarch) found her dead body. Now they proceed to dress her in the appropriate attire. Death steals upon her slowly—too slowly! Cleopatra prepares herself for a consummation which will be both spiritual and physical, but there is no time to waste. A momentary (and entirely characteristic) flash of jealousy is less important than the urgent need to outwit Caesar's strategies; and then a gentle peace overcomes all other feelings. Cleopatra has won, and Charmian prepares to display her in the splendour of her own triumph.

Caesar's Guards, joined by Dolabella, are not really surprised at what they see, and Caesar himself expresses only admiration: Cleopatra is 'Bravest at the last'. As he searches for the cause of death and finds no outward signs, he can only remark that

> she looks like sleep,
> As she would catch another Antony
> In her strong toil of grace.

At last, it seems, Caesar can understand what it was that kept Antony from his Roman concerns.

The excitement of Plutarch

It's not easy to get enthusiastic about Plutarch's 'Life of Marcus Antonius' when you have only the extracts printed 'for critical comparison' at the back of an edition of *Antony and Cleopatra*! But the 'Life' in its entirety, even today, makes 'a good read'—whether you read it in the translation by Sir Thomas North that Shakespeare knew, or in some modern version[1]. Plutarch tells a great story which is exciting, action-packed, amusing and amazing. A story that would be incredible if it were not true—and Shakespeare seems to have been enthralled by it.

From the very beginning of his writing career, Shakespeare shows an easy familiarity with classical literature. As a boy at Stratford Grammar School he would have been taught Latin and perhaps Greek, and he would have studied works of the major authors in these languages. He gives no indication of having read Plutarch, however, until 1599, when the *Parallel Lives* provided the source for *Julius Caesar*, and also the inspiration for one of the comic scenes of *Henry V* (*Act 4*, Scene 2) where the Welsh captain, Llewellyn, drawing a parallel between the lives of Alexander the Great and Henry V, attempts (and fails) to imitate Plutarch's comparisons.

In the *Lives* Shakespeare found the plots and main characters for four plays: as well as *Julius Caesar* and *Antony and Cleopatra* there were *Coriolanus* and much of *Timon of Athens*. In Plutarch he found a writer after his own heart, interested—as Shakespeare himself was—in the minute particulars that best distinguish individuals:

> . . . my intent is not to write histories, but only lives. For the noblest deeds do not always show men's virtues and vices; but oftentimes a light occasion, a word or some sport makes men's natural dispositions and manners appear more plain than the famous battles won wherein are slain ten thousand men, or great armies, or the cities won by siege or assault.
>
> ('The Life of Alexander')

---

[1] *Makers of Rome*, by Ian Scott-Kilvert (London, 1965).

The 'Life of Marcus Antonius' is the longest and easily the best of all the 'Lives'. Mark Antony's first biographer was not very far removed from his subject, and he could write of Antony and Cleopatra—legends in their own lifetime—with all the authority of hearsay: 'My grandfather told me . . . ' Plutarch's grandfather could tell, if only at second-hand, of conspicuous expense and riotous living; and the old man also knew of the hardships and privations endured by those who were too close to the action, for his own father had lived near Actium when the villages were constrained to supply men and sustenance for Antony's armies.

Shakespeare moves easily around the 'Life', selecting from Plutarch's comprehensive narrative the episodes and details, no matter how trivial, which suit his own purpose and changing them, as though by magic, into poetry. Plutarch remarks that Cleopatra's

> voice and words were marvellous pleasant: for her tongue was an instrument of music to divers sports and pastimes

—and Antony embraces Cleopatra with the delighted 'My nightingale!' (4, 8, 18).

When Antony is careless of Caesar's messenger and anxious to divert Cleopatra's thoughts, he makes the somewhat unusual proposal that:

> all alone
> Tonight we'll wander through the streets and note
> The qualities of people.

> (1, 1, 53–5)

The dramatist has remembered the biographer's account of how, in Alexandria, the Roman triumvir

> would go up and down the city disguised like a slave in the night, and would peer into poor men's windows and their shops, and scold and brawl with them within the house: Cleopatra would be also in a chambermaid's array, and amble up and down the streets with him.

Only very careful, and probably very frequent, reading of this unwieldy book—a leather-bound folio of more than a thousand leaves—could have given Shakespeare such control over Plutarch's discursive narrative and such intimacy with its details. And the words of the English translation caught his attention and fixed themselves in his memory. Shakespeare so respected the vigorous colloquial prose of Sir Thomas North that he often retained its phraseology and idioms, making a few slight adjustments for the purposes of rhythm and emphasis—as a comparison of 'Life' and play will show (see 'Plutarch', p. 143).

Shakespeare's encounter with Plutarch, through the mediation of North, was a coincidence of rare talents, generating in *Antony and Cleopatra* a work of imagination where we can almost see the fancy outworking nature (2, 2, 210), and which might even perhaps be called (see 5, 2, 98) 'fancy's piece 'gainst nature'!

Shakespeare's Verse

Shakespeare's plays are written mainly in 'blank verse', the form preferred by most dramatists in the sixteenth and early seventeenth centuries. It is a very flexible medium, which is capable—like the human speaking voice—of a wide range of tones. Basically, the lines, which are unrhymed, are ten syllables long. The syllables have alternating stresses, just like normal English speech; and they divide into five 'feet'. The technical name for this is 'iambic pentameter'.

Philo initiates this rhythm for the play. The anger of his disillusionment beats on our ears in regular pentameters with a distinct mid-line break (a 'caesura') making for added emphasis:

> Nay, bút this dótage óf our génerál's
> O'erflóws the méasure. Thóse his góodly éyes,
> That ó'er the files and músters óf the wár
> Have glówed like pláted Márs, now bénd, now túrn
> The óffice ánd devótion óf their víew
> Upón a táwny frónt . . .

The same rhythm is taken up, but in a greatly relaxed manner, by the happy teasing of Antony and Cleopatra:

> **Cleopatra**
> If ít be lóve indéed, tell mé how múch.
> **Antony**
> There's béggary ín the lóve that cán be réckoned.

In Philo's speech the sense of his words does not stop at the end of the line: like the 'dotage' he is speaking of, it overflows the pentameter measure. At the beginning of his career Shakespeare wrote mainly regular, 'end-stopped', lines (such as those spoken here by Cleopatra and Antony) where the grammatical unit of meaning is contained within each verse line. Now, in *Antony and Cleopatra*, Shakespeare is completely in control of every aspect of his medium, and the flexibility of his verse, in which the thought often runs effortlessly between the lines, allowing the characters to talk, argue and persuade; to abuse and to console each other, to proclaim their public thoughts for all to hear, and to whisper their private sentiments 'aside' for the understanding of none but the audience.

A line can be shared between different characters without losing its rhythm; as in everyday speech, syllables may be elided ('o'er', 'Perform't'); and occasionally an incomplete pentameter will compel an eloquent silence:

Cleopatra
                                        who knóws
If thé scarce-béarded Cáesar háve not sént
His pówerful mándate tó you: 'Do thís, or thís;
Take ín that kíngdom ánd enfránchise thát.
Perfórm't, or élse we dámn thee.'
        Antony
                                        Hów, my lóve?
        Cleopatra
Perchánce? Nay, ánd most líke.

Sometimes the verse makes its own demands, requiring an extra syllable or even an unusual emphasis or stress—as in these lines:

Pompey
For théy have éntertáinèd cáuse enóugh
To dráw their swórds. But hów the féar of ús
May cément théir divísions, ánd bind úp
The pétty differencés, we yét not knów.

                                        (2, 1, 47-50)

Here it is necessary for 'entertained' to have *four* syllables, and to stress 'cement' unusually on its first syllable.

Source, Date, and Text

Shakespeare's main source for *Antony and Cleopatra*, as for *Julius Caesar*, was Plutarch's *Parallel Lives of the Greeks and Romans*. This was written in Greek in the first century AD; translated into French by Jacques Amyot (1559); and then into English by Sir Thomas North (1579). No precise date has yet been established for the writing of Shakespeare's play, but evidence from the work of a contemporary writer, Samuel Daniel, suggests that it could have been as early as 1604. The play was not published until it appeared in the First Folio of 1623.

This edition makes use of the text established by John Wilders in 1995 for the Arden Shakespeare Series.

Characters in the Play

ROME

Mark Antony
Octavius Caesar   *the triumvirs*
Lepidus

Octavia   *sister of* Octavius Caesar

Pompey   *leader of the opposition faction*

Domitius Enobarbus
Ventidius
Eros
Schoolmaster
Demetrius
Silius   *officers and followers of* Mark Antony
Dercetus
Soothsayer
Philo
Canidius
Scarus

Maecenas
Thidias
Proculeius
Agrippa   *officers and followers of* Caesar
Dolabella
Taurus
Gallus

Menas
Menacretes   *followers of* Pompey
Varrus

EGYPT

Cleopatra   *queen of Egypt*

Charmian
Iras   *her personal attendants*

Alexas   *her minister*

Mardian   *a eunuch*

Seleucus   *her treasurer*

Diomedes   *a servant*

Clown   *a countryman*

Messengers, servants, officers, soldiers, sentries, guards, watchmen

The action takes place in Egypt, Rome, Athens and other regions of the Roman empire

Act I

Two officers lament the change that has come over their leader, and we see the man himself when Antony arrives with Cleopatra and her entourage. Antony flirts with the queen, refusing to hear the messengers from Caesar.

1 *Nay*: The play opens in the middle of a conversation.
   dotage: infatuation, folly.
2 *O'erflows the measure*: goes beyond the limit.
3 *files and musters*: assembled ranks.
4 *plated*: in full armour.
   Mars: the Roman god of war.
5 *office*: service.
6 *front*: forehead, face.
8 *breast*: breastplate.
   reneges all temper: abandons all restraint, goes completely soft.
9 *bellows . . . fan*: stimulation and satisfaction.
10 *gipsy*: Gipsies were thought to have come from Egypt.
10s.d. *Flourish*: fanfare of trumpets (usually heralding a royal or military procession).
   Eunuchs: castrated male slaves, often employed to guard and serve high-born Eastern ladies.
12 *triple pillar*: Antony was one of the three rulers ('the triumvirs') who governed the Roman empire.
12–13 *transform'd . . . fool*: so much changed that he's allowed that whore to make a fool of him.
15 'It's a miserably poor love that can be counted up'; Antony takes Cleopatra's 'tell' in the sense of 'calculate'.
16 'I'll fix the limits on how far you must love me.'
17 *new . . . earth*: i.e. new boundaries.

Scene 1

Alexandria: enter Demetrius *and* Philo

Philo
Nay, but this dotage of our general's
O'erflows the measure. Those his goodly eyes,
That o'er the files and musters of the war
Have glowed like plated Mars, now bend, now turn
5 The office and devotion of their view
Upon a tawny front. His captain's heart,
Which in the scuffles of great fights hath burst
The buckles on his breast, reneges all temper
And is become the bellows and the fan
10 To cool a gipsy's lust.

> *Flourish. Enter* Antony, Cleopatra, *her*
> ladies, Charmian *and* Iras, *the train, with*
> Eunuchs *fanning her*

                Look where they come!
Take but good note, and you shall see in him
The triple pillar of the world transform'd
Into a strumpet's fool. Behold and see.
    Cleopatra
If it be love indeed, tell me how much.
    Antony
15 There's beggary in the love that can be reckon'd.
    Cleopatra
I'll set a bourn how far to be belov'd.
    Antony
Then must thou needs find out new heaven, new earth.

Enter a Messenger

    Messenger
News, my good lord, from Rome.

19 *Grates me*: grates on my ears.
   The sum: be brief.

21 *Fulvia*: Antony's wife (see 'Events in history', p. vii).
   perchance: perhaps.
22 *scarce-bearded*: At the time the play opens, Caesar was twenty-three and Antony forty-two.
24 *Take in*: occupy, take possession of.
   enfranchise: liberate.
25 *we*: Cleopatra, speaking in parody of Caesar, uses the 'royal plural', expressing sovereignty and authority.
   How: what do you mean?
27 *dismission*: order to withdraw [from Egypt].
29 *process*: summons to appear in a court of law.

32 *homager*: dutiful servant.
   else so: or else.
34 *Tiber*: the river flowing through Rome.
   arch: Shakespeare develops the idea beginning with 'the triple pillar of the world' (line 12).
35 *rang'd*: ordered.
36 *dungy earth*: dunghill of a world.
38 *thus*: Antony's gesture embraces the entirety of his new lifestyle with Cleopatra.
   mutual: well-matched.
39 *twain*: couple.
   bind: charge, command; Antony issues a public proclamation.
40 *On pain*: for fear.
   weet: recognize, admit.
41 *Excellent falsehood*: Cleopatra tries to provoke Antony, who returns her taunts in such a way as to flatter her.
43 *seem*: pretend to be.
44 *himself*: i.e. the fool that he really is.
   But . . . Cleopatra: only if I am inspired by Cleopatra.
46 *confound*: waste.
   conference harsh: argumentation.
48 *pleasure now*: instant, immediate, delight.
   sport: entertainment, pastime.

Antony
Grates me! The sum.
Cleopatra
20 Nay, hear them, Antony.
Fulvia perchance is angry, or who knows
If the scarce-bearded Caesar have not sent
His powerful mandate to you: 'Do this, or this;
Take in that kingdom and enfranchise that.
25 Perform't, or else we damn thee.'
Antony
                    How, my love?
Cleopatra
Perchance? Nay, and most like.
You must not stay here longer; your dismission
Is come from Caesar; therefore hear it, Antony.
Where's Fulvia's process?—Caesar's, I would say.
   Both?
30 Call in the messengers! As I am Egypt's queen,
Thou blushest, Antony, and that blood of thine
Is Caesar's homager; else so thy cheek pays shame
When shrill-tongued Fulvia scolds. The messengers!
Antony
Let Rome in Tiber melt, and the wide arch
35 Of the rang'd empire fall! Here is my space!
Kingdoms are clay! Our dungy earth alike
Feeds beast as man. The nobleness of life
Is to do thus, when such a mutual pair
And such a twain can do't, in which I bind,
40 On pain of punishment, the world to weet
We stand up peerless.
Cleopatra
                    Excellent falsehood!
Why did he marry Fulvia and not love her?
I'll seem the fool I am not. Antony
Will be himself.
Antony
                    But stirr'd by Cleopatra.
45 Now, for the love of Love and her soft hours,
Let's not confound the time with conference harsh.
There's not a minute of our lives should stretch
Without some pleasure now. What sport tonight?
Cleopatra
Hear the ambassadors.

Antony

                        Fie, wrangling queen,
50 Whom everything becomes—to chide, to laugh,
To weep; whose every passion fully strives
To make itself, in thee, fair and admir'd!
No messenger but thine, and all alone
Tonight we'll wander through the streets and note

55 *The qualities of people*: what people are like.

55 The qualities of people. Come, my queen!
Last night you did desire it. [*To the* Messenger]
    Speak not to us.

56s.d. *train*: retinue.

           [*Exeunt* Antony *and* Cleopatra *with the train*

Demetrius

Is Caesar with Antonius priz'd so slight?

57 *priz'd*: valued, respected.

Philo

Sir, sometimes, when he is not Antony,
He comes too short of that great property

59 *property*: distinctive quality.
60 *still*: always.

60 Which still should go with Antony.

Demetrius

                  I am full sorry

61 *approves . . . liar*: confirms the truth of what is common gossip.

63 *Rest you happy*: good luck to you.

That he approves the common liar who
Thus speaks of him at Rome, but I will hope
Of better deeds tomorrow. Rest you happy!

                     [*Exeunt*

Act 1   Scene 2

In the idle luxury of the Egyptian court, Cleopatra's maidservants, watched by Enobarbus and some Roman officers, await the coming of their mistress and her lover. Cleopatra appears first, sends for Antony— and leaves the stage as soon as he arrives! Antony, however, has heard the news from Rome, and determines to get away from Egypt and Cleopatra.

Scene 2

Alexandria: enter Enobarbus *and other*
Roman Officers, *a* Soothsayer, Charmian,
Iras, Mardian the Eunuch, *and* Alexas

Charmian

Lord Alexas, sweet Alexas, most anything Alexas, almost most absolute Alexas, where's the soothsayer that you praised so to th'queen? O, that I knew this husband which you say must charge his horns with
5 garlands!

4 *this husband*: Apparently the Soothsayer has already predicted marriage for Charmian.
4–5 *charge . . . garlands*: hang a bridal wreath on his cuckold's horns: even before she finds him, Charmian is planning to cheat on her husband. The Elizabethans often joked about the horns which (they said) would grow on the head of a cuckold (= a man whose wife is unfaithful).

Alexas
Soothsayer!
Soothsayer
Your will?
Charmian
Is this the man? Is't you, sir, that know things?
Soothsayer
In nature's infinite book of secrecy
10 A little I can read.
Alexas
                                        Show him your hand.
Enobarbus

11 *banquet*: refreshments, 'running buffet' of wine, fruit, and sweets.

Bring in the banquet quickly; wine enough
Cleopatra's health to drink.

Enter Servants *with wine and other refreshments and exeunt*

Charmian
[*Gives her hand to the* Soothsayer] Good sir, give me good fortune.
Soothsayer
15 I make not, but foresee.
Charmian
Pray then, foresee me one.
Soothsayer
You shall be yet far fairer than you are.
Charmian
He means in flesh.
Iras

19 *paint*: use cosmetics.

No, you shall paint when you are old.
Charmian
20 Wrinkles forbid!
Alexas

21 *prescience*: foreknowledge.

Vex not his prescience. Be attentive.
Charmian
Hush!
Soothsayer
You shall be more beloving than belov'd.
Charmian

24 *heat my liver*: get worked up: love, like drink, was thought to inflame the liver.

I had rather heat my liver with drinking.
Alexas
25 Nay, hear him.

27-9 *three kings . . . homage*: Shakespeare alludes to the biblical story of the birth of Christ, with the visitation of the three kings and the passion of Herod of Judaea.
forenoon: morning.

32-3 *outlive . . . figs*: An audience familiar with the story would recognize Shakespeare's anticipation of the play's last scene—but in her reference to 'figs' Charmian may well be thinking of their resemblance to the male genitals.
34 *prov'd*: experienced.

36 *have no names*: i.e. be bastards.

40 *forgive . . . witch*: acquit you of any charge of witchcraft: Charmian scorns the prophetic powers of the Soothsayer.
41 *privy to*: aware of.

46 *drunk to bed*: to go to bed drunk.
49 *E'en as*: just as much as.
the o'erflowing . . . famine: By overflowing its banks, the river Nile irrigates the soil and makes the land fertile.

51 *oily palm*: It was popularly thought that a moist hand indicated sexual willingness.
52 *scratch mine ear*: I'll never believe my ears: to have itching or burning ears was said to be a sign that gossip is being spoken.

Charmian
Good now, some excellent fortune! Let me be married to three kings in a forenoon and widow them all. Let me have a child at fifty to whom Herod of Jewry may do homage. Find me to marry me with
30 Octavius Caesar and companion me with my mistress.
    Soothsayer
You shall outlive the lady whom you serve.
    Charmian
O, excellent! I love long life better than figs.
    Soothsayer
You have seen and prov'd a fairer former fortune
35 Than that which is to approach.
    Charmian
Then belike my children shall have no names. Prithee, how many boys and wenches must I have?
    Soothsayer
If every of your wishes had a womb,
And fertile every wish, a million.
    Charmian
40 Out, fool! I forgive thee for a witch.
    Alexas
You think none but your sheets are privy to your wishes.
    Charmian
Nay, come, tell Iras hers.
    Alexas
We'll know all our fortunes.
    Enobarbus
45 Mine, and most of our fortunes tonight, shall be drunk to bed.
    Iras
[*Holds out her hand*] There's a palm presages chastity, if nothing else.
    Charmian
E'en as the o'erflowing Nilus presageth famine.
    Iras
50 Go, you wild bedfellow, you cannot soothsay!
    Charmian
Nay, if an oily palm be not a fruitful prognostication, I cannot scratch mine ear. Prithee, tell her but a workaday fortune.

Soothsayer
Your fortunes are alike.
    Iras
55 But how? But how? Give me particulars!
    Soothsayer
I have said.
    Iras
Am I not an inch of fortune better than she?
    Charmian
Well, if you were but an inch of fortune better than
I, where would you choose it?
    Iras
60 Not in my husband's nose.
    Charmian
Our worser thoughts heavens mend! Alexas—come,
his fortune, his fortune! O, let him marry a woman
that cannot go, sweet Isis I beseech thee, and let her
die too, and give him a worse, and let worse follow
65 worse, till the worst of all follow him laughing to his
grave, fiftyfold a cuckold! Good Isis, hear me this
prayer, though thou deny me a matter of more
weight; good Isis, I beseech thee!
    Iras
Amen. Dear goddess, hear that prayer of the people!
70 For as it is a heartbreaking to see a handsome man
loose-wived, so it is a deadly sorrow to behold a foul
knave uncuckolded. Therefore, dear Isis, keep
decorum and fortune him accordingly!
    Charmian
Amen.
    Alexas
75 Lo now, if it lay in their hands to make me a cuckold,
they would make themselves whores, but they'd do't.

Enter Cleopatra

    Enobarbus
Hush, here comes Antony.
    Charmian
Not he, the queen.
    Cleopatra
Saw you my lord?
    Enobarbus
80 No, lady.

60 *nose*: Iras would probably prefer the extra inch to be on her husband's penis.

63 *go*: enjoy sex.
Isis: the Egyptian goddess controlling the moon, the earth, and all fertility.

68 *weight*: importance.

69 *of the people*: from everybody.

72 *knave*: wretch, rotter.
72–3 *keep decorum*: act properly.
73 *fortune . . . accordingly*: give him an appropriate fortune.

77 *Antony*: Enobarbus pretends to mistake Cleopatra.

Cleopatra

Was he not here?

Charmian

No, madam.

Cleopatra

He was disposed to mirth, but on the sudden

A Roman thought hath struck him. Enobarbus!

Enobarbus

85 Madam?

Cleopatra

Seek him and bring him hither. [*Exit* Enobarbus

Where's Alexas?

Alexas

Here, at your service. My lord approaches.

Enter Antony *with a* Messenger

Cleopatra

We will not look upon him. Go with us.

[*Exeunt all but* Antony *and* Messenger

Messenger

Fulvia thy wife first came into the field.

Antony

90 Against my brother Lucius?

Messenger

Ay,

But soon that war had end, and the time's state

Made friends of them, jointing their force 'gainst Caesar,

Whose better issue in the war from Italy

95 Upon the first encounter drave them.

Antony

Well, what worst?

Messenger

The nature of bad news infects the teller.

Antony

When it concerns the fool or coward. On!

Things that are past are done with me. 'Tis thus:

100 Who tells me true, though in his tale lie death,

I hear him as he flatter'd.

Messenger

Labienus—

This is stiff news—hath with his Parthian force

Extended Asia. From Euphrates

89 *field*: battlefield; see 'Events in history' p. vii.

92 *time's state*: situation at that time.

93 *jointing*: uniting.

94 *better issue*: greater success.

94–5 *from Italy . . . them*: drove them out of Italy.

96 *what worst*: what's the worst news.

101 *as*: just as though.
Labienus: In the events before the opening of the play, Labienus had been sent by Cassius into Parthia in order to raise troops to fight against Antony and Octavius (see 'Events in history' p. vii).

103 *Extended*: taken possession of (a legal term).
Euphrates: The stress is on the first syllable.

His conquering banner shook, from Syria
105 To Lydia, and to Ionia,
Whilst—

Antony
'Antony', thou wouldst say—
Messenger
O, my lord!
Antony
Speak to me home; mince not the general tongue;
Name Cleopatra as she is called in Rome;
Rail thou in Fulvia's phrase, and taunt my faults
110 With such full licence as both truth and malice
Have power to utter. Oh, then we bring forth weeds
When our quick minds lie still, and our ills told us
Is as our earing. Fare thee well awhile.
Messenger
At your noble pleasure.   [*Exit* Messenger

Enter another Messenger

Antony
115 From Sicyon how the news? Speak there!
Second Messenger
The man from Sicyon—
Antony
Is there such a one?
Second Messenger
He stays upon your will.
Antony
Let him appear.
                    [*Exit* Second Messenger
These strong Egyptian fetters I must break,
Or lose myself in dotage.

Enter another Messenger *with a letter*

What are you?
Third Messenger
120 Fulvia thy wife is dead.
Antony
Where died she?
Third Messenger
In Sicyon.
Her length of sickness, with what else more serious
Importeth thee to know, this bears.

107   *home*: plainly, frankly.
      mince . . . tongue: don't tone down what
      everybody is saying.
109   *Rail thou*: you abuse me.

111–13   *Oh, then . . . earing*: when energetic
         spirits are idle they go to waste like
         fields that lie fallow, but when the faults
         are pointed out to us it is like ploughing
         up ('earing') the land again.

116   *Sicyon*: a Greek city, north-west of
      Corinth.

117   *stays upon your will*: waits upon your
      orders.

124   *Importeth*: concerns you.

Gives him the letter

Antony

                                Forbear me.
                            [*Exit* Third Messenger

124 *Forbear me*: leave me alone.

125 There's a great spirit gone! Thus did I desire it.
What our contempts doth often hurl from us
We wish it ours again. The present pleasure,
By revolution lowering, does become
The opposite of itself. She's good, being gone.
130 The hand could pluck her back that shoved her on.
I must from this enchanting queen break off.
Ten thousand harms, more than the ills I know,
My idleness doth hatch. How now, Enobarbus!

126–7 *What . . . again*: we often wish we still
had those things which we once
despised and rejected.
128 *By revolution*: in course of time, as the
wheel of Fortune turns.
130 *could*: would like to; Antony begins to
feel guilty about his neglect of Fulvia.

Enter Enobarbus

Enobarbus
What's your pleasure, sir?

Antony
135 I must with haste from hence.

Enobarbus
Why then we kill all our women. We see how mortal
an unkindness is to them. If they suffer our
departure, death's the word.

136 *mortal*: deadly.

Antony
I must be gone.

Enobarbus
140 Under a compelling occasion let women die. It were
pity to cast them away for nothing, though between
them and a great cause they should be esteemed
nothing. Cleopatra, catching but the least noise of
this, dies instantly. I have seen her die twenty times
145 upon far poorer moment. I do think there is mettle
in death which commits some loving act upon her,
she hath such a celerity in dying.

140 *die*: Enobarbus prepares for word-play
on 'die' = achieve orgasm.

145 *mettle*: spirit, stimulation.

Antony
She is cunning past man's thought.

Enobarbus
Alack, sir, no; her passions are made of nothing but
150 the finest part of pure love. We cannot call her winds
and waters sighs and tears; they are greater storms
and tempests than almanacs can report. This cannot
be cunning in her. If it be, she makes a shower of rain
as well as Jove.

152 *almanacs*: weather forecasts (which were
printed, together with calendars and
astronomical predictions, in diaries sold
by pedlars).
154 *Jove*: Jupiter, the god responsible for the
rain and storms.

155 *Would*: I wish.

158 *discredited your travel*: lowered your reputation as a traveller.

164–8 *When . . . new*: Antony should take comfort at the thought that a dead wife, like a worn-out garment, can easily be replaced with a new one.

168–70 *members . . . cut . . . case*: Enobarbus continues his word-play with sexual innuendoes referring to the male organs . . . castration . . . vagina.

171 *smock*: woman's petticoat (= here, the woman herself).

174 *broached*: started off—but Enobarbus takes up the sense 'pierced, thrust through'.

179 *light*: smutty.
180 *break*: reveal, explain.
181 *expedience*: haste, urgency.
183 *touches*: concerns.
185 *contriving*: collaborating.

186 *at home*: to come home.
    Sextus Pompeius: the son of Pompey the Great—see 'Events in history' p. vii.

Antony
155 Would I had never seen her!
Enobarbus
O, sir, you had then left unseen a wonderful piece of work, which not to have been blest withal would have discredited your travel.
Antony
Fulvia is dead.
Enobarbus
160 Sir?
Antony
Fulvia is dead.
Enobarbus
Fulvia?
Antony
Dead.
Enobarbus
Why, sir, give the gods a thankful sacrifice. When it
165 pleaseth their deities to take the wife of a man from him, it shows to man the tailors of the earth; comforting therein, that when old robes are worn out, there are members to make new. If there were no more women but Fulvia, then had you indeed a
170 cut, and the case to be lamented. This grief is crowned with consolation: your old smock brings forth a new petticoat, and indeed the tears live in an onion that should water this sorrow.
Antony
The business she hath broached in the state
175 Cannot endure my absence.
Enobarbus
And the business you have broached here cannot be without you, especially that of Cleopatra's, which wholly depends on your abode.
Antony
No more light answers. Let our officers
180 Have notice what we purpose. I shall break
The cause of our expedience to the queen
And get her leave to part. For not alone
The death of Fulvia, with more urgent touches,
Do strongly speak to us, but the letters too
185 Of many our contriving friends in Rome
Petition us at home. Sextus Pompeius

187 *given the dare to*: acted in defiance of.
188 *slippery*: unreliable, fickle.

190 *throw*: give the title.
193 *blood and life*: spirit and energy.
    stands up: presents himself as.
194 *the main*: the greatest.
    whose . . . on: if he continues in this
    way.
195 *The . . . danger*: may threaten the
    international balance of power.
196 *the courser's hair*: Antony refers to the
    belief that a single horse-hair, put into a
    bucket of river water, moves and comes
    alive.
197-8 *Say . . . hence*: tell my officers—those
    who need to know—that we must get
    away from here quickly.

Hath given the dare to Caesar and commands
The empire of the sea. Our slippery people,
Whose love is never link'd to the deserver
190 Till his deserts are past, begin to throw
'Pompey the Great' and all his dignities
Upon his son, who, high in name and power,
Higher than both in blood and life, stands up
For the main soldier; whose quality going on,
195 The sides o'th' world may danger. Much is breeding
Which, like the courser's hair, hath yet but life
And not a serpent's poison. Say our pleasure,
To such whose place is under us, requires
Our quick remove from hence.
          Enobarbus
200 I shall do't.
                              [*Exeunt*

Act 1   Scene 3

Cleopatra reveals some of her tactics for
keeping a man—but Antony is resolute and
eventually Cleopatra resigns herself to his
departure.

4 *I . . . you*: don't tell him I sent you.

8 *hold*: practise, follow.

Scene 3

        Alexandria: enter Cleopatra, Charmian,
        Alexas, *and* Iras
    Cleopatra
Where is he?
    Charmian
I did not see him since.
    Cleopatra
[*To* Alexas] See where he is, who's with him, what
    he does.
I did not send you. If you find him sad,
5 Say I am dancing; if in mirth, report
That I am sudden sick. Quick, and return.
                              [*Exit* Alexas
    Charmian
Madam, methinks if you did love him dearly,
You do not hold the method to enforce
The like from him.
    Cleopatra
                    What should I do I do not?
    Charmian
10 In each thing give him way; cross him in nothing.

Cleopatra
Thou teachest like a fool: the way to lose him.
Charmian
Tempt him not so too far; I wish, forbear.
In time we hate that which we often fear.

Enter Antony

But here comes Antony.
Cleopatra
                          I am sick and sullen.
Antony
15 I am sorry to give breathing to my purpose—
Cleopatra
Help me away, dear Charmian! I shall fall!
It cannot be thus long; the sides of nature
Will not sustain it.
Antony
                          Now, my dearest queen—
Cleopatra
Pray you, stand farther from me!
Antony
                                        What's the matter?
Cleopatra
20 I know by that same eye there's some good news.
What, says the married woman you may go?
Would she had never given you leave to come!
Let her not say 'tis I that keep you here.
I have no power upon you; hers you are.
Antony
25 The gods best know—
Cleopatra
                          Oh, never was there queen
So mightily betray'd! Yet at the first
I saw the treasons planted.
Antony
                                        Cleopatra—
Cleopatra
Why should I think you can be mine and true—
Though you in swearing shake the throned gods—
30 Who have been false to Fulvia? Riotous madness,
To be entangled with those mouth-made vows
Which break themselves in swearing!

12 *Tempt*: provoke.

14 *sullen*: depressed.

15 *to give . . . purpose*: to have to tell you, say what I'm going to do.

17–18 *the sides . . . sustain it*: I can only take so much.

20 *that same eye*: the way you're looking at me.
21 *the married woman*: i.e. Fulvia.

29 *Though . . . gods*: When Jupiter swore an oath, a tremor shook Mount Olympus, the habitation of the gods.
31 *mouth-made*: merely verbal.

Antony

Most sweet queen—

Cleopatra

Nay, pray you seek no colour for your going,
But bid farewell and go. When you sued staying,
35 Then was the time for words; no going then.
Eternity was in our lips and eyes,
Bliss in our brows' bent; none our parts so poor
But was a race of heaven. They are so still,
Or thou, the greatest soldier of the world,
40 Art turn'd the greatest liar.

Antony

How now, lady?

Cleopatra

I would I had thy inches! Thou shouldst know
There were a heart in Egypt!

Antony

Hear me, queen.
The strong necessity of time commands
Our services awhile, but my full heart
45 Remains in use with you. Our Italy
Shines o'er with civil swords; Sextus Pompeius
Makes his approaches to the port of Rome;
Equality of two domestic powers
Breed scrupulous faction; the hated, grown to
    strength,
50 Are newly grown to love; the condemn'd Pompey,
Rich in his father's honour, creeps apace
Into the hearts of such as have not thriv'd
Upon the present state, whose numbers threaten;
And quietness, grown sick of rest, would purge
55 By any desperate change. My more particular,
And that which most with you should safe my going,
Is Fulvia's death.

Cleopatra

Though age from folly could not give me freedom,
It does from childishness. Can Fulvia die?

Antony

60 She's dead, my queen. [*Gives her the letters*]
Look here, and at thy sovereign leisure read
The garboils she awak'd. At the last, best,
See when and where she died.

33 *colour*: pretext, excuse.

34 *sued staying*: begged to be allowed to stay.

36–8 *Eternity . . . heaven*: Cleopatra is quoting Antony's own words to her.

36 *our*: my; Cleopatra uses the royal plural.

37 *our brows' bent*: the arch of my eyebrows.

38 *race of heaven*: heavenly in its origin.

42 *a heart in Egypt*: some courage here; Cleopatra may refer either to the country or to its queen, herself.

45 *in use with you*: in your keeping.

46 *civil swords*: the swords of civil war.

47 *the port of Rome*: i.e. Ostia, the sea-port serving Rome.

48–9 'To have two equal parties within one country creates factions that will disagree over the smallest detail.'

49 *grown to strength*: now that they have become powerful.

50 *condemn'd*: outlawed; Sextus Pompeius was conquered by Julius Caesar soon after the battle of Pharsalia (see 'Events in history' p. vii).

51 *Rich . . . honour*: Sextus Pompeius is benefiting from the reputation of his father, Pompey the Great.
apace: rapidly.

53 *Upon . . . state*: under the present administration.

54 *quietness*: peace.
rest: idleness.

54–5 *would . . . change*: must be cured by drastic means.

55 *particular*: personal motive.

56 *safe my going*: guarantee that my going will not affect you.

62 *garboils*: troubles, disturbances.
best: best news; *or* (if the word is addressed to Cleopatra) my dearest.

64 *sacred vials*: tear-bottles, lachrymatories. Such bottles have been found in Roman tombs and are thought to have contained the tears of mourners, offered in tribute to the dead.

68 *bear*: intend.

69 *the fire*: i.e. the sun (which dries up the floodwater and thus fertilizes the Nile valley).

72 *as thou affects*: whichever way you want it.
    Cut my lace: i.e. the lace of her tightly fitting bodice; Cleopatra struggles for breath.

74 *So Antony loves*: as long as Antony loves me—*or*, depending on whether or not Antony loves me.

76 *So Fulvia told me*: so I can see from the way you behave about Fulvia.

79 *Egypt*: i.e. the queen of Egypt.

82 *meetly*: pretty good.

83 *target*: shield.
    mends: is getting better.

85 *Herculean*: Plutarch says that there was a tradition that Antony's family was descended from the mythical superman Hercules.

85–6 *does . . . chafe*: acts out his performance of anger.

91 *I would*: I wanted to say.

92 'My forgetfulness is as unreliable as Antony himself.'

93 *I am all forgotten*: I've forgotten everything, *and/or*, I've been completely forgotten.

93–4 *But . . . subject*: if it were not for the fact that your majesty is completely in control of all this silliness.

95–7 *sweating labour . . . this*: Cleopatra compares the heartache she is suffering (which Antony calls 'idleness') to the pains of a woman in childbirth.

98 *becomings*: charms, attractions.

99 *Eye well*: look good in your eyes.

Cleopatra

                O most false love!
Where be the sacred vials thou shouldst fill
65 With sorrowful water? Now I see, I see,
In Fulvia's death how mine receiv'd shall be.

    Antony
Quarrel no more, but be prepar'd to know
The purposes I bear; which are, or cease,
As you shall give th'advice. By the fire
70 That quickens Nilus' slime, I go from hence
Thy soldier, servant, making peace or war
As thou affects.

    Cleopatra
             Cut my lace, Charmian, come!
But let it be; I am quickly ill and well—
So Antony loves.

    Antony
           My precious queen, forbear,
75 And give true evidence to his love, which stands
An honourable trial.

    Cleopatra
           So Fulvia told me.
I prithee, turn aside and weep for her,
Then bid adieu to me, and say the tears
Belong to Egypt. Good now, play one scene
80 Of excellent dissembling, and let it look
Like perfect honour.

    Antony
          You'll heat my blood. No more.

    Cleopatra
You can do better yet, but this is meetly.

    Antony
Now by my sword—

    Cleopatra
          And target. Still he mends,
But this is not the best. Look, prithee, Charmian,
85 How this Herculean Roman does become
The carriage of his chafe.

    Antony
I'll leave you, lady.

    Cleopatra
Courteous lord, one word:
Sir, you and I must part, but that's not it;

101–3 *Upon . . . feet*: Cleopatra pictures
    Antony as the conquering hero, bearing
    a laurel wreath and treading on the
    rushes strewn in the path of his
    triumphal procession.
102 *laurel victory*: the laurel wreath of
    victory.
104–6 *Our separation . . . thee*: Although they
    will be physically separated, they will be
    together in spirit.

90 Sir, you and I have lov'd, but there's not it;
That you know well. Something it is I would—
Oh, my oblivion is a very Antony,
And I am all forgotten!
    Antony
                        But that your royalty
Holds idleness your subject, I should take you
95 For idleness itself.
    Cleopatra
                    'Tis sweating labour
To bear such idleness so near the heart
As Cleopatra this. But, sir, forgive me,
Since my becomings kill me when they do not
Eye well to you. Your honour calls you hence;
100 Therefore be deaf to my unpitied folly,
And all the gods go with you! Upon your sword
Sit laurel victory, and smooth success
Be strew'd before your feet!
    Antony
                        Let us go. Come.
Our separation so abides and flies
105 That thou, residing here, goes yet with me,
And I, hence fleeting, here remain with thee.
Away!

                                    [*Exeunt*

Act 1   Scene 4

Caesar and Lepidus, the other members of the Roman triumvirate, discuss the reports of Antony's conduct in Egypt. Caesar is censorious but Lepidus, mindful of Antony's accomplishments, can be tolerant of his failings. When they hear the latest news of threats to Rome, Caesar calls for action.

3 *competitor*: associate, colleague.

5 *the . . . night*: This could be a poetic expression for the stars—but the prosaic and economical Caesar is probably thinking of oil-burning lamps.

6 *queen of Ptolemy*: Cleopatra was a member of the Ptolemy dynasty and (in accordance with Egyptian custom) had been married to two of her own brothers.

7 *gave audience*: listened to my messengers.

8 *there*: i.e. in the letter.

9 *abstract*: embodiment, epitome.

12 *spots of heaven*: i.e. the stars.

14 *purchas'd*: acquired, of his own choosing. Lepidus uses the legal terms that make distinction between property that has been inherited and that which is obtained by other means.

18 *mirth*: joke.

19 *keep . . . tippling*: share the drinking rounds.

20 *reel*: stagger about.
    stand the buffet: knock about.

22 *As . . . indeed*: although it would be a most remarkable personality.

24 *foils*: failings, disgrace.

25 *weight*: responsibility.
    in his lightness: because of his frivolity.

26 *vacancy*: spare time.
    voluptuousness: riotous living.

27–8 *Full surfeits . . . for't*: let him pay the price for it with upset stomachs and venereal diseases (drying of the bones was thought to be an effect of syphillis).

28 *confound*: waste.

29 *drums*: summons (as with a drum).

Scene 4

> *Rome: enter* Octavius Caesar *reading a letter,* Lepidus, *and their train*

Caesar
You may see, Lepidus, and henceforth know,
It is not Caesar's natural vice to hate
Our great competitor. From Alexandria
This is the news: he fishes, drinks, and wastes
5 The lamps of night in revel; is not more manlike
Than Cleopatra, nor the queen of Ptolemy
More womanly than he; hardly gave audience, or
Vouchsaf'd to think he had partners. You shall find there
A man who is the abstract of all faults
10 That all men follow.

Lepidus
                              I must not think there are
Evils enough to darken all his goodness.
His faults, in him, seem as the spots of heaven,
More fiery by night's blackness; hereditary
Rather than purchas'd; what he cannot change
15 Than what he chooses.

Caesar
You are too indulgent. Let's grant it is not
Amiss to tumble on the bed of Ptolemy,
To give a kingdom for a mirth, to sit
And keep the turn of tippling with a slave,
20 To reel the streets at noon, and stand the buffet
With knaves that smells of sweat. Say this becomes him—
As his composure must be rare indeed
Whom these things cannot blemish—yet must Antony
No way excuse his foils, when we do bear
25 So great weight in his lightness. If he fill'd
His vacancy with his voluptuousness,
Full surfeits and the dryness of his bones
Call on him for't. But to confound such time
That drums him from his sport, and speaks as loud

30 *his . . . ours*: all our positions (as
   triumvirs).
   'tis to be chid: it must be reprimanded.
31 *rate*: scold, chide.
   mature in knowledge: old enough to
   know better.
32 *Pawn . . . pleasure*: sacrifice everything
   they have learned for the sake of some
   immediate pleasure.
33 *to*: against.

40 *Give him*: say that he [Pompey] is.

41 *from . . . state*: ever since government
   began.
42 *he which . . . were*: the man who is now
   in power had his supporters until he
   reached that power.
43 *the ebb'd man*: the man who is on his
   way out—i.e. losing power.
44 *common body*: general public.
45 *vagabond flag*: drifting reed.
46–7 *Goes . . . motion*: floats forwards and
   backwards according to the ebb and
   flow of the tide, like a page ('lackey') at
   his master's heels.
47 *motion*: movement.
49 *famous*: notorious.
50 *ear*: plough.
51 *keels*: ships.
   hot inroads: destructive raids.
52 *borders maritime*: coastal areas.
53 *Lack blood*: turn pale (with fear).
   flush youth revolt: hotheaded young men;
   Plutarch says these were 'desirous of
   gain and service, not caring under
   whom they went.'
55–6 *Pompey's name . . . resisted*: the very
   name of Pompey causes more damage
   than if we had declared war and fought
   against him.
57 *wassails*: orgies, revelry.
57–69 Caesar recalls Antony's former glory;
   see 'Plutarch', p. 143.

30 As his own state and ours, 'tis to be chid
As we rate boys who, being mature in knowledge,
Pawn their experience to their present pleasure
And so rebel to judgement.

Enter a Messenger

Lepidus
                              Here's more news.
Messenger
Thy biddings have been done, and every hour,
35 Most noble Caesar, shalt thou have report
How 'tis abroad. Pompey is strong at sea,
And it appears he is belov'd of those
That only have fear'd Caesar. To the ports
The discontents repair, and men's reports
40 Give him much wrong'd.
Caesar
                    I should have known no less.
It hath been taught us from the primal state
That he which is was wish'd until he were,
And the ebb'd man, ne'er lov'd till ne'er worth love,
Comes dear'd by being lack'd. This common body,
45 Like to a vagabond flag upon the stream,
Goes to and back, lackeying the varying tide,
To rot itself with motion.

Enter another Messenger

Second Messenger
Caesar, I bring thee word
Menecrates and Menas, famous pirates,
50 Makes the sea serve them, which they ear and
   wound
With keels of every kind. Many hot inroads
They make in Italy—the borders maritime
Lack blood to think on't—and flush youth revolt.
No vessel can peep forth but 'tis as soon
55 Taken as seen; for Pompey's name strikes more
Than could his war resisted.
Caesar
                    Antony,
Leave thy lascivious wassails! When thou once
Was beaten from Modena, where thou slew'st
Hirtius and Pansa, consuls, at thy heel

63 *stale*: urine.
  gilded: golden in colour.
64 *deign*: condescend to eat.

65 *rudest*: wildest, least cultivated.

67 *browsed*: browsèd.

72 *So . . . not*: didn't even get thin.

79–80 *Both . . . time*: what forces I can
  muster, both by sea and by land, to
  deal with this present situation.

83 *stirs*: stirrings, events.

85 *I knew . . . bond*: I know what is my
  duty.

60 Did famine follow, whom thou fought'st against,
Though daintily brought up, with patience more
Than savages could suffer. Thou didst drink
The stale of horses and the gilded puddle
Which beasts would cough at. Thy palate then did
    deign
65 The roughest berry on the rudest hedge.
Yea, like the stag when snow the pasture sheets,
The barks of trees thou browsed. On the Alps,
It is reported, thou didst eat strange flesh
Which some did die to look on. And all this—
70 It wounds thine honour that I speak it now—
Was borne so like a soldier that thy cheek
So much as lank'd not.
        Lepidus
'Tis pity of him.
        Caesar
                    Let his shames quickly
Drive him to Rome. 'Tis time we twain
75 Did show ourselves i'th'field, and to that end
Assemble we immediate council. Pompey
Thrives in our idleness.
        Lepidus
                        Tomorrow, Caesar,
I shall be furnish'd to inform you rightly
Both what by sea and land I can be able
80 To front this present time.
        Caesar
                        Till which encounter,
It is my business too. Farewell.
        Lepidus
Farewell, my lord. What you shall know meantime
Of stirs abroad, I shall beseech you, sir,
To let me be partaker.
        Caesar
                    Doubt not, sir.
85 I knew it for my bond.
                    [*Exeunt by different doors*

Act 1   Scene 5

Cleopatra's lonely boredom is relieved when
Alexas brings greetings from Antony, sent as
he started his journey to Rome.

Scene 5

> *Alexandria: enter* Cleopatra, Charmian,
> Iras, *and* Mardian

Cleopatra
Charmian!

Charmian
Madam?

Cleopatra
[*Yawns*] Ha, ha.
Give me to drink mandragora.

4 *mandragora*: a narcotic derived from the
flower of the mandrake plant.

Charmian
                                      Why, madam?

Cleopatra
5 That I might sleep out this great gap of time
My Antony is away.

Charmian
You think of him too much.

Cleopatra
Oh, 'tis treason!

Charmian
                          Madam, I trust not so.

Cleopatra
Thou, eunuch Mardian!

Mardian
                                  What's your highness' pleasure?

10 *sing*: The eunuch's voice (castrato) was
highly valued in courts and choirs.

Cleopatra
10 Not now to hear thee sing. I take no pleasure
In aught an eunuch has. 'Tis well for thee
That, being unseminar'd, thy freer thoughts
May not fly forth of Egypt. Hast thou affections?

12 *unseminar'd*: castrated, emasculated.
freer: less restrained, unrepressed.
13 *affections*: feelings, desires.

Mardian
Yes, gracious madam.

Cleopatra
15 Indeed?

Mardian
Not in deed, madam, for I can do nothing
But what indeed is honest to be done.
Yet have I fierce affections, and think
What Venus did with Mars.

16 *do*: perform.
17 *honest*: chaste.
19 *What . . . Mars*: Venus (the goddess of
love) and Mars (the god of war) were
trapped together in the act of love when
Vulcan (Venus's husband) threw a net
over their bed and called all the other
gods to witness their ignominy.

Cleopatra
                                  O, Charmian,
20 Where think'st thou he is now? Stands he, or sits he?

23 *bravely*: magnificently.
   wot'st thou: are you aware of.
24 *demi-Atlas*: In classical mythology, Atlas
   was said to support the whole world on
   his shoulders; Cleopatra recognizes that
   Antony shares *his* responsibility with
   Caesar (she ignores Lepidus).
24–5 *arm And burgonet*: i.e. the complete
   soldier to champion and defend.
25 *burgonet*: helmet with visor so fitted to
   the head-piece that the head could be
   turned without exposing the neck.
28–30 *Think . . . time*: Cleopatra may be
   questioning her own self-delusion (i.e.
   'why should he be thinking about
   me . . . ?'). The Folio text has no
   question mark, which could possibly
   make the words an injunction to
   Antony.
29 *Phoebus*: Phoebus Apollo, god of the
   sun.
30–2 *Broad-fronted Caesar . . . great Pompey*:
   Cleopatra's lovers had included both
   Julius Caesar (who is usually depicted
   with a broad forehead) and Gnaeus
   Pompey, the son of Pompey the Great,
   and brother to the play's Sextus
   Pompey.
34 *aspect*: (stressed on the second syllable)
   gaze.
   die: faint with ecstasy, have an orgasm.

Or does he walk? Or is he on his horse?
O happy horse, to bear the weight of Antony!
Do bravely, horse, for wot'st thou whom thou
   mov'st?
The demi-Atlas of this earth, the arm
25 And burgonet of men! He's speaking now,
Or murmuring 'Where's my serpent of old Nile?'
For so he calls me. Now I feed myself
With most delicious poison. Think on me
That am with Phoebus' amorous pinches black
30 And wrinkled deep in time? Broad-fronted Caesar,
When thou wast here above the ground, I was
A morsel for a monarch; and great Pompey
Would stand and make his eyes grow in my brow;
There would he anchor his aspect, and die
35 With looking on his life.

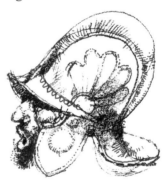

Enter Alexas *from* Antony

Alexas
Sovereign of Egypt, hail!
   Cleopatra
How much unlike art thou Mark Antony!
Yet, coming from him, that great medicine hath
With his tinct gilded thee.
40 How goes it with my brave Mark Antony?
   Alexas
Last thing he did, dear queen,
He kiss'd—the last of many doubled kisses—
This orient pearl. His speech sticks in my heart.
   Cleopatra
Mine ear must pluck it thence.

38 *that great medicine*: Cleopatra refers to
   the elixir of life—a term from alchemy
   for the concoction that would (if it were
   ever found) change base metal into
   gold.
39 *tinct*: colouring.

43 *orient*: lustrous—a description usually
   given to pearls from the East, which
   had a deeper sheen than those found in
   the West.

Alexas

                                    'Good friend,' quoth he,
45 'Say the firm Roman to great Egypt sends
This treasure of an oyster, at whose foot,
To mend this petty present, I will piece
Her opulent throne with kingdoms. All the East,
Say thou, shall call her mistress.' So he nodded
50 And soberly did mount an arm-gaunt steed
Who neigh'd so high that what I would have spoke
Was beastly dumb'd by him.
    Cleopatra
What, was he sad or merry?
    Alexas
Like to the time o'th' year between the extremes
55 Of hot and cold, he was nor sad nor merry.
    Cleopatra
O well-divided disposition! Note him,
Note him, good Charmian, 'tis the man; but note
    him!
He was not sad, for he would shine on those
That make their looks by his; he was not merry,
60 Which seem'd to tell them his remembrance lay
In Egypt with his joy; but between both.
O heavenly mingle! Be'st thou sad or merry,
The violence of either thee becomes,
So does it no man else. Met'st thou my posts?
    Alexas
65 Ay, madam, twenty several messengers.
Why do you send so thick?
    Cleopatra
                                    Who's born that day
When I forget to send to Antony
Shall die a beggar. Ink and paper, Charmian!
Welcome, my good Alexas! Did I, Charmian,
70 Ever love Caesar so?
    Charmian
                                    O that brave Caesar!
    Cleopatra
Be chok'd with such another emphasis!
Say, 'the brave Antony'.
    Charmian
                                    The valiant Caesar!

45 *firm*: constant, loyal.

47 *piece*: reinforce, complete.

50 *arm-gaunt steed*: noble war-horse; Shakespeare's adjective seems to defy definition—or perhaps the compositors of the Folio text misread their manuscript!

52 *beastly dumb'd*: rendered inaudible by the creature, *or*, reduced to beast-like silence.

57 *'tis the man*: that's just like him.

59 *That make . . . his*: whose attitudes are guided by his.

63 *thee becomes*: is becoming to you, suits you.
64 *posts*: messengers.

65 *several*: different.
66 *so thick*: in such numbers.

70 *brave*: splendid.

74 *paragon*: set side by side as a model.

76 *I . . . you*: I'm only saying what you said
   yourself.
   salad days: In the next line Cleopatra
   herself explains the meaning of her
   expression.
77 *green*: inexperienced.
   cold in blood: sexually immature.

80 *several*: separate.

Cleopatra
By Isis, I will give thee bloody teeth
If thou with Caesar paragon again
75 My man of men!
   Charmian
                  By your most gracious pardon,
I sing but after you.
   Cleopatra
                  My salad days,
When I was green in judgement, cold in blood,
To say as I said then. But come, away,
Get me ink and paper!
80 He shall have every day a several greeting
Or I'll unpeople Egypt!
                                          [*Exeunt*

Act 2

The pirate Pompey, unaware of the new
solidarity between Caesar and Antony,
rejoices in his own naval strength—until he
hears the news from Rome.

3   *they*: i.e. the gods; Menecrates speaks a
proverb: 'Delays are not denials'.
4–5 *Whiles . . . sue for*: whilst we are
praying to the gods, the thing that we
pray for is wasting away.
5–8 *We . . . prayers*: Shakespeare gives to
Menecrates the words of the Bible:
'Likewise the spirit also helpeth our
infirmities. For we know not what we
should pray for as we ought' (Romans
8:26).

10 *crescent*: swelling; Pompey's metaphor of
the moon is developed in the next line.
auguring: prophetic.
13 *without doors*: out of doors (i.e. away
from Cleopatra's bed).
13–14 *Caesar . . . hearts*: Caesar's heavy
taxes are losing him supporters.
15 *neither loves*: loves neither.

17 *in the field*: already engaged in military
operations.

18 *Where . . . this*: where did you learn this.

Scene 1

> *Sicily*: *enter* Pompey, Menecrates, *and*
> Menas *in warlike manner*

Pompey
If the great gods be just, they shall assist
The deeds of justest men.
Menecrates
                              Know, worthy Pompey,
That what they do delay they not deny.
Pompey
Whiles we are suitors to their throne, decays
5 The thing we sue for.
Menecrates
                              We, ignorant of ourselves,
Beg often our own harms, which the wise powers
Deny us for our good; so find we profit
By losing of our prayers.
Pompey
                              I shall do well.
The people love me, and the sea is mine;
10 My powers are crescent, and my auguring hope
Says it will come to th' full. Mark Antony
In Egypt sits at dinner, and will make
No wars without doors; Caesar gets money where
He loses hearts; Lepidus flatters both,
15 Of both is flatter'd; but he neither loves,
Nor either cares for him.
Menas
                              Caesar and Lepidus
Are in the field. A mighty strength they carry.
Pompey
Where have you this? 'Tis false.

Menas

From Silvius, sir.

Pompey

He dreams. I know they are in Rome together,
20 Looking for Antony. But all the charms of love,
Salt Cleopatra, soften thy wan'd lip!
Let witchcraft join with beauty, lust with both;
Tie up the libertine in a field of feasts;
Keep his brain fuming. Epicurean cooks
25 Sharpen with cloyless sauce his appetite
That sleep and feeding may prorogue his honour
Even till a Lethe'd dullness—

Enter Varrius

How now, Varrius?

Varrius

This is most certain that I shall deliver:
Mark Antony is every hour in Rome
30 Expected. Since he went from Egypt 'tis
A space for farther travel.

Pompey

I could have given less matter
A better ear. Menas, I did not think
This amorous surfeiter would have donn'd his helm
35 For such a petty war. His soldiership
Is twice the other twain. But let us rear
The higher our opinion, that our stirring
Can from the lap of Egypt's widow pluck
The ne'er-lust-wearie'd Antony.

Menas

I cannot hope
40 Caesar and Antony shall well greet together.
His wife that's dead did trespasses to Caesar;
His brother warr'd upon him, although I think
Not mov'd by Antony.

Pompey

I know not, Menas,
How lesser enmities may give way to greater.
45 Were't not that we stand up against them all,
'Twere pregnant they should square between them-
selves,
For they have entertained cause enough
To draw their swords. But how the fear of us

---

20 *Looking for*: hoping for, expecting.
21 *Salt*: lecherous, raunchy.
   wan'd: Pompey applies his moon metaphor to describe Cleopatra's fading charms.
24 *fuming*: befuddled (with alcohol).
   Epicurean cooks: gourmet chefs.
25 *cloyless sauce*: sauce that never satiates.
26 *prorogue*: stall, baulk.
   his honour: what his sense of honour will force him to do.
27 *a Lethe'd dullness*: Those who drank from the river Lethe (in the Underworld of classical mythology) became completely oblivious of everything in their past lives.

31 *A . . . travel*: time to travel even farther than Rome.
32-3 *I could . . . ear*: I would rather have heard some better news.

35 *soldiership*: military experience.
36-7 *rear . . . opinion*: raise our opinion of ourselves.
38 *Egypt's widow*: See note to *Act 1, Scene 4, line 6*.
39 *ne'er-lust-wearie'd*: sexually insatiable.
   hope: expect.
40 *well greet*: get on well.
41-3 *his wife . . . Antony*: see 1, 2, 89–95 and 'Events in history', p. vii.
41 *trespasses to*: offences against.
43 *mov'd*: encouraged.

45 *stand up against*: oppose.
46 *'Twere . . . square*: it would be pretty obvious that they would fall out.
47 *entertained . . . enough*: entertainèd; given each other enough provocation.

49 *cement*: cément.

51–2 *It only . . . hands*: all we can do now is
to fight with all we've got in a matter of
life and death.

> May cement their divisions, and bind up
> 50 The petty difference, we yet not know.
> Be't as our gods will have't! It only stands
> Our lives upon to use our strongest hands.
> Come, Menas.
>
> [Exeunt

Act 2   Scene 2

Cautiously Caesar and Antony make their
first approaches to each other, watched by
their supporters. Both are reluctant to
disclose the thoughts that are uppermost in
their minds, but they are eventually
persuaded to forget their quarrels in the face
of the present crisis. Agrippa's proposal of a
marriage between Antony and Octavia is
generally welcomed as being a more lasting
solution to their differences. But Enobarbus
ends the scene with a powerful reminder of
Cleopatra.

4 *like himself*: in his own way.
move: anger.
5–8 *Let . . . today*: Antony can afford to
treat Caesar with contempt because he
has the power of Mars, the god of war,
and could dare Caesar to pluck his
beard (a sign of defiance). Enobarbus
uses the familiar form, 'Antonio', in
affectionate respect.
9 *private stomaching*: personal resentments.
9–10 *Every . . . in't*: there's always a right
time for everything.

14/15s.d. Antony and Caesar enter from
different sides of the stage, each
apparently deep in conversation.

Scene 2

Rome: enter Enobarbus and Lepidus

Lepidus
Good Enobarbus, 'tis a worthy deed,
And shall become you well, to entreat your captain
To soft and gentle speech.
Enobarbus
                                   I shall entreat him
To answer like himself. If Caesar move him,
5 Let Antony look over Caesar's head
And speak as loud as Mars. By Jupiter,
Were I the wearer of Antonio's beard,
I would not shave't today!
Lepidus
                                   'Tis not a time
For private stomaching.
Enobarbus
                                   Every time
10 Serves for the matter that is then born in't.
Lepidus
But small to greater matters must give way.
Enobarbus
Not if the small come first.
Lepidus
                                   Your speech is passion;
But pray you stir no embers up. Here comes
The noble Antony.

Enter Antony and Ventidius

Enobarbus
                                   And yonder Caesar.

Enter Caesar, Maecenas, *and* Agrippa

Antony

15 If we compose well here, to Parthia.
Hark, Ventidius.

Caesar

I do not know, Maecenas. Ask Agrippa.

Lepidus

Noble friends,
That which combin'd us was most great, and let not

20 A leaner action rend us. What's amiss,
May it be gently heard. When we debate
Our trivial difference loud, we do commit
Murder in healing wounds. Then, noble partners,
The rather for I earnestly beseech,

25 Touch you the sourest points with sweetest terms,
Nor curstness grow to th' matter.

Antony

                           'Tis spoken well.

Were we before our armies, and to fight,
I should do thus.

Flourish

Caesar

Welcome to Rome.

Antony

30 Thank you.

Caesar

Sit.

Antony

Sit, sir.

Caesar

Nay then.

Caesar sits, then Antony

Antony

I learn you take things ill which are not so,

35 Or being, concern you not.

Caesar

                         I must be laugh'd at

If, or for nothing or a little, I
Should say myself offended, and with you

---

15 'If we can come to some satisfactory agreement here, we can set out for Parthia.'

20 *leaner*: less important.

23 *healing*: trying to heal.
24 'Especially since it is I who am asking it in all earnestness.'
25 *Touch*: discuss.
26 'And don't add your bad temper to our problems.'

27 *to*: ready to.
28 *thus*: Antony offers some gesture of peace and reconciliation, which is signalled by a fanfare on the trumpets.

34 *take . . . so*: find faults where there are none.
35 *Or being . . . not*: or if there is something wrong, it's none of your business.
I must . . . at: I would be a fool.
36 *or . . . or*: either . . . or.
37 *say myself*: say that I was.

38 *more laugh'd at*: even more of a fool.

39 *derogately*: disparagingly, disrespectfully.

44 *practise on my state*: plot against my authority.

45 *my question*: be of some concern to me.
   intend: mean by.

46 *catch at*: get some idea of.

47 *befall me*: happen to me.

48–9 *their . . . war*: their uprising was all on account of you; you gave them the cause to fight.

51 *urge . . . act*: use me as a pretext for what he was doing.
   enquire: look into.

52 *true reports*: reliable sources.

53 *drew . . . with you*: were fighting against you.

54 *Discredit*: flout, defy.
   with: along with, as well as.

55 *stomach*: wishes, inclinations.

56 *Having . . . cause*: having the same interests as you.

57 *satisfy*: assure, inform.

57–9 *If you'll . . . this*: if you are determined to pick a quarrel, you have plenty of material to do it with and you must not use this scrap.

61 *patch'd up*: worked up, concocted.

62 *lack*: fail to understand.

65–6 *Could . . . peace*: could not look favourably on wars that threatened my own security.

Chiefly i'th' world; more laugh'd at that I should
Once name you derogately when to sound your
    name
40 It not concern'd me.
        Antony   My being in Egypt, Caesar,
What was't to you?
        Caesar
No more than my residing here at Rome
Might be to you in Egypt. Yet if you there
Did practise on my state, your being in Egypt
45 Might be my question.
        Antony   How intend you, 'practis'd'?
        Caesar
You may be pleas'd to catch at mine intent
By what did here befall me. Your wife and brother
Made wars upon me, and their contestation
Was theme for you; you were the word of war.
        Antony
50 You do mistake your business. My brother never
Did urge me in his act. I did enquire it,
And have my learning from some true reports
That drew their swords with you. Did he not rather
Discredit my authority with yours,
55 And make the wars alike against my stomach,
Having alike your cause? Of this my letters
Before did satisfy you. If you'll patch a quarrel,
As matter whole you have to make it with,
It must not be with this.
        Caesar   You praise yourself
60 By laying defects of judgement to me, but
You patch'd up your excuses.
        Antony   Not so, not so!
I know you could not lack—I am certain on't—
Very necessity of this thought, that I,
Your partner in the cause 'gainst which he fought,
65 Could not with graceful eyes attend those wars
Which fronted mine own peace. As for my wife,
I would you had her spirit in such another.

68 *snaffle*: the lightest bridle-bit.
69 *pace*: control, direct.

The third o'th' world is yours, which with a snaffle
You may pace easy, but not such a wife.
                    Enobarbus
70 Would we had all such wives, that the men might go
    to wars with the women!
                    Antony
    So much uncurbable, her garboils, Caesar,

72 *uncurbable*: uncontrollable (even with a
    curbed bit).
    garboils: troubles, disturbances.
73–4 *not . . . policy*: were not without some
    political acumen.
75–6 *you . . . say*: you have to admit.

    Made out of her impatience—which not wanted
    Shrewdness of policy too—I grieving grant
75 Did you too much disquiet. For that, you must
    But say I could not help it.
                    Caesar
                            I wrote to you
    When rioting in Alexandria. You

78 *pocket up*: just put in your pocket (i.e.
    without reading).
79 *gibe . . . audience*: scorn my messenger
    out of your presence.

    Did pocket up my letters, and with taunts
    Did gibe my missive out of audience.
                    Antony
                                    Sir,

80 *fell . . . then*: at that moment he took me
    by surprise when he had not been
    properly admitted to me.
81–2 *did want . . . morning*: had a hangover
    the next morning.
83 *of myself*: what a state I had been in.
84–6 *Let . . . wipe him*: don't bring that
    fellow into it; if we're going to argue,
    leave him out of the business.

80 He fell upon me ere admitted, then.
    Three kings I had newly feasted, and did want
    Of what I was i'th' morning. But next day
    I told him of myself, which was as much
    As to have ask'd him pardon. Let this fellow
85 Be nothing of our strife; if we contend,
    Out of our question wipe him.
                    Caesar
                            You have broken
    The article of your oath, which you shall never
    Have tongue to charge me with.
                    Lepidus

89 *Soft*: carefully, go easy.

    Soft, Caesar!
                    Antony
90 No, Lepidus, let him speak.
    The honour is sacred which he talks on now,

92 *Supposing . . . it*: suggesting that I am
    deficient in it.
94–5 *To lend . . . rather*: This is Caesar's
    main charge against Antony—and
    Antony is evasive.

    Supposing that I lack'd it. But on, Caesar:
    'The article of my oath—'
                    Caesar
    To lend me arms and aid when I requir'd them,
95 The which you both denied.
                    Antony
                            Neglected, rather;

96–7 *bound . . . knowledge*: got me so
    incapacitated that I didn't know what
    was going on.
97 *As . . . may*: as far as I can.
98 *play the penitent*: apologize.
    honesty: i.e. in acknowledging my fault.
99 *make . . . greatness*: diminish my
    authority.
99–100 *my power . . . without it*: my
    authority will not be used without
    honesty.

105 *enforce*: urge, press.
106 *griefs*: grievances.
106–8 *to forget . . . you*: if you could forget
    them completely, it would show that
    you understand how the present crisis
    demands that you should be at one with
    each other.

109 *instant*: present.

115 *presence*: distinguished gathering.
116 *considerate*: perceptive, contemplative.
118 *his*: i.e. Enobarbus's.
119 *conditions*: dispositions.
121 *hoop . . . staunch*: bond could keep us
    together; the image is of the iron hoop
    circling a barrel ('staunch' = watertight).

122 *Give me leave*: if I may be allowed to
    speak.

And then when poison'd hours had bound me up
From mine own knowledge. As nearly as I may
I'll play the penitent to you, but mine honesty
Shall not make poor my greatness, nor my power
100 Work without it. Truth is that Fulvia,
To have me out of Egypt, made wars here,
For which myself, the ignorant motive, do
So far ask pardon as befits mine honour
To stoop in such a case.

Lepidus
                                   'Tis noble spoken.

Maecenas
105 If it might please you to enforce no further
The griefs between ye; to forget them quite
Were to remember that the present need
Speaks to atone you.

Lepidus
                         Worthily spoken, Maecenas.

Enobarbus
Or, if you borrow one another's love for the instant,
110 you may, when you hear no more words of Pompey,
return it again. You shall have time to wrangle in
when you have nothing else to do.

Antony
Thou art a soldier only. Speak no more.

Enobarbus
That truth should be silent, I had almost forgot.

Antony
115 You wrong this presence; therefore speak no more.

Enobarbus
Go to, then! Your considerate stone.

Caesar
I do not much dislike the matter but
The manner of his speech; for't cannot be
We shall remain in friendship, our conditions
120 So differing in their acts. Yet, if I knew
What hoop should hold us staunch, from edge to
    edge
O'th' world I would pursue it.

Agrippa
                                   Give me leave, Caesar.

Caesar
Speak, Agrippa.
    Agrippa
Thou hast a sister by the mother's side,
125 Admir'd Octavia. Great Mark Antony
Is now a widower.
    Caesar
                Say not so, Agrippa.
If Cleopatra heard you, your reproof
Were well deserv'd of rashness.
    Antony
I am not married, Caesar. Let me hear
130 Agrippa further speak.
    Agrippa
To hold you in perpetual amity,
To make you brothers, and to knit your hearts
With an unslipping knot, take Antony
Octavia to his wife; whose beauty claims
135 No worse a husband than the best of men;
Whose virtue and whose general graces speak
That which none else can utter. By this marriage
All little jealousies which now seem great,
And all great fears which now import their dangers
140 Would then be nothing. Truths would be tales,
Where now half-tales be truths. Her love to both
Would each to other, and all loves to both
Draw after her. Pardon what I have spoke,
For 'tis a studied, not a present thought,
145 By duty ruminated.
    Antony
                Will Caesar speak?
    Caesar
Not till he hears how Antony is touch'd
With what is spoke already.
    Antony
What power is in Agrippa,
If I would say, 'Agrippa, be it so',
150 To make this good?
    Caesar
                The power of Caesar, and
His power unto Octavia.
    Antony
                May I never,

124 *by . . . side*: In historical fact, Octavia was a true sister of Octavius Caesar; the mistake was made by Plutarch.

127–8 *your . . . rashness*: you would well have deserved the reproof of your rashness.

133 *take Antony*: let Antony take.

136–7 *speak . . . utter*: reveal qualities such as no other woman can show.

138 *jealousies*: suspicions.

139 *import*: carry with them, involve.

140–1 *Truths . . . truths*: unpleasant facts would then be dismissed as mere fabrications, whereas now rumours are taken to be truths.

144 *studied*: carefully considered.
    present: impulsive.

146 *is touch'd*: has reacted.

153 *impediment*: The word resonates with echoes of the marriage service in the *Book of Common Prayer*, 'if either of you do know any impediment, why you may not be lawfully joined together in Matrimony, that ye confess it'.
thy: Welcoming Caesar as a brother, Antony adopts the familiar pronoun— but Caesar persists with the formality of 'you'.

154 *Further*: promote, help forward.

159–60 *never . . . again*: may our affections never desert us.

162–3 *laid . . . upon me*: recently done me some unusual and very big favours.

163–4 *only . . . report*: just so that I don't get a bad reputation for forgetfulness.

165 *At heel of*: following.

166 *Of us*: by us; Caesar will not allow time for Antony's courteousness.
presently: immediately.

169 *Misena*: a promontory, town, and harbour in the Bay of Naples.

172 *fame*: rumour, report.

173 *Would . . . together*: You and I should have had some conference about this (instead of quarrelling).

176 *my sister's view*: to see my sister.

177 *straight*: at once.

To this good purpose that so fairly shows,
Dream of impediment! Let me have thy hand.
Further this act of grace, and from this hour
155 The heart of brothers govern in our loves
And sway our great designs!

Caesar
                                    There's my hand.

They clasp hands

A sister I bequeath you, whom no brother
Did ever love so dearly. Let her live
To join our kingdoms and our hearts; and never
160 Fly off our loves again!

Lepidus
                                    Happily, amen!

Antony
I did not think to draw my sword 'gainst Pompey,
For he hath laid strange courtesies and great
Of late upon me. I must thank him, only
Lest my remembrance suffer ill report;
165 At heel of that, defy him.

Lepidus
                                    Time calls upon's.
Of us must Pompey presently be sought
Or else he seeks out us.

Antony
Where lies he?

Caesar
About the Mount Misena.

Antony
170 What is his strength by land?

Caesar
Great and increasing, but by sea
He is an absolute master.

Antony
                                    So is the fame.
Would we had spoke together! Haste we for it.
Yet, ere we put ourselves in arms, dispatch we
175 The business we have talk'd of.

Caesar
                                    With most gladness,
And do invite you to my sister's view,
Whither straight I'll lead you.

Antony
Let us, Lepidus, not lack your company.
Lepidus
Noble Antony, not sickness should detain me.

Flourish

[*Exeunt all except* Enobarbus, Agrippa, Maecenas
Maecenas
180 Welcome from Egypt, sir.
Enobarbus
Half the heart of Caesar, worthy Maecenas! My
honourable friend, Agrippa!
Agrippa
Good Enobarbus!
Maecenas
We have cause to be glad that matters are so well
185 digested. You stayed well by't in Egypt.
Enobarbus
Ay, sir, we did sleep day out of countenance and
made the night light with drinking.
Maecenas
Eight wild boars roasted whole at a breakfast, and
but twelve persons there. Is this true?
Enobarbus
190 This was but as a fly by an eagle. We had much more
monstrous matter of feast, which worthily deserved
noting.
Maecenas
She's a most triumphant lady, if report be square to
her.
Enobarbus
195 When she first met Mark Antony, she pursed up his
heart upon the river of Cydnus.
Agrippa
There she appeared indeed! Or my reporter devised
well for her.
Enobarbus
I will tell you.
200 The barge she sat in, like a burnish'd throne,
Burn'd on the water; the poop was beaten gold;
Purple the sails, and so perfumed that
The winds were love-sick with them; the oars were
silver,

181 *Half the heart*: Maecenas and Agrippa were Caesar's 'two chief friends' (Plutarch).

185 *digested*: settled.
stayed well by't: fought a good fight, had a good time.
186 *sleep . . . countenance*: put day to shame by sleeping through it.
187 *made . . . light*: the night was brightened by their oil-lamps (see *1*, 4, 5–6); and they themselves were 'lit up' with alcohol.

190 *fly . . . eagle*: i.e. not worth mentioning; see p. 143.

193 *square to*: accurate about.

195–6 *pursed . . . heart*: got his heart in her pocket.
196 *Cydnus*: a river in the south-east of Turkey.
197 *devised*: invented.

200–27 *The . . . nature*: In this passage Shakespeare follows Plutarch more closely than anywhere else in the play. See 'Plutarch', p. 144.
202 *perfumed*: perfumèd.

204 *kept stroke*: kept their strokes in rhythm.

206 *strokes*: beat of the oars, *and* caresses.

208 *cloth-of-gold of tissue*: a rich fabric interwoven with gold.
209–10 *O'erpicturing . . . nature*: excelling that picture of Venus in which the artist's imagination surpasses the real goddess.

213 *glow*: make glow.

215 *Nereides*: sea-nymphs, daughters of the sea-god Nereus; the word is pronounced with four syllables, with stress on the first.
216–17 *tended . . . adornings*: Plutarch says that these handmaidens were in the bows ('eyes') of the vessel, 'some steering the helm, others tending the tackle and ropes ('bends' = knots) of the barge'. Some critics, however, suggest that Enobarbus is describing the graceful movements of the gentlewomen as they bow before Cleopatra.
218 *tackle*: rigging and sails.
220 *yarely . . . office*: perform their tasks efficiently.
222 *wharfs*: banks of the river.
225 *but for vacancy*: except that it would have created a vacuum.
226 *Had*: would have.

234 *ordinary*: simple meal.

237 *cropp'd*: Cleopatra bore a son (Caesarion) to Julius Caesar.

Which to the tune of flutes kept stroke, and made
205 The water which they beat to follow faster,
    As amorous of their strokes. For her own person,
    It beggar'd all description: she did lie
    In her pavilion, cloth-of-gold of tissue,
    O'erpicturing that Venus where we see
210 The fancy outwork nature. On each side her
    Stood pretty dimpled boys, like smiling cupids,
    With divers-colour'd fans, whose wind did seem
    To glow the delicate cheeks which they did cool,
    And what they undid did.

Agrippa
                                    O, rare for Antony!

Enobarbus
215 Her gentlewomen, like the Nereides,
    So many mermaids, tended her i'th' eyes,
    And made their bends adornings. At the helm
    A seeming mermaid steers. The silken tackle
    Swell with the touches of those flower-soft hands
220 That yarely frame the office. From the barge
    A strange invisible perfume hits the sense
    Of the adjacent wharfs. The city cast
    Her people out upon her, and Antony,
    Enthron'd i'th' market-place, did sit alone,
225 Whistling to th'air, which, but for vacancy,
    Had gone to gaze on Cleopatra, too,
    And made a gap in nature.

Agrippa
                                    Rare Egyptian!

Enobarbus
    Upon her landing, Antony sent to her;
    Invited her to supper. She replied
230 It should be better he became her guest,
    Which she entreated. Our courteous Antony,
    Whom ne'er the word of 'No' woman heard speak,
    Being barber'd ten times o'er, goes to the feast,
    And, for his ordinary, pays his heart
235 For what his eyes eat only.

Agrippa
                                    Royal wench!
    She made great Caesar lay his sword to bed.
    He plough'd her, and she cropp'd.

Enobarbus

                                    I saw her once
Hop forty paces through the public street
And, having lost her breath, she spoke and panted,
240 That she did make defect perfection,
And, breathless, pour breath forth.

Maecenas

Now Antony must leave her utterly.

Enobarbus

Never! He will not.
Age cannot wither her, nor custom stale
245 Her infinite variety. Other women cloy
The appetites they feed, but she makes hungry
Where most she satisfies; for vilest things
Become themselves in her, that the holy priests
Bless her when she is riggish.

Maecenas

250 If beauty, wisdom, modesty can settle
The heart of Antony, Octavia is
A blessed lottery to him.

Agrippa

                              Let us go.
Good Enobarbus, make yourself my guest
Whilst you abide here.

Enobarbus

                            Humbly, sir, I thank you.
                                            [*Exeunt*

241 *breathless . . . forth*: even her breathlessness spoke for her.

244 *stale*: make stale.

248 *Become themselves*: are attractive.
249 *riggish*: lascivious, wanton.

252 *blessed*: blessèd.
lottery: prize.

Act 2   Scene 3

Antony, newly married to Octavia, is beginning to regret his actions and to look again towards Egypt. At the end of the scene his mind is made up—and his future determined.

Scene 3

        Rome: enter Antony *and* Caesar *with*
        Octavia *between them*

Antony

The world and my great office will sometimes
Divide me from your bosom.

Octavia

                            All which time
Before the gods my knee shall bow my prayers
To them for you.

Antony

                    Good night, sir. My Octavia,

5 'Don't believe everything that people
tell you about me.'
6 *kept my square*: always done everything
by the book; the image is from the set-
square used in carpentry.

10 *sirrah*: A form of address used only to
inferiors.

11 *Would*: I wish.

13 *in my motion*: intuitively.
14 *hie you*: hurry, get yourself off.

21 *afeard*: afraid.

23 *no . . . when*: only when.

26 *lustre*: brilliance.
thickens: grows dim.

5 Read not my blemishes in the world's report.
I have not kept my square, but that to come
Shall all be done by th' rule. Good night, dear lady.
Octavia
Good night, sir.
Caesar
Good night.   [*Exeunt* Caesar *and* Octavia

Enter Soothsayer

Antony
10 Now, sirrah! You do wish yourself in Egypt?
Soothsayer
Would I had never come from thence, nor you
thither!
Antony
If you can, your reason?
Soothsayer
I see it in my motion; have it not in my tongue.
But yet hie you to Egypt again.
Antony
                    Say to me,
15 Whose fortunes shall rise higher, Caesar's or mine?
Soothsayer
Caesar's.
Therefore, O Antony, stay not by his side.
Thy daemon—that thy spirit which keeps thee—is
Noble, courageous, high unmatchable,
20 Where Caesar's is not. But near him, thy angel
Becomes afeard, as being o'erpower'd; therefore
Make space enough between you.
Antony
                    Speak this no more.
Soothsayer
To none but thee; no more but when to thee.
If thou dost play with him at any game,
25 Thou art sure to lose; and of that natural luck
He beats thee 'gainst the odds. Thy lustre thickens
When he shines by. I say again, thy spirit
Is all afraid to govern thee near him;
But, he away, 'tis noble.
Antony
                    Get thee gone.

31 *Be . . . hap*: whether it is by magical art
or just by chance.
33 *better cunning*: superior skill.
34 *chance*: luck.
speeds: wins.
35 *still*: always.
36 *quails*: little fighting birds.

37 *inhoop'd*: hooped round, closed in a
circle (to prevent the birds from
escaping).

40 *commission*: warrant, authorization (of
command in Parthia).

Act 2   Scene 4

The Romans prepare to do battle with
Pompey.

3 *e'en but*: only just.

6 *the Mount*: i.e. Mount Misena, where
Pompey's fleet is anchored: see *2, 2,*
169.

30 Say to Ventidius I would speak with him.
                              [*Exit* Soothsayer
He shall to Parthia. Be it art or hap,
He hath spoken true. The very dice obey him,
And in our sports my better cunning faints
Under his chance. If we draw lots, he speeds;
35 His cocks do win the battle still of mine
When it is all to naught, and his quails ever
Beat mine, inhoop'd, at odds. I will to Egypt;
And though I make this marriage for my peace,
I'th' East my pleasure lies.

                    Enter Ventidius

                              O come, Ventidius.
40 You must to Parthia. Your commission's ready.
Follow me and receive't.
                              [*Exeunt*

Scene 4

          Rome: enter Lepidus, Maecenas, *and*
          Agrippa

     Lepidus
Trouble yourselves no further. Pray you hasten
Your generals after.
          Agrippa
                              Sir, Mark Antony
Will e'en but kiss Octavia, and we'll follow.
          Lepidus
Till I shall see you in your soldiers' dress,
5 Which will become you both, farewell.
          Maecenas
                              We shall,
As I conceive the journey, be at the Mount
Before you, Lepidus.
          Lepidus
                    Your way is shorter;

8 'My plans will take me a longer way
   round.'
9 *win*: gain.

My purposes do draw me much about.
You'll win two days upon me.
        Maecenas and **Agrippa**
10 Sir, good success!
        Lepidus
Farewell.

                                        [*Exeunt*

Act 2   Scene 5

Ignorant of events in Rome, Cleopatra
continues to languish in boredom. But she is
stirred to violent action when she hears the
news brought by a messenger (who seems to
have left Rome shortly after the decisions of
Scene 2).

1 *moody*: melancholy, temperamental.

Scene 5

        Alexandria: *enter* Cleopatra, Charmian,
        Iras, *and* Alexas

    Cleopatra
Give me some music—music, moody food
Of us that trade in love.
        All
                        The music, ho!

    Enter Mardian the Eunuch

    Cleopatra
Let it alone. Let's to billiards. Come, Charmian.
        Charmian
My arm is sore. Best play with Mardian.
        Cleopatra
5 As well a woman with an eunuch play'd
As with a woman. Come, you'll play with me, sir?
        Mardian
As well as I can, madam.
        Cleopatra

8 *come too short*: has something missing.

9 *I'll none*: I don't want to do that.
10 *angle*: fishing rod.
11 *betray*: trap, catch.

And when good will is show'd, though't come too
   short,
The actor may plead pardon. I'll none now.
10 Give me mine angle; we'll to th' river. There,
My music playing far off, I will betray
Tawny-finn'd fishes. My bended hook shall pierce
Their slimy jaws, and, as I draw them up,
I'll think them every one an Antony,
15 And say 'Ah, ha! You're caught!'
        Charmian
                        'Twas merry when
You wager'd on your angling; when your diver

17 *salt*: dried (or pickled) in salt.

18 *That time*: See 'Plutarch' p. 144.
19 *that*: the same.
22 *tires*: head-dresses.

23 *sword Philippan*: the sword used by
    Antony at the Battle of Philippi; see
    'Events in history', p. vii.
26 *Antonio*: Cleopatra speaks with
    affection.
27 *free*: i.e. not captured by Caesar.
28 *yield*: report.

30 *lipp'd*: touched with their lips.

32 *we use*: it's customary.

33 *Bring it to that*: if you're going to say
    that.

35 *ill-uttering*: announcing bad news, *and*,
    selling rotten goods (see below, line 54).

38 *tart*: sour, miserable.
    favour: expression, face.
39 *trumpet*: herald.
40 *Fury . . . snakes*: In Greek mythology
    the Furies were avenging spirits,
    represented with snakes springing from
    their heads.
41 *formal*: normal, sane.

Did hang a salt fish on his hook, which he
With fervency drew up.
      Cleopatra
                      That time? O times!
I laugh'd him out of patience, and that night
20 I laugh'd him into patience, and next morn,
Ere the ninth hour, I drunk him to his bed,
Then put my tires and mantles on him, whilst
I wore his sword Philippan.

        Enter a Messenger

                      Oh, from Italy!
Ram thou thy fruitful tidings in mine ears,
25 That long time have been barren!
      Messenger
                      Madam, madam—
      Cleopatra
Antonio's dead! If thou say so, villain,
Thou kill'st thy mistress; but well and free,
If thou so yield him, there is gold, and here
My bluest veins to kiss, a hand that kings
30 Have lipp'd, and trembled, kissing.
      Messenger
First, madam, he is well.
      Cleopatra
                  Why, there's more gold.
But sirrah, mark, we use
To say the dead are well. Bring it to that,
The gold I give thee will I melt and pour
35 Down thy ill-uttering throat.
      Messenger
                  Good madam, hear me.
      Cleopatra
Well, go to, I will.
But there's no goodness in thy face if Antony
Be free and healthful. So tart a favour
To trumpet such good tidings! If not well,
40 Thou shouldst come like a Fury crown'd with snakes,
Not like a formal man.
      Messenger
                  Will't please you hear me?
      Cleopatra
I have a mind to strike thee ere thou speak'st.

Yet if thou say Antony lives, is well,
Or friends with Caesar, or not captive to him,
45 I'll set thee in a shower of gold and hail
Rich pearls upon thee.

Messenger   Madam, he's well.

Cleopatra
                                                            Well said!

Messenger
And friends with Caesar.

Cleopatra
                                          Thou'rt an honest man!

47 *honest*: worthy.

Messenger
Caesar and he are greater friends than ever.

Cleopatra
Make thee a fortune from me!

Messenger
                                                      But yet, madam—

Cleopatra
50 I do not like 'But yet'. It does allay
The good precedence. Fie upon 'But yet'!
'But yet' is as a gaoler to bring forth
Some monstrous malefactor. Prithee, friend,
Pour out the pack of matter to mine ear,
55 The good and bad together. He's friends with
    Caesar,
In state of health, thou say'st, and, thou sayst, free.

50–1 *allay . . . precedence*: spoil the good
news that's gone before ('precedence' is
stressed on the second syllable, which is
pronounced with long 'e' as in
'precéde').

54 *pack*: Cleopatra thinks of the messenger
with his news as a pedlar with his pack
(see above, line 35), and she returns to
the image in lines 104–6.

Messenger
Free, madam? No. I made no such report.
He's bound unto Octavia.

58 *bound*: married, committed—but
Cleopatra interprets the word as
meaning 'indebted'.

Cleopatra
                                          For what good turn?

Messenger
For the best turn i'th' bed.

Cleopatra
                                          I am pale, Charmian.

Messenger
60 Madam, he's married to Octavia.

Cleopatra
The most infectious pestilence upon thee!

                    Strikes him down

Messenger
Good madam, patience!
  Cleopatra
                              What say you?

Strikes him

                                        Hence,

63 *spurn*: kick.

Horrible villain, or I'll spurn thine eyes
Like balls before me! I'll unhair thy head!

64s.d. *hales*: hauls, drags.

She hales him up and down

66 *pickle*: brine.

65 Thou shalt be whipp'd with wire and stew'd in brine,
Smarting in lingering pickle!
  Messenger
                              Gracious madam,
I that do bring the news made not the match.
  Cleopatra
Say 'tis not so, a province I will give thee,
And make thy fortunes proud. The blow thou hadst
70 Shall make thy peace for moving me to rage,

71 *boot*: reward.

And I will boot thee with what gift beside
Thy modesty can beg.
  Messenger
                              He's married, madam.
  Cleopatra
Rogue, thou hast lived too long!

Draws a knife

  Messenger
                              Nay then, I'll run.
What mean you, madam? I have made no fault.
                                        [*Exit*
  Charmian
75 Good madam, keep yourself within yourself.
The man is innocent.
  Cleopatra
Some innocents 'scape not the thunderbolt.

78 *Melt . . . Nile*: Compare *1*, 1, 34, 'Let
Rome in Tiber melt'.
kindly: natural; Cleopatra wants to turn
all normal creatures into monsters.

Melt Egypt into Nile, and kindly creatures
Turn all to serpents! Call the slave again!
80 Though I am mad, I will not bite him. Call!
  Charmian
He is afeard to come.

Cleopatra

I will not hurt him.

[*Exit* Charmian

These hands do lack nobility that they strike

83 *A meaner than*: one socially inferior to.

A meaner than myself, since I myself

Have given myself the cause.

Enter the Messenger *again with* Charmian

Come hither, sir.

85 Though it be honest, it is never good

To bring bad news. Give to a gracious message

An host of tongues, but let ill tidings tell

Themselves when they be felt.

Messenger

I have done my duty.

Cleopatra

Is he married?

90 I cannot hate thee worser than I do

If thou again say 'Yes'.

Messenger

He's married, madam.

Cleopatra

The gods confound thee! Dost thou hold there still?

92 *hold there*: stick to that story.

Messenger

Should I lie, madam?

Cleopatra

Oh, I would thou didst,

94 *So*: even if.

So half my Egypt were submerg'd and made

95 *cistern*: pond.

95 A cistern for scal'd snakes! Go, get thee hence!

96 *Narcissus*: the ideal of male beauty. In classical mythology he was a young man who fell in love with his own reflection seen in a fountain.

Hadst thou Narcissus in thy face, to me

Thou wouldst appear most ugly. He is married?

Messenger

I crave your highness' pardon.

Cleopatra

He is married?

Messenger

Take no offence that I would not offend you.

99 'Don't be angry just because I am reluctant to offend you again.'

100 To punish me for what you make me do

101 *much unequal*: very unfair.

Seems much unequal. He's married to Octavia.

Cleopatra

Oh, that his fault should make a knave of thee

103 *act . . . sure of*: do not commit the offence that you are so certain about.

That act not what thou'rt sure of! Get thee hence!

104 *merchandise*: i.e. the news brought in the messenger's 'pack' (line 54).

105 *upon thy hand*: unsold.

106 *undone*: ruined.

The merchandise which thou hast brought from
        Rome
105 Are all too dear for me. Lie they upon thy hand
        And be undone by 'em.   [*Exit* Messenger
    Charmian
                            Good your highness, patience.
    Cleopatra
In praising Antony, I have disprais'd Caesar.
    Charmian
Many times, madam.
    Cleopatra
                            I am paid for't now.
        Lead me from hence;
110 I faint! O Iras, Charmian! 'Tis no matter.
        Go to the fellow, good Alexas, bid him

112 *feature*: appearance.

113 *inclination*: disposition, personality.

116–17 *he . . . Mars*: Cleopatra describes a 'perspective' picture, in which the image can be seen from different angles: looked at in one way, Antony resembles the god of war—but from another point of view he appears as the Gorgon Medusa (who was depicted with a crown of snakes and whose gaze turned men to stone).

        Report the feature of Octavia, her years,
        Her inclination; let him not leave out
        The colour of her hair. Bring me word quickly.
                                    [*Exit* Alexas
115 Let him for ever go! Let him not, Charmian.
        Though he be painted one way like a Gorgon,
        The other way's a Mars. [*To* Iras] Bid you Alexas
        Bring me word how tall she is. Pity me, Charmian,
        But do not speak to me. Lead me to my chamber.
                                    [*Exeunt*

Act 2   Scene 6

On the military front, meanwhile, events are taking a surprising turn. The three Roman leaders have encountered Pompey, their common enemy, and are now holding peace talks. Pompey tries to justify his rebellion: he wanted to avenge his father's death, and to oppose the centralization of power in Rome. A treaty is negotiated, and the former adversaries prepare to celebrate. Enobarbus and Menas are both sceptical!

Scene 6

Mount Misena. Flourish. Enter Pompey
and Menas *at one door with drum and
trumpet; at another* Caesar, Lepidus,
Antony, Enobarbus, Maecenas, Agrippa,
with Soldiers *marching*

    Pompey
Your hostages I have, so have you mine,
And we shall talk before we fight.
    Caesar
                            Most meet
That first we come to words, and therefore have we

4 *purposes*: proposals.

Our written purposes before us sent,

7 *tall*: valiant.

9 *senators alone*: only senators; Pompey is rebelling against the triumvirs because he believes that political power should be more widely distributed.

10 *factors*: agents, deputies.

11 *my father*: Pompey the Great, who had been defeated by Julius Caesar at the Battle of Pharsalus (see 'Events in history', p. vii).
   want: lack, be in need of.

13–14 *Who . . . for him*: The ghost of Julius Caesar appeared at Philippi where Octavius Caesar and Antony were fighting on *his* behalf against Cassius and Brutus (see 'Events in history', p. vii).

15 *pale*: pale-faced; Julius Caesar (according to Plutarch) was suspicious of his enemy's 'pale looks'.

16 *honest*: honourable.

17 *courtiers of*: i.e. those who loved, desired, and served.

18 *drench*: i.e. in the blood of Julius Caesar.

19 *but a man*: just an ordinary man (not a king or a dictator).

20 *burden*: load, freight.

22 *despiteful*: scornful.

23 *Take your time*: don't hurry, calm down.

24 *fear*: frighten.

25 *speak*: contend.

26 *o'ercount*: outnumber.

27 *Thou . . . house*: Pompey is bitter because Antony had bought at auction the house of Pompey the Great—and then refused to pay for it!

28 *the cuckoo*: The cuckoo does not build a nest itself but lays its eggs in the nests of other birds.

29 *as thou may'st*: while you can.

30 *from the present*: beside the point.
   take: react to.

32 *entreated to*: persuaded about.
   weigh: consider.

33 *embrac'd*: if it is accepted.

5 Which if thou hast consider'd, let us know
If 'twill tie up thy discontented sword
And carry back to Sicily much tall youth
That else must perish here.

Pompey
                              To you all three,
The senators alone of this great world,
10 Chief factors for the gods: I do not know
Wherefore my father should revengers want,
Having a son and friends, since Julius Caesar,
Who at Philippi the good Brutus ghosted,
There saw you labouring for him. What was't
15 That mov'd pale Cassius to conspire? And what
Made the all-honour'd, honest Roman, Brutus,
With the arm'd rest, courtiers of beauteous freedom,
To drench the Capitol, but that they would
Have one man but a man? And that is it
20 Hath made me rig my navy, at whose burden
The anger'd ocean foams, with which I meant
To scourge th'ingratitude that despiteful Rome
Cast on my noble father.

Caesar
                              Take your time.

Antony
Thou canst not fear us, Pompey, with thy sails.
25 We'll speak with thee at sea. At land thou know'st
How much we do o'ercount thee.

Pompey
                              At land indeed
Thou dost o'ercount me of my father's house;
But since the cuckoo builds not for himself,
Remain in't as thou mayst.

Lepidus
                              Be pleas'd to tell us—
30 For this is from the present—how you take
The offers we have sent you.

Caesar
                              There's the point.

Antony
Which do not be entreated to, but weigh
What it is worth embrac'd.

34 *try . . . fortune*: attempt something more
ambitious. Caesar is warning Pompey
not to fight.

35 *I must*: i.e. in return I must.

38 *part*: withdraw.
edges: swords (literally, the cutting edges
of their swords).
39 *targes*: targets (= shields); the word is
monosyllabic, with hard 'g'.

43–6 *you must . . . friendly*: Pompey
addresses Antony, referring to the wars
begun by Fulvia and Antony's brother—
see *1, 2,* 89–95.
46 *I . . . it*: Antony has already referred to
this courtesy in *2, 2,* 162–3.
47 *studied for*: prepared to give.
51 *timelier . . . purpose*: sooner than I had
intended.
54 *counts*: amounts, charges.
casts: reckons up; Pompey compares his
face to the slate in a tavern on which
the inn-keeper has marked the price (in
lines or scars) which Pompey has had to
pay for his experience.

55–6 'I'm never going to let bad luck affect
me and get the better of me.' ('vassal' =
serf, slave)

Caesar
　　　　　　　　　　　　　　And what may follow
To try a larger fortune.
　　Pompey
　　　　　　　　　　　　You have made me offer
35 Of Sicily, Sardinia; and I must
Rid all the sea of pirates; then to send
Measures of wheat to Rome. This 'greed upon,
To part with unhack'd edges, and bear back
Our targes undinted.
　　Caesar, Antony, Lepidus
　　　　　　　　　　　That's our offer.
　　Pompey
　　　　　　　　　　　　　　Know, then,
40 I came before you here a man prepar'd
To take this offer, but Mark Antony
Put me to some impatience. Though I lose
The praise of it by telling, you must know
When Caesar and your brother were at blows,
45 Your mother came to Sicily and did find
Her welcome friendly.
　　Antony
　　　　　　　　　　I have heard it, Pompey,
And am well studied for a liberal thanks
Which I do owe you.
　　Pompey
　　　　　　　　　　Let me have your hand.

　　　　　　They shake hands

I did not think, sir, to have met you here.
　　Antony
50 The beds i'th' East are soft; and thanks to you
That call'd me timelier than my purpose hither,
For I have gain'd by't.
　　Caesar
　　　　　　　　　　Since I saw you last,
There is a change upon you.
　　Pompey
　　　　　　　　　　　　Well, I know not
What counts harsh Fortune casts upon my face,
55 But in my bosom shall she never come
To make my heart her vassal.

Lepidus
                                        Well met here!

Pompey
I hope so, Lepidus. Thus we are agreed.
I crave our composition may be written
And seal'd between us.

Caesar
                              That's the next to do.

Pompey
60 We'll feast each other ere we part, and let's
Draw lots who shall begin.

Antony
                                   That will I, Pompey.

Pompey
No, Antony, take the lot.
But, first or last, your fine Egyptian cookery
Shall have the fame. I have heard that Julius Caesar
65 Grew fat with feasting there.

Antony
                                        You have heard much.

Pompey
I have fair meanings, sir.

Antony
                                   And fair words to them.

Pompey
Then so much have I heard.
And I have heard Apollodorus carried—

Enobarbus
No more of that! He did so.

Pompey
                                   What, I pray you?

Enobarbus
70 A certain queen to Caesar in a mattress.

Pompey
I know thee now. How far'st thou, soldier?

Enobarbus
                                                        Well;
And well am like to do, for I perceive
Four feasts are toward.

Pompey
                              Let me shake thy hand.

They shake hands

Margin notes:

58 *composition*: agreement; i.e. the peace treaty.

62 *take the lot*: accept the result of the lottery.

64–6 *I have . . . them*: Pompey hints at the relationship between Julius Caesar and Cleopatra—but Antony is sensitive!

70 The short answer from Enobarbus indicates that Pompey should change the subject (See 'Plutarch', p. 145).

73 *toward*: imminent, impending; the word is stressed 'tóward'.

I never hated thee. I have seen thee fight
75 When I have envied thy behaviour.
    Enobarbus
                          Sir,
I never lov'd you much, but I have prais'd ye
When you have well deserv'd ten times as much
As I have said you did.
    Pompey

78 *Enjoy*: continue to indulge.

                     Enjoy thy plainness;
It nothing ill becomes thee.
80 Aboard my galley I invite you all.
Will you lead, lords?
    Caesar, Antony, Lepidus
                  Show's the way, sir.
    Pompey
                              Come.
    [*Exeunt all but* Enobarbus *and* Menas
    Menas
[*Aside*] Thy father, Pompey, would ne'er have made

83 *known*: known each other.

this treaty. [*To* Enobarbus] You and I have known,
sir.
    Enobarbus
85 At sea, I think.
    Menas
We have, sir.
    Enobarbus

87 *done well*: fought bravely, *and*, made
   good profit from plunder.

You have done well by water.
    Menas
And you by land.
    Enobarbus
I will praise any man that will praise me, though it
90 cannot be denied what I have done by land.
    Menas
Nor what I have done by water.
    Enobarbus
Yes, something you can deny for your own safety:
you have been a great thief by sea.
    Menas
And you by land.

95 *land service*: Enobarbus will deny that
   robbery was any part of his military
   service.
97 *take*: catch, arrest.
   two thieves: i.e. their hands.

    Enobarbus
95 There I deny my land service. But give me your
hand, Menas! [*They shake hands*] If our eyes had
authority, here they might take two thieves kissing.

Menas

All men's faces are true, whatsome'er their hands are.

Enobarbus

100 But there is never a fair woman has a true face.

Menas

No slander. They steal hearts.

Enobarbus

We came hither to fight with you.

Menas

For my part, I am sorry it has turned to a drinking. Pompey doth this day laugh away his fortune.

Enobarbus

105 If he do, sure he cannot weep't back again.

Menas

You've said, sir. We looked not for Mark Antony here. Pray you, is he married to Cleopatra?

Enobarbus

Caesar's sister is called Octavia.

Menas

True, sir. She was the wife of Caius Marcellus.

Enobarbus

110 But she is now the wife of Marcus Antonius.

Menas

Pray ye, sir?

Enobarbus

'Tis true.

Menas

Then is Caesar and he for ever knit together.

Enobarbus

If I were bound to divine of this unity, I would not
115 prophesy so.

Menas

I think the policy of that purpose made more in the marriage than the love of the parties.

Enobarbus

I think so too. But you shall find the band that seems to tie their friendship together will be the very
120 strangler of their amity. Octavia is of a holy, cold and still conversation.

Menas

Who would not have his wife so?

---

100 *true*: i.e. not changed with cosmetics.

101 *No slander*: that's quite true.

106 *said*: said it.
     looked not for: didn't expect.

109 *Caius Marcellus*: Octavia's first husband.

114 *bound to divine*: asked to make a prediction.

116 *The policy . . . purpose*: the political motives for that proposal.

119 *be the very*: actually be the.

121 *still*: gentle, passive.
     conversation: disposition.

Enobarbus

Not he that himself is not so; which is Mark Antony.
He will to his Egyptian dish again. Then shall the
125 sighs of Octavia blow the fire up in Caesar, and, as I
said before, that which is the strength of their amity
shall prove the immediate author of their variance.
Antony will use his affection where it is. He married
but his occasion here.

Menas

130 And thus it may be. Come, sir, will you aboard? I
have a health for you.

Enobarbus

I shall take it, sir. We have used our throats in Egypt.

Menas

Come, let's away.

[*Exeunt*

Act 2   Scene 7

On Pompey's barge, the guests have just
dined and are proceeding, unsteadily, to a
different cabin for their dessert. The waiting
servants discuss their masters. When these
heads of state do appear, they are in various
stages of intoxication, and the merriment
continues. Pompey's new-found sense of
amity and honour forces him to reject a
scheme proposed by Menas. Lepidus,
senseless, is carried ashore, but the revelry
reaches new heights with song and dance. At
last Caesar calls a halt—though Antony and
Pompey resolve to carry on drinking in
private.

os.d. *banquet*: dessert with wine.
1–2 *some . . . ill-rooted*: The servant makes
   play with 'plants' (= seedlings, schemes,
   and footholds) and 'rooted' (= set down,
   based).
4 *high-coloured*: red in the face.
5 *alms-drink*: The expression is
   unfamiliar—but the meaning is
   explained in the lines that follow.
6 *pinch*: provoke, rub up the wrong way.
   by the disposition: characteristically. The
   Servant recognizes that the leaders are
   temperamentally incompatible.

127 *author*: cause.
128 *use his affection*: satisfy his [sexual]
   appetite.
129 *occasion*: political opportunity.
130–1 *I . . . you*: I want to drink your health.

132 *used*: trained.

Scene 7

Pompey's *barge. Music plays. Enter two or
three* Servants *with a banquet*

First Servant

Here they'll be man. Some o' their plants are ill-
rooted already; the least wind i'th' world will blow
them down.

Second Servant

Lepidus is high-coloured.

First Servant

5 They have made him drink alms-drink.

Second Servant

As they pinch one another by the disposition, he
cries out 'No more', reconciles them to his entreaty,
and himself to th' drink.

First Servant

But it raises the greater war between him and his
10 discretion.

Second Servant

Why, this it is to have a name in great men's
fellowship. I had as lief have a reed that will do me
no service as a partisan I could not heave.

7 *No more*: i.e. no more fighting.
entreaty: plea for peace.

9 *it*: i.e. the drink.

10 *discretion*: prudence, sobriety.

11–12 *a name . . . fellowship*: be a party to
the alliance of great men.

11 *had as lief*: would as soon as.

13 *partisan*: long-handled spear.

14–15 *To be . . . in't*: to be called to a high
position and then be seen to have no
function there. The servant alludes to
the doctrine of Ptolemaic astronomy
describing the movement of the planets,
which circled the earth in crystalline
'spheres' driven by 'intelligences',
influencing everything beneath them.

15 *are . . . be*: is like having eye-sockets
with no eyes in them.

16 *pitifully*: sadly, *and*, by being full of pits
or sockets.
disaster: strike with calamity (an
astrological term), ruin.

16s.d. *sennet*: trumpeting call to announce a
ceremonial entrance.

17 *Thus do they*: this is how they do it.

17–18 *take . . . pyramid*: The Egyptians
calculate ('take') the rise and fall of the
water by the observation of a scale
inscribed on a pillar ('pyramid').

19 *mean*: median, medium.
dearth: famine.

20 *foison*: plenty, abundance.

26 *Your*: Lepidus, now very drunk, is
showing off his knowledge.

26–7 *serpent . . . crocodile*: It was widely
believed that creatures such as snakes
and flies could be generated out of
vegetable matter.

First Servant
To be called into a huge sphere and not to be seen to
15 move in't, are the holes where eyes should be, which
pitifully disaster the cheeks.

> *A sennet sounded. Enter* Caesar, Antony,
> Pompey, Lepidus, Agrippa, Maecenas,
> Enobarbus, Menas *with other* Captains
> *and a* Boy Singer

Antony
Thus do they, sir: they take the flow o'th' Nile
By certain scales i'th' pyramid. They know
By th'height, the lowness, or the mean, if dearth
20 Or foison follow. The higher Nilus swells,
The more it promises. As it ebbs, the seedsman
Upon the slime and ooze scatters his grain,
And shortly comes to harvest.
Lepidus
You've strange serpents there?
Antony
25 Ay, Lepidus.
Lepidus
Your serpent of Egypt is bred, now, of your mud by
the operation of your sun; so is your crocodile.

Antony
They are so.
Pompey
Sit, and some wine! A health to Lepidus!

They sit and drink

Lepidus
30 I am not so well as I should be, but I'll ne'er out.

30 *ne'er out*: not drop out (of the drinking).

31 *in*: indoors, *and*, in drink, drunk.

33 *pyramises*: Lepidus tries to say
    'pyramids'.
34 *goodly*: impressive.

39 *Forbear . . . anon*: leave it until a little
    later.

43–4 *it own*: its own.

45 *elements*: life.
    it transmigrates: Antony is alluding to
    the doctrine of Pythagoras that after
    death the soul of one creature passes
    into the body of another.

51–2 'He would have to be a real sceptic
    not to believe it after all the drink that
    Pompey has given him.' Epicurus and
    his followers, refusing to believe in any
    after-life, rejected the teaching of
    Pythagoras.

Enobarbus
[*Aside*] Not till you have slept. I fear me you'll be in
till then.
Lepidus
Nay, certainly, I have heard the Ptolemies' pyramises
are very goodly things. Without contradiction I have
35 heard that.
Menas
[*Aside to* Pompey] Pompey, a word.
Pompey
[*Aside to* Menas]   Say in my ear what is't
Menas
[*Whispers in his ear*] Forsake thy seat, I do beseech
    thee, captain,
And hear me speak a word.
Pompey
[*Aside to* Menas] Forbear me till anon.—This wine
40 for Lepidus!
Lepidus
What manner o' thing is your crocodile?
Antony
It is shaped, sir, like itself, and it is as broad as it hath
breadth. It is just so high as it is, and moves with it
own organs. It lives by that which nourisheth it, and
45 the elements once out of it, it transmigrates.
Lepidus
What colour is it of?
Antony
Of it own colour too.
Lepidus
'Tis a strange serpent.
Antony
'Tis so, and the tears of it are wet.
Caesar
50 Will this description satisfy him?
Antony
With the health that Pompey gives him, else he is a
very epicure.

Menas whispers again

Pompey
[*Aside to* Menas] Go hang, sir, hang! Tell me of
    that? Away!

Do as I bid you.—Where's this cup I called for?
Menas

55 merit: my earlier services.

55 [*Aside to* Pompey] If for the sake of merit thou wilt
      hear me,
    Rise from thy stool.
        Pompey
    [*Aside to* Menas] I think thou'rt mad. The matter?

                Rises and walks aside with Menas

        Menas

57 'I have always been a loyal servant to
    you.' (Servants were always bareheaded
    in the presence of their masters.)

    I have ever held my cap off to thy fortunes.
        Pompey
    Thou hast serv'd me with much faith. What's else
      to say?—
    Be jolly, lords.
        Antony
                  These quicksands, Lepidus,

59 quicksands: Lepidus is lurching around;
    by line 86 he has collapsed completely.

60 Keep off them, for you sink.
        Menas
    Wilt thou be lord of all the world?
        Pompey
    What sayst thou?
        Menas
                  Wilt thou be lord of the whole world?
    That's twice.
        Pompey
                  How should that be?
        Menas

63 But entertain it: just give it a thought.

                              But entertain it,
    And, though thou think me poor, I am the man
65 Will give thee all the world.
        Pompey
                              Hast thou drunk well?
        Menas
    No, Pompey, I have kept me from the cup.
    Thou art, if thou dar'st be, the earthly Jove,

68 pales: fences in (as with pales or stakes).
    inclips: encircles.

    Whate'er the ocean pales or sky inclips
    Is thine, if thou wilt ha't.
        Pompey
                              Show me which way.
        Menas

70 competitors: associates, colleagues.

70 These three world-sharers, these competitors,

71 *cable*: rope or chain attached to the anchor.

Are in thy vessel. Let me cut the cable,
And when we are put off, fall to their throats.
All then is thine.

Pompey
                                    Ah, this thou shouldst have done
And not have spoke on't. In me 'tis villainy;
75 In thee't had been good service. Thou must know
'Tis not my profit that does lead mine honour;

77 *Mine honour, it*: my honour leads my profit.

Mine honour, it. Repent that e'er thy tongue
Hath so betray'd thine act. Being done unknown,
I should have found it afterwards well done,
80 But must condemn it now. Desist and drink.

Returns to the others

Menas
[*Aside*] For this,
I'll never follow thy pall'd fortunes more.

82 *pall'd*: weakened, enfeebled.

Who seeks and will not take, when once 'tis offer'd,
Shall never find it more.

Pompey
                                    This health to Lepidus!

Antony

85 *pledge it*: respond to it (by sharing the toast).

85 Bear him ashore. I'll pledge it for him, Pompey.

Enobarbus
Here's to thee, Menas!

Menas
                                    Enobarbus, welcome!

Pompey
Fill till the cup be hid.

Enobarbus
[*Points to the* Attendant *who carries off* Lepidus]
There's a strong fellow, Menas.

Menas
Why?

90 *'A*: he.
third part: i.e. one of the three triumvirs, rulers of the known world.

Enobarbus
90 'A bears the third part of the world, man. Seest not?

Menas

92 *go on wheels*: spin round.

The third part then he is drunk. Would it were all,
That it might go on wheels!

Enobarbus

93 *reels*: revels, *and/or*, giddiness.

Drink thou! Increase the reels!

Menas
Come!

96 *Strike the vessels*: clash the cups together, *or*, tap the wine-casks.

97 *forbear't*: abstain from drinking the toast.

98 *wash my brain*: i.e. with liquor.

100 *child o'th' time*: i.e. one of us. *'Possess it'* . . . *answer*: Caesar prefers to be master, not child, of the time.

103 *Bacchanals*: riotous dances celebrating Bacchus, the Roman god of wine.

105 *ha't*: get on with it.

107 *Lethe*: the river of forgetfulness (see note to 2, 1, 27).

108 *Make battery to*: make an assault on.

109 *The while*: in the meantime.

110–11 'Every man will stamp out the chorus ('holding') with all his might, like a volley of firearms.'

112–17 The song calls to the god Bacchus— perhaps in parody of other [Christian] invocations of the divine spirit.

113 *Plumpy . . . eyne*: Fatty Bacchus with little pink eyes; the '-*y*' suffix and the archaic plural seem to indicate disrespect.

116 *Cup us*: fill our cups.

Pompey

95 This is not yet an Alexandrian feast.

   Antony

It ripens towards it. Strike the vessels, ho!
Here's to Caesar!

   Caesar

               I could well forbear't.
It's monstrous labour when I wash my brain
And it grows fouler.

   Antony

100 Be a child o'th' time.

   Caesar

              'Possess it', I'll make answer.
But I had rather fast from all, four days,
Than drink so much in one.

   Enobarbus

[*To* Antony]   Ha, my brave emperor,
Shall we dance now the Egyptian Bacchanals
And celebrate our drink?

   Pompey

105 Let's ha't, good soldier.

   Antony

              Come, let's all take hands
Till that the conquering wine hath steep'd our sense
In soft and delicate Lethe.

   Enobarbus

               All take hands.
Make battery to our ears with the loud music,
The while I'll place you; then the boy shall sing.

110 The holding every man shall beat as loud
As his strong sides can volley.

     Music plays. Enobarbus *places them hand in hand*

   Boy

[*sings*] Come, thou monarch of the vine,
     Plumpy Bacchus with pink eyne!
     In thy vats our cares be drown'd;

115   With thy grapes our hairs be crown'd.

   All

     Cup us till the world go round!
     Cup us till the world go round!

118 *brother*: brother-in-law.
119 *off*: to come off the barge.

121 *burnt our cheeks*: drunk until we are red
     in the face.

123 *Splits*: slurs, mispronounces.
     wild disguise: disorderly performance.
124 *Antick'd us all*: made us all look
     ridiculous.

126 *try you*: see how you drink.

128–9 *you . . . friends*: See 2, 6, 27 and *note*;
       Pompey's hostility has been dispelled by
       drink and laughter.
129   *boat*: i.e. the boat that will take them
      ashore.

131–3 *These drums . . . out*: Menas gives a
       confused order to the [off-stage]
       musicians to salute the departing guests
       with a ceremonial fanfare.

Caesar
What would you more? Pompey, good night. Good
    brother,
Let me request you off. Our graver business
120 Frowns at this levity. Gentle lords, let's part.
You see we have burnt our cheeks. Strong Enobarb
Is weaker than the wine, and mine own tongue
Splits what it speaks. The wild disguise hath almost
Antick'd us all. What needs more words? Good
    night.
125 Good Antony, your hand.
    Pompey
I'll try you on the shore.
    Antony
And shall, sir. Give's your hand.
    Pompey
O, Antony, you have my father's house.
But what? We are friends! Come down into the boat.
    Enobarbus
130 Take heed you fall not.
                    [*Exeunt all but* Enobarbus *and* Menas
                         Menas, I'll not on shore.
    Menas
No, to my cabin! These drums, these trumpets,
    flutes! What!
Let Neptune hear we bid a loud farewell
To these great fellows. Sound and be hang'd!
    Sound out!

         Sound a flourish with drums

    Enobarbus
Hoo, says 'a! There's my cap!

         Flings his cap in the air

    Menas
135 Hoo! Noble captain, come!
                                        [*Exeunt*

Act 3

Act 3   Scene 1

After the drunken festivity on Pompey's barge, the scene changes, momentarily, to an extreme outpost of the Roman empire where fighting is still going on. The Romans had wanted revenge on the army of Pacorus, son of the king of Parthia, which had defeated that of Marcus Crassus, a member of the first triumvirate (see 'Events in history', p. vii). A subordinate officer, Ventidius, has successfully carried out his orders. Ventidius, although he is obedient and loyal, has no illusions about his present service.

os.d. *as in triumph*: i.e. rejoicing over a victory: this is not a formal 'triumph' (= the victory parade of a conquering hero).
1 *darting Parthia*: The cavalry of Parthia, when apparently in retreat, turned in the saddle and discharged flights of arrows at their enemy.
struck: punished.
2 *Marcus Crassus*: a member (with Pompey the Great and Julius Caesar) of the First Triumvirate.
4 *Orodes*: king of Parthia.
7 *The . . . follow*: follow the fleeing Parthians.
Spur: spur on your horse (and troops).
10 *triumphant*: triumphal; Silius visualizes a victory parade.
12 *lower place*: subordinate.
15 *him we serve*: i.e. Antony.
16 *ever*: always.
17 *in their officer*: through the fighting of their officers.
18 *place*: rank.
lieutenant: the officer holding command under Antony.
20 *by th' minute*: every minute.
23–4 *rather . . . him*: would prefer to lose rather than win when the victory brings him out of favour.

Scene 1

Syria: enter Ventidius *as in triumph, with* Silius *and other* Romans, Officers, *and* Soldiers, *the dead body of* Pacorus *borne before him*

Ventidius
Now, darting Parthia, art thou struck, and now
Pleas'd Fortune does of Marcus Crassus' death
Make me revenger. Bear the king's son's body
Before our army. Thy Pacorus, Orodes,
5 Pays this for Marcus Crassus.
Silius
                        Noble Ventidius,
Whilst yet with Parthian blood thy sword is warm,
The fugitive Parthians follow. Spur through Media,
Mesopotamia, and the shelters whither
The routed fly. So thy grand captain Antony
10 Shall set thee on triumphant chariots and
Put garlands on thy head.
Ventidius
                        O Silius, Silius,
I have done enough. A lower place, note well,
May make too great an act. For learn this, Silius:
Better to leave undone than, by our deed,
15 Acquire too high a fame when him we serve's away.
Caesar and Antony have ever won
More in their officer than person. Sossius,
One of my place in Syria, his lieutenant,
For quick accumulation of renown,
20 Which he achiev'd by th' minute, lost his favour.
Who does i'th' wars more than his captain can,
Becomes his captain's captain; and ambition,
The soldier's virtue, rather makes choice of loss
Than gain which darkens him.

25 *Antonius*: the Latin form of 'Antony'.

26 *in his offence*: by taking offence.

27 *perish*: come to nothing.

28 *that*: that quality, i.e. discretion.

30 *Grants scarce distinction*: can hardly be distinguished from each other.

31–2 *I'll . . . effected*: Ventidius will not claim the achievement for himself but attribute the victory to the magical effects of the name of Antony.

34 *horse*: cavalry.

35 *jaded*: exhausted; a 'jade' is a worn-out horse.

36 *purposeth*: intends to go.

37 *weight*: baggage.

---

25 I could do more to do Antonius good,
   But 'twould offend him, and in his offence
   Should my performance perish.
          Silius
   Thou hast, Ventidius, that
   Without the which a soldier and his sword
30 Grants scarce distinction. Thou wilt write to Antony?
          Ventidius
   I'll humbly signify what in his name,
   That magical word of war, we have effected;
   How, with his banners and his well-paid ranks,
   The ne'er-yet-beaten horse of Parthia
35 We have jaded out o'th' field.
          Silius
                              Where is he now?
          Ventidius
   He purposeth to Athens, whither, with what haste
   The weight we must convey with's will permit,
   We shall appear before him. On there! Pass along!
                                    [*Exeunt*

Act 3   Scene 2

The 'morning after' feeling! At the summit conference festivities are over and normal life begins again. The critical commentators, Enobarbus and Agrippa, prepare the way for the world leaders—and offer derisive comments about Lepidus, the weakest of the triumvirate. Antony and Octavia are about to leave for Athens, and there is an emotional parting from Caesar—but again, the commentators are sceptical.

1 *brothers*: Caesar and Antony, now brothers-in-law—or perhaps Agrippa speaks ironically of all the members of the triumvirate, who made such show of love for each other at the feast on Pompey's barge.

2 *dispatch'd with Pompey*: settled the business with Pompey and sent him away.

3 *sealing*: i.e. the contracts.

4 *sad*: serious.

Scene 2

          Rome: enter Agrippa *at one door,*
          Enobarbus *at another*

     Agrippa
   What, are the brothers parted?
     Enobarbus
   They have dispatch'd with Pompey; he is gone.
   The other three are sealing. Octavia weeps
   To part from Rome; Caesar is sad, and Lepidus
5 Since Pompey's feast, as Menas says, is troubled
   With the green-sickness.
     Agrippa
                         'Tis a noble Lepidus.
     Enobarbus
   A very fine one. Oh, how he loves Caesar!
     Agrippa
   Nay, but how dearly he adores Mark Antony!

6 *green-sickness*: the anaemic sickness of young girls—in fact Lepidus has a hangover.

7 *fine one*: Enobarbus plays with the word: '*lepidus*' is the Latin word for 'fine, elegant'.

11 *nonpareil*: incomparable.

12 *Arabian bird*: i.e. the phoenix. The mythological bird was said to be the only one of its kind; after living for several hundred years in the Arabian desert, it burned itself to death then rose again out of its own ashes.

14 *plied*: loaded.

16–17 *Hearts . . . number*: The sequence of nouns is paralleled by the corresponding sequence of verbs—a poetic device familiar to Elizabethan love poets.

16 *figures*: figures of speech.

17 *cast*: count, calculate.
number: versify, put into 'numbers' (= verses).

20 *They . . . beetle*: they are no more than the dung on which he feeds; an allusion to the proverb 'the beetle flies over many sweet flowers and lights in a cow-shard'.

21 *This . . . horse*: this trumpet-call is telling us to get on our horses.

23 *No further*: you need go no further; Caesar and Antony have been in conversation before they come on to the stage.

25 *Use*: treat.

26–7 *As my thoughts . . . approof*: as I am sure you will be, and such as I could stake everything on your proving to be.

26 *bond*: security, pawn.

27 *pass*: pledge.
approof: trial, approval.

28 *piece*: masterpiece, example.

29 *cement*: cément.

Enobarbus
Caesar? Why he's the Jupiter of men!
Agrippa
10 What's Antony? The god of Jupiter!
Enobarbus
Spake you of Caesar? Hoo! The nonpareil!
Agrippa
O Antony! O thou Arabian bird!
Enobarbus
Would you praise Caesar, say 'Caesar'. Go no further.
Agrippa
Indeed, he plied them both with excellent praises.
Enobarbus
15 But he loves Caesar best. Yet he loves Antony.
Hoo! Hearts, tongues, figures, scribes, bards, poets, cannot
Think, speak, cast, write, sing, number—hoo!—
His love to Antony! But as for Caesar,
Kneel down, kneel down, and wonder!
Agrippa
                                        Both he loves.
Enobarbus
20 They are his shards and he their beetle.

Trumpet within

                                        So,
This is to horse. Adieu, noble Agrippa.
Agrippa
Good fortune, worthy soldier, and farewell.

Enter Caesar, Antony, Lepidus, *and* Octavia

Antony
No further, sir.
Caesar
You take from me a great part of myself.
25 Use me well in't. Sister, prove such a wife
As my thoughts make thee, and as my farthest bond
Shall pass on thy approof. Most noble Antony,
Let not the piece of virtue which is set
Betwixt us, as the cement of our love
30 To keep it builded, be the ram to batter
The fortress of it. For better might we

32 *mean*: go-between, mediator.

Have lov'd without this mean, if on both parts
This be not cherish'd.

Antony
                          Make me not offended
In your distrust.

Caesar
                     I have said.

Antony
                          You shall not find,

35 *be therein curious*: make the most
searching enquiries.

35 Though you be therein curious, the least cause
For what you seem to fear. So the gods keep you,
And make the hearts of Romans serve your ends.
We will here part.

Caesar
Farewell, my dearest sister, fare thee well.

40 *elements*: seasons, weather.

40 The elements be kind to thee, and make
Thy spirits all of comfort! Fare thee well.

Octavia
My noble brother!

She weeps

43–4 *The April . . . on*: Antony alludes
poetically to Octavia's tears as the April
showers that, proverbially, 'bring forth
May flowers'.

Antony
The April's in her eyes; it is love's spring
And these the showers to bring it on. Be cheerful.

Octavia
45 Sir, look well to my husband's house, and—

Caesar
What, Octavia?

Octavia
                     I'll tell you in your ear.

She whispers to Caesar

48 *inform*: instruct, direct.

49 *at . . . tide*: on still water, just before the
tide turns.

Antony
Her tongue will not obey her heart, nor can
Her heart inform her tongue—the swan's-down
        feather
That stands upon the swell at full of tide,
50 And neither way inclines.

51 *cloud in's face*: looks sorrowful.

52–3 *He were . . . man*: A cloud (= a dark
     spot on the face) lessened the value of a
     horse; Enobarbus seems to scorn
     Caesar's show of emotion.

54–6 In *Julius Caesar* Antony had wept, and
     moved others to tears, at the sight of
     the murdered Caesar (*Act 3*, Scene 1),
     but he displayed no grief at the death of
     Brutus (*Act 5*, Scene 5).

57 *rheum*: watering of the eyes.
58 *confound*: destroy.
     wail'd: lamented.

60 *still*: regularly.
60–1 *The time . . . you*: there will never be a
     time when I do not think of you.

Enobarbus
[*Aside to* Agrippa] Will Caesar weep?
    Agrippa
[*Aside to* Enobarbus]   He has a cloud in's face.
    Enobarbus
[*Aside to* Agrippa] He were the worse for that were
     he a horse;
So is he, being a man.
    Agrippa
[*Aside to* Enobarbus]   Why, Enobarbus,
When Antony found Julius Caesar dead,
55 He cried almost to roaring and he wept
When at Philippi he found Brutus slain.
    Enobarbus
[*Aside to* Agrippa] That year, indeed, he was
     troubled with a rheum.
What willingly he did confound he wail'd,
Believe't, till I wept too.
    Caesar
                   No, sweet Octavia,
60 You shall hear from me still. The time shall not
Outgo my thinking on you.
    Antony
                Come, sir, come,
I'll wrestle with you in my strength of love.
Look, here I have you [*Embracing him*]; thus I let
     you go,
And give you to the gods.
    Caesar
                Adieu. Be happy!
    Lepidus
65 Let all the number of the stars give light
To thy fair way!
    Caesar
             Farewell, farewell! [*Kisses* Octavia]
    Antony
                 Farewell!

        Trumpets sound   [*Exeunt*

Act 3   Scene 3

In Alexandria time has been standing still: this scene is a continuation of *Act 2, Scene 5*, in which Cleopatra first heard the news of Antony's marriage. She is still struggling to overcome the hurt of the apparent betrayal— but the audience is better informed! Cleopatra questions the messenger about Octavia.

2   *Go to*: nonsense.
2s.d.   *as before*: i.e. the same messenger (bringing the news from Rome about Antony's marriage to Octavia).
3   *Herod of Jewry*: i.e. the most ferocious tyrant. The ruler of Judaea at the time of Cleopatra was Herod the Great, but the reputation for murderous tyranny was earned by another Herod, his successor, who ordered the Slaughter of the Innocents at the time of the birth of Christ.

5   *how*: i.e. how can I have it.

12   *shrill-tongued*: i.e. like Fulvia (see *1, 1, 33*).

Scene 3

> *Alexandria*: *enter* Cleopatra, Charmian, Iras, *and* Alexas

Cleopatra
Where is the fellow?

Alexas
                              Half afeard to come.

Cleopatra
Go to, go to.

> *Enter the* Messenger *as before*

              Come hither, sir.

Alexas
                                        Good majesty,
Herod of Jewry dare not look upon you
But when you are well pleas'd.

Cleopatra
                                        That Herod's head
5   I'll have! But how, when Antony is gone,
Through whom I might command it?—Come thou near.

Messenger
Most gracious majesty!

Cleopatra
                                        Didst thou behold Octavia?

Messenger
Ay, dread queen.

Cleopatra
                    Where?

Messenger
                                        Madam, in Rome.
I look'd her in the face, and saw her led
10   Between her brother and Mark Antony.

Cleopatra
Is she as tall as me?

Messenger
                                        She is not, madam.

Cleopatra
Didst hear her speak? Is she shrill-tongued or low?

Messenger
Madam, I heard her speak; she is low-voiced.

Cleopatra
That's not so good. He cannot like her long.
　　　　Charmian
15 Like her? O Isis! 'Tis impossible.
　　　　Cleopatra
I think so, Charmian. Dull of tongue and dwarfish.
What majesty is in her gait? Remember,
If e'er thou look'dst on majesty.
　　　　Messenger
　　　　　　　　　　　　She creeps.
Her motion and her station are as one.
20 She shows a body rather than a life,
A statue than a breather.
　　　　Cleopatra
　　　　　　　　　　Is this certain?
　　　　Messenger
Or I have no observance.
　　　　Charmian
　　　　　　　　　　Three in Egypt
Cannot make better note.
　　　　Cleopatra
　　　　　　　　　He's very knowing;
I do perceiv't. There's nothing in her yet.
25 The fellow has good judgement.
　　　　Charmian
　　　　　　　　　　　Excellent.
　　　　Cleopatra
Guess at her years, I prithee.
　　　　Messenger
　　　　　　　　　　Madam,
She was a widow—
　　　　Cleopatra
　　　　　　　Widow? Charmian, hark!
　　　　Messenger
And I do think she's thirty.
　　　　Cleopatra
Bear'st thou her face in mind? Is't long or round?
　　　　Messenger
30 Round, even to faultiness.
　　　　Cleopatra
For the most part, too, they are foolish that are so.
Her hair, what colour?

17 *gait*: manner of walking, deportment.

19 *station*: standing still.
20 *shows . . . life*: looks more dead than
    alive.

27 *widow*: Octavia had first been married
    to Caius Marcellus (see 2, 6, 109).

28 *thirty*: Cleopatra makes no comment. In
    historical fact, the Egyptian queen was
    herself 29 at the time of this action.

Messenger

            Brown, madam, and her forehead
As low as she would wish it.

Cleopatra

            There's gold for thee.
Thou must not take my former sharpness ill.
35 I will employ thee back again; I find thee
Most fit for business. Go, make thee ready;
Our letters are prepar'd.   [*Exit* Messenger

Charmian

            A proper man.

Cleopatra

Indeed, he is so. I repent me much
That so I harried him. Why methinks, by him,
40 This creature's no such thing.

Charmian

            Nothing, madam.

Cleopatra

The man hath seen some majesty, and should know.

Charmian

Hath he seen majesty? Isis else defend,
And serving you so long!

Cleopatra

I have one thing more to ask him yet, good
   Charmian.
45 But 'tis no matter; thou shalt bring him to me
Where I will write. All may be well enough.

Charmian

I warrant you, madam.

                      [*Exeunt*

Scene 4

    Athens: enter Antony *and* Octavia

Antony

Nay, nay, Octavia, not only that.
That were excusable—that, and thousands more
Of semblable import—but he hath wag'd
New wars 'gainst Pompey; made his will, and read it
5 To public ear;
Spoke scantly of me; when perforce he could not

---

33 *As low . . . it*: i.e. she wouldn't want it to be any lower; a low forehead was considered unattractive.

35 *back*: to go back.

37 *proper*: excellent, first class.

39 *harried*: harassed.
  by him: according to what he says.
40 *no such thing*: nothing very special.

42 *Isis else defend*: may Isis forbid that he should say anything else.
43 *And serving you*: since he has been serving you; the implication is that Cleopatra had sent the messenger to spy on Antony.

Act 3   Scene 4

Now living in Athens (see *3, 1, 36*), Antony has learned that Caesar is breaking the terms of the peace treaty and has declared war again on Pompey. He is angry, and threatens to join battle. Octavia volunteers to act as a mediator between her husband and her brother.

  3 *semblance*: similar.

4   *New wars*: The peace treaty made in 2, 6, 34–5 granted Sicily and Sardinia to Pompey, but now Caesar has made war against him 'to get Sicilia into his hands' (Plutarch).

4–5   *made . . . ear*: Presumably the will of Octavius Caesar, like that of his uncle, made generous bequests to the Roman citizens (see *Julius Caesar, Act 2, Scene 1*).

6   *scantly*: grudgingly.
     perforce: of necessity.
8   *vented*: uttered, expressed.
9   *hint*: cue, opportunity.
10 *from his teeth*: with clenched teeth.
12 *Stomach not*: don't take offence at.
13 *division chance*: split occurs.
     between: i.e. between Antony and Caesar.
15 *presently*: at once.
17 *Undo*: and then undo.

21 *draw . . . point*: turn you in the direction; Antony uses the image of the compass needle.

24 *so branchless*: destitute of that honour—i.e. not wearing the crown of oak or laurel leaves which would be awarded to a hero.
26 *preparation of*: combat forces for.
27 *stain*: darken, eclipse.
27–8 *Make . . . yours*: make as much haste as you can, provided that is what you want.

31 *cleave*: split apart.

33 *where this begins*: where all this started.
34 *our faults*: i.e. those of Antony and Caesar.
36 *move*: be angry.
     Provide your going: make all preparations for your departure.
37 *what cost*: whatever expenses.

But pay me terms of honour, cold and sickly
He vented them; most narrow measure lent me;
When the best hint was given him, he not took't,
10 Or did it from his teeth.
>   **Octavia**
>   O, my good lord,
Believe not all, or if you must believe,
Stomach not all. A more unhappy lady,
If this division chance, ne'er stood between,
Praying for both parts.
15 The good gods will mock me presently
When I shall pray 'O, bless my lord and husband!';
Undo that prayer by crying out as loud
'O, bless my brother!' Husband win, win brother,
Prays and destroys the prayer; no midway
20 'Twixt these extremes at all.
>   **Antony**
>   Gentle Octavia,
Let your best love draw to that point which seeks
Best to preserve it. If I lose mine honour,
I lose myself; better I were not yours
Than yours so branchless. But, as you requested,
25 Yourself shall go between's. The meantime, lady,
I'll raise the preparation of a war
Shall stain your brother. Make your soonest haste,
So your desires are yours.
>   **Octavia**
>   Thanks to my lord.
The Jove of power make me, most weak, most weak,
30 Your reconciler! Wars 'twixt you twain would be
As if the world should cleave, and that slain men
Should solder up the rift.
>   **Antony**
When it appears to you where this begins,
Turn your displeasure that way, for our faults
35 Can never be so equal that your love
Can equally move with them. Provide your going;
Choose your own company, and command what cost
Your heart has mind to.
>   [*Exeunt*

Enobarbus and Eros meet to exchange
news—and to bring the audience up to date.
Caesar has triumphed over Pompey; Lepidus
is imprisoned on Caesar's accusation; and
Pompey has been murdered.

5 *old*: Antony has learned of this at the
beginning of *Act 3, Scene 4*.
success: outcome.
6 *him*: i.e. Lepidus.
7 *presently*: immediately.
rivality: partnership, equality.

10 *upon . . . appeal*: on Caesar's own
accusation—i.e. with no other evidence.
11 *third*: i.e. of the triumvirate.
up: shut up, imprisoned.
enlarge: sets him free from.
12 *chaps*: jaws.
14 *grind . . . other*: grind against each
other.
15 *thus*: Eros demonstrates Antony's gait as
he kicks at the rushes strewn on the
floor of the stage.
17 *that his officer*: that particular officer of
his; Shakespeare is evasive about the
details of Pompey's death—see
'Commentary', p. xxvi.

20 *presently*: at once.
21 *hereafter*: later.

Scene 5

> Antony's *house*: *enter* Enobarbus *and* Eros,
> *meeting*

Enobarbus
How now, friend Eros?
Eros
There's strange news come, sir.
Enobarbus
What, man?
Eros
Caesar and Lepidus have made wars upon Pompey.
Enobarbus
5 This is old. What is the success?
Eros
Caesar, having made use of him in the wars 'gainst
Pompey, presently denied him rivality; would not let
him partake in the glory of the action, and, not
resting here, accuses him of letters he had formerly
10 wrote to Pompey; upon his own appeal, seizes him.
So the poor third is up, till death enlarge his confine.
Enobarbus
Then, world, thou hast a pair of chaps, no more,
And throw between them all the food thou hast,
They'll grind the one the other. Where's Antony?
Eros
15 He's walking in the garden, thus, and spurns
The rush that lies before him; cries, 'Fool Lepidus!',
And threats the throat of that his officer
That murder'd Pompey.
Enobarbus
      Our great navy's rigg'd.
Eros
For Italy and Caesar. More, Domitius:
20 My lord desires you presently. My news
I might have told hereafter.
Enobarbus
      'Twill be naught,
But let it be. Bring me to Antony.
Eros
Come, sir.
           [*Exeunt*

Act 3   Scene 6

Now it is Caesar's turn to accuse Antony—
who has returned to Egypt and to Cleopatra,
and is giving away large portions of the
Roman empire to his Egyptian family.
Octavia arrives from Athens, and Caesar tells
her how she has been betrayed and deserted
by Antony.

1 *Contemning*: contemptuous of.
3 *tribunal*: raised platform.

6 *Caesarion . . . son*: i.e. Caesarion,
   Cleopatra's son by Julius Caesar;
   Octavius himself had been adopted by
   Caesar as his son and heir.
9 *stablishment*: confirmed possession.

Scene 6

> *Rome: enter* Agrippa, Maecenas, *and*
> Caesar

Caesar
Contemning Rome, he has done all this, and more
In Alexandria. Here's the manner of't:
I'th' market-place, on a tribunal silver'd,
Cleopatra and himself in chairs of gold
5 Were publicly enthron'd. At the feet sat
Caesarion, whom they call my father's son,
And all the unlawful issue that their lust
Since then hath made between them. Unto her
He gave the stablishment of Egypt; made her
10 Of lower Syria, Cyprus, Lydia,
Absolute queen.

Maecenas
                    This in the public eye?
Caesar
I'th' common showplace where they exercise.
His sons he there proclaim'd the kings of kings:
Great Media, Parthia and Armenia
15 He gave to Alexander; to Ptolemy he assign'd
Syria, Cilicia and Phoenicia. She
In th'habiliments of the goddess Isis

12 *common . . . exercise*: public exercise
    ground.

17 *habiliments*: attire.

19 *so*: dressed like this.

20 *Rome*: i.e. the senate and populace of
Rome.

21 *queasy with*: sick of.

23 *knows*: Shakespeare often gives an '*s*'
ending to verbs in the third person
plural.

26 *spoil'd*: stripped of his possession.
rated: allotted.

30 *being*: having been deposed.
31 *revenue*: revénue.

35 *change*: change of fortune—from
triumvir to captive.

39s.d. *train*: retinue.

41 *castaway*: rejected, discarded.

That day appear'd, and oft before gave audience
As 'tis reported, so.

Maecenas

20 Let Rome be thus inform'd.

Agrippa

Who, queasy with his insolence already,
Will their good thoughts call from him.

Caesar

The people knows it, and have now receiv'd
His accusations.

Agrippa   Who does he accuse?

Caesar

25 Caesar; and that having in Sicily
Sextus Pompeius spoil'd, we had not rated him
His part o'th' isle. Then does he say he lent me
Some shipping, unrestor'd. Lastly, he frets
That Lepidus of the triumvirate

30 Should be depos'd and, being, that we detain
All his revenue.

Agrippa   Sir, this should be answer'd.

Caesar

'Tis done already, and the messenger gone.
I have told him Lepidus was grown too cruel,
That he his high authority abus'd

35 And did deserve his change. For what I have
    conquer'd,
I grant him part; but then in his Armenia
And other of his conquer'd kingdoms, I
Demand the like.

Maecenas   He'll never yield to that.

Caesar

Nor must not then be yielded to in this.

Enter Octavia *with her train*

Octavia

40 Hail, Caesar, and my lord! Hail, most dear Caesar!

Caesar

That ever I should call thee castaway!

Octavia

You have not call'd me so, nor have you cause.

Caesar
Why have you stolen upon us thus? You come not
Like Caesar's sister. The wife of Antony
45 Should have an army for an usher, and
The neighs of horse to tell of her approach
Long ere she did appear. The trees by th' way
Should have borne men, and expectation fainted,
Longing for what it had not. Nay, the dust
50 Should have ascended to the roof of heaven,
Rais'd by your populous troops. But you are come
A market maid to Rome, and have prevented
The ostentation of our love which, left unshown,
Is often left unlov'd. We should have met you
55 By sea and land, supplying every stage
With an augmented greeting.

Octavia
                              Good my lord,
To come thus was I not constrain'd, but did it
On my free will. My lord Mark Antony,
Hearing that you prepar'd for war, acquainted
60 My grieved ear withal, whereon I begg'd
His pardon for return.

Caesar
                         Which soon he granted,
Being an abstract 'tween his lust and him.

Octavia
Do not say so, my lord.

Caesar
                         I have eyes upon him,
And his affairs come to me on the wind.
65 Where is he now?

Octavia
                    My lord, in Athens.

Caesar
                                        No,
My most wronged sister. Cleopatra hath
Nodded him to her. He hath given his empire
Up to a whore, who now are levying
The kings o'th' earth for war. He hath assembled
70 Bocchus the king of Libya, Archelaus
Of Cappadocia, Philadelphos king
Of Paphlagonia, the Thracian king Adallas,
King Manchus of Arabia, king of Pont,

47 *by th' way*: along the roadside.
48–9 *expectation . . . not*: the waiting crowds should have grown weak with longing before they could see her.

51 *populous*: numerous.
52 *A market maid*: like a maid going to market.
   prevented: forestalled.
53 *ostentation*: public demonstration.
54 *left unlov'd*: taken for lack of love.
55 *stage*: stopping-place.

60 *grieved*: grievèd.
61 *pardon*: permission.

62 *Being an abstract*: because it removed an obstacle.

67 *Nodded him*: summoned him with a nod of her head.
68 *who now are*: and they are now.
69–77 *He . . . sceptres*: The list is taken from Plutarch.

Herod of Jewry, Mithridates king
75 Of Comagene, Polemon and Amyntas,
The kings of Mede and Lycaonia,
With a more larger list of sceptres.
  Octavia
Ay me, most wretched,
That have my heart parted betwixt two friends
80 That does afflict each other!
  Caesar
        Welcome hither.
Your letters did withhold our breaking forth
Till we perceiv'd both how you were wrong led
And we in negligent danger. Cheer your heart.
Be you not troubled with the time, which drives
85 O'er your content these strong necessities,
But let determin'd things to destiny
Hold unbewail'd their way. Welcome to Rome,
Nothing more dear to me! You are abus'd
Beyond the mark of thought, and the high gods,
90 To do you justice, makes his ministers
Of us and those that love you. Best of comfort,
And ever welcome to us.
  Agrippa
        Welcome, lady.
  Maecenas
Welcome, dear madam.
Each heart in Rome does love and pity you.
95 Only th'adulterous Antony, most large
In his abominations, turns you off
And gives his potent regiment to a trull
That noises it against us.
  Octavia
        Is it so, sir?
  Caesar
Most certain. Sister, welcome. Pray you
100 Be ever known to patience. My dear'st sister!
            [*Exeunt*

---

77 *sceptres*: crowned heads, rulers.

80 *does*: do; for the third-person plural with 's' compare 'knows' *3, 6, 23*.

81 *breaking forth*: rising up.

83 *negligent danger*: danger through being negligent.

85 *strong necessities*: cruel inevitabilities.

86–7 *determin'd . . . way*: events whose destiny has been foreordained proceed without regret. Plutarch explained that 'it was predestined that the government of all the world should fall into Octavius Caesar's hands'.

88 *abus'd*: exploited, deceived.

89 *mark of thought*: beyond what could be thought.

90 *makes . . . ministers*: make us their agents.

95 *large*: unrestrained.

96 *off*: away.

97 *potent regiment*: mighty authority. *trull*: whore.

98 *noises it*: is making an uproar.

Act 3   Scene 7

Antony's forces are assembling on the north-east coast of Greece—and Cleopatra insists on being present to see the action, despite the hostility of Enobarbus. She supports Antony's rash decision to fight by sea, although this is opposed by experienced soldiers.

3 *forspoke*: argued against, opposed.

5 *denounc'd*: declared.

8 *merely lost*: lost completely; Enobarbus perhaps makes a pun with 'merely' and 'marely'.
bear: carry—*and*, copulate with.

10 *puzzle*: fluster, confuse.

13 *Traduc'd*: censured, condemned.
14 *eunuch*: i.e. Mardian.

16 *charge*: expense, cost.

18 *for*: just like.

19 *I have done*: Enobarbus acknowledges defeat: it was Canidius (according to Plutarch) who argued that Cleopatra should remain because she 'defrayed so great a charge' in the war.

Scene 7

Actium: enter Cleopatra *and* Enobarbus

Cleopatra
I will be even with thee, doubt it not.
Enobarbus
But why, why, why?
Cleopatra
Thou hast forspoke my being in these wars
And say'st it is not fit.
Enobarbus
                    Well, is it, is it?
Cleopatra
5 Is't not denounc'd against us? Why should not we
Be there in person?
Enobarbus
                    Well, I could reply
If we should serve with horse and mares together,
The horse were merely lost. The mares would bear
A soldier and his horse.
Cleopatra
                    What is't you say?
Enobarbus
10 Your presence needs must puzzle Antony,
Take from his heart, take from his brain, from's time
What should not then be spar'd. He is already
Traduc'd for levity, and 'tis said in Rome
That Photinus, an eunuch and your maids
15 Manage this war.
Cleopatra
                    Sink Rome, and their tongues rot
That speak against us! A charge we bear i'th' war,
And, as the president of my kingdom, will
Appear there for a man. Speak not against it!
I will not stay behind.

Enter Antony *and* Canidius

Enobarbus
                    Nay, I have done.
20 Here comes the emperor.

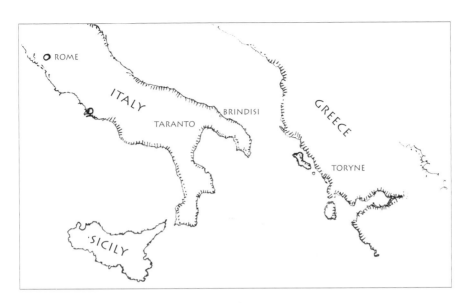

Antony

Is it not strange, Canidius,
That from Tarentum and Brundusium
He could so quickly cut the Ionian sea
And take in Toryne? You have heard on't, sweet?

Cleopatra

Celerity is never more admir'd

25 Than by the negligent.

Antony

A good rebuke,
Which might have well becomed the best of men,
To taunt at slackness. Canidius, we
Will fight with him by sea.

Cleopatra

By sea—what else?

Canidius

Why will my lord do so?

Antony

For that he dares us to't.

Enobarbus

30 So hath my lord dar'd him to single fight.

Canidius

Ay, and to wage this battle at Pharsalia,
Where Caesar fought with Pompey. But these offers,
Which serve not for his vantage, he shakes off,
And so should you.

21–3 Caesar has led his army from Rome down to Taranto and Brindisi at the southern tip of Italy, then across the Adriatic ('Ionian') to Toryne, on the west coast of Greece; see map, above.

23 *take in*: occupy.

24 *admir'd*: wondered at.

29 *For that*: because.

31 *Pharsalia*: the site of the battle in which Julius Caesar fought and defeated Pompey the Great; see 'Events in history', p. vii.

32 *offers*: challenges.

35 *muleteers*: mule-drivers.
36 *Engross'd . . . impress*: got together by hurried conscription.
38 *yare*: trim, light and easily manageable.

42 *absolute soldiership*: excellent military force.
43 *Distract*: split up.
most: mainly.
44 *war-mark'd footmen*: veteran infantrymen.
unexecuted: unused, redundant.
46 *assurance*: certainty of success.
47 *merely*: completely.

49 *sails*: ships.

50 *overplus of*: surplus.
51 *head*: headland, promontory.

Enobarbus
                          Your ships are not well mann'd,
35 Your mariners are muleteers, reapers, people
Engross'd by swift impress. In Caesar's fleet
Are those that often have 'gainst Pompey fought;
Their ships are yare, yours heavy. No disgrace
Shall fall you for refusing him at sea,
40 Being prepar'd for land.
Antony
                          By sea, by sea.
Enobarbus
Most worthy sir, you therein throw away
The absolute soldiership you have by land;
Distract your army, which doth most consist
Of war-mark'd footmen; leave unexecuted
45 Your own renowned knowledge; quite forgo
The way which promises assurance; and
Give up yourself merely to chance and hazard
From firm security.
Antony
                          I'll fight at sea.
Cleopatra
I have sixty sails, Caesar none better.
Antony
50 Our overplus of shipping will we burn
And with the rest full-mann'd, from th'head of
    Actium
Beat th'approaching Caesar. But if we fail,
We then can do't at land.

Enter a Messenger

                                    Thy business?
Messenger
The news is true, my lord; he is descried.
55 Caesar has taken Toryne.
        Antony
Can he be there in person? 'Tis impossible;
Strange that his power should be. Canidius,
Our nineteen legions thou shalt hold by land
And our twelve thousand horse. We'll to our ship.
60 Away, my Thetis!

            Enter a Soldier

                        How now, worthy soldier?
        Soldier
O noble emperor, do not fight by sea.
Trust not to rotten planks. Do you misdoubt
This sword and these my wounds? Let th'Egyptians
And the Phoenicians go a-ducking; we
65 Have us'd to conquer standing on the earth
And fighting foot to foot.
        Antony
                        Well, well, away!
            [*Exeunt* Antony, Cleopatra, *and* Enobarbus

54   *is descried*: has been sighted.

57   *power*: forces, army.

59   *horse*: cavalry.
     to: get to.
60   *Thetis*: The name of a sea-goddess,
     mother of Achilles.

62   *misdoubt*: mistrust.

64   *Phoenicians*: the seafaring nation living
     in what is now called Lebanon.
     go a-ducking: take to the water, be
     ducked in the sea.
65   *have us'd*: are accustomed.

67 *Hercules*: the classical superman whom
Antony claimed as ancestor.

68–9 *his . . . on't*: his entire strategy is being
founded on those capacities in which he
is not strong.

70 *women's men*: the servants of women.
keep: command.

71 *whole*: undivided.

72–3 The names are taken from Plutarch.

75 *Carries*: shoots him forward.

76 *power*: troops.
distractions: detachments, separate
divisions.
77 *Beguil'd*: deceived.
spies: observers.

78 *Taurus*: This mention of the general in
command of Caesar's land forces
prepares for the character's appearance
in the next scene.

80–1 'Every minute some more news is
delivered.'

Soldier
By Hercules, I think I am i'th' right.
    Canidius
Soldier, thou art. But his whole action grows
Not in the power on't. So our leader's led,
70 And we are women's men.
    Soldier
                    You keep by land
The legions and the horse whole, do you not?
    Canidius
Marcus Octavius, Marcus Justeius,
Publicola and Caelius are for sea,
But we keep whole by land. This speed of Caesar's
75 Carries beyond belief.
    Soldier
                    While he was yet in Rome,
His power went out in such distractions as
Beguil'd all spies.
    Canidius
                Who's his lieutenant, hear you?
    Soldier
They say one Taurus.
    Canidius
                Well I know the man.

Enter a Messenger

    Messenger
The emperor calls Canidius.
    Canidius
80 With news the time's in labour, and throws forth
Each minute some.
                                    [*Exeunt*

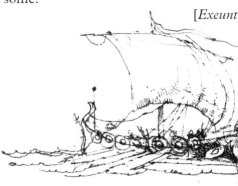

Act 3 Scenes 8, 9, 10

The battle of Actium is about to begin, and there will be fierce fighting throughout the next three scenes—offshore and off-stage! Caesar gives orders.

3 *whole*: together.

5 *prescript*: instructions.

6 *jump*: gamble, venture.

Scene 8

> *Actium*: *enter* Caesar *and* Taurus *with his army, marching*

Caesar
Taurus!
　　Taurus
My lord?
　　Caesar
Strike not by land; keep whole; provoke not battle
Till we have done at sea. Do not exceed
5 The prescript of this scroll. [*Gives him a scroll*] Our fortune lies
Upon this jump.

　　　　　　　　　　　　　　　　[*Exeunt*

Act 3   Scene 9

Antony issues directives.

2 *eye*: sight.
　 battle: main forces, battalion.

Scene 9

> *Actium*: *enter* Antony *and* Enobarbus

Antony
Set we our squadrons on yond side o'th' hill
In eye of Caesar's battle, from which place
We may the number of the ships behold
And so proceed accordingly.

　　　　　　　　　　　　　　　　[*Exeunt*

Act 3   Scene 10

Quick movements, curt directives, and the noises of battle have been sufficient to keep the audience informed at first, and now—suddenly—it is all over! We learn, through Enobarbus and Scarus, the shameful events that have already occurred, and we learn, from Canidius, of the desertion of Antony's followers.

os.d. *Alarum*: battle call to arms; the fighting is about to begin.
1 *Naught*: lost, ruined.
2 *Antoniad . . . admiral*: The flagship of Cleopatra was called *The Antoniad*.
4 *blasted*: struck blind.

5 *synod*: assembly, parliament.

Scene 10

Actium: Canidius *marcheth with his land army one way over the stage, and* Taurus, *the lieutenant of* Caesar, *the other way. After their going in, is heard the noise of a sea fight*

Alarum. Enter Enobarbus

Enobarbus
Naught, naught, all naught! I can behold no longer!
Th'Antoniad, the Egyptian admiral,
With all their sixty, fly and turn the rudder.
To see't mine eyes are blasted.

Enter Scarus

Scarus
                                    Gods and goddesses!
5 All the whole synod of them!

Enobarbus

What's thy passion?

Scarus

The greater cantle of the world is lost
With very ignorance. We have kiss'd away
Kingdoms and provinces.

Enobarbus

How appears the fight?

Scarus

On our side, like the token'd pestilence
10 Where death is sure. Yon ribaudred nag of Egypt—
Whom leprosy o'ertake!—i'th' midst o'th' fight
When vantage like a pair of twins appear'd
Both as the same—or, rather, ours the elder—
The breeze upon her, like a cow in June,
15 Hoists sails and flies.

6 *cantle*: segment (of a circle or sphere).
7 *With very ignorance*: through sheer stupidity.
9 *token'd pestilence*: spotted plague.
10 *ribaudred nag*: The disgust and contempt of Scarus can find no other expression: translation is impossible! Both 'ribaldry' and 'debauchery' are contained in *ribaudred*, and the kind of horse described as a *nag* was likely to have had many riders.
11 *leprosy*: This was believed to be a sexually transmitted disease.
12 *vantage*: advantage, chances of success.
13 *elder*: i.e. therefore stronger.
14 *breeze*: gadfly (= an insect that attacks cattle).

Enobarbus

That I beheld.
Mine eyes did sicken at the sight and could not
Endure a further view.

Scarus

              She once being loof'd,
The noble ruin of her magic, Antony,
20 Claps on his sea-wing and, like a doting mallard,
Leaving the fight in height, flies after her.
I never saw an action of such shame.
Experience, manhood, honour, ne'er before
Did violate so itself.

Enobarbus

              Alack, alack!

Enter Canidius

Canidius

25 Our fortune on the sea is out of breath
And sinks most lamentably. Had our general
Been what he knew—himself—it had gone well.
Oh, he has given example for our flight
Most grossly by his own!

Enobarbus

              Ay, are you thereabouts?
30 Why then, good night indeed.

Canidius

Toward Peloponnesus are they fled.

Scarus

'Tis easy to't, and there I will attend
What further comes.

Canidius

              To Caesar will I render
My legions and my horse. Six kings already
35 Show me the way of yielding.

Enobarbus

              I'll yet follow

18 *loof'd*: luffed. Shakespeare used Plutarch's nautical term (= sailed into the wind), but the sense seems to demand something like 'aloof, at a distance'.

20 *sea-wing*: sails.

27 *Been . . . himself*: behaved like the leader that he knew he was.

29 *grossly*: blatantly, conspicuously.
    are you thereabouts: is that what you are thinking.

30 *good night indeed*: it is really all over.

32 *'Tis easy to't*: it's easy to get there—see 'The world of the play', p. x.
    attend: wait and see.

33 *render*: hand over, surrender.

34 *legions . . . horse*: foot soldiers and cavalry.

36 *wounded chance*: ruined fortunes.

37 *Sits . . . me*: is warning me against it.

The wounded chance of Antony, though my reason
Sits in the wind against me.
[*Exit at one door* Canidius, *at the other* Scarus *and*
Enobarbus

Act 3   Scene 11

Two episodes from Plutarch's narrative are
here conflated into a single scene. On board
Cleopatra's vessel Antony, defeated and
depressed, dismisses his attendants. He is
sunk in misery when Cleopatra approaches
him, but his recriminations are more in
sorrow than anger. When Cleopatra weeps,
however, Antony begins to recover his spirits.

1 *Hark*: Antony's footsteps echo as he
   treads the boards.
3 *lated*: belated, overcome by the dark.

12 *that*: that which (i.e. Cleopatra).

17 *Sweep your way*: smooth your path.
18 *loathness*: reluctance.
19 *that*: i.e. himself.
20 *leaves itself*: is no longer what it was.
21 *possess you*: let you have possession.

Scene 11

On Cleopatra's *ship*; *Taenarus.*

Enter Antony *with* Attendants

Antony
Hark! The land bids me tread no more upon't;
It is asham'd to bear me. Friends, come hither.
I am so lated in the world that I
Have lost my way for ever. I have a ship
5 Laden with gold. Take that, divide it. Fly
And make your peace with Caesar.
All
                                   Fly? Not we.
Antony
I have fled myself and have instructed cowards
To run and show their shoulders. Friends, be gone.
I have myself resolv'd upon a course
10 Which has no need of you. Be gone.
My treasure's in the harbour. Take it. Oh,
I follow'd that I blush to look upon.
My very hairs do mutiny, for the white
Reprove the brown for rashness, and they them
15 For fear and doting. Friends, be gone. You shall
Have letters from me to some friends that will
Sweep your way for you. Pray you, look not sad
Nor make replies of loathness; take the hint
Which my despair proclaims. Let that be left
20 Which leaves itself. To the sea-side straightway.
I will possess you of that ship and treasure.
Leave me, I pray, a little—pray you, now;
Nay, do so; for indeed I have lost command;
Therefore, I pray you. I'll see you by and by.
                                   [*Exeunt* Attendants

Antony *sits down*

Enter Cleopatra *led by* Charmian, Iras, *and* Eros

Eros
25 Nay, gentle madam, to him! Comfort him.
Iras
Do, most dear queen.
Charmian
Do? Why, what else?
Cleopatra
Let me sit down. O, Juno!
Antony
No, no, no, no, no!
Eros
30 See you here, sir?
Antony
O fie, fie, fie!
Charmian
Madam!
Iras
Madam! O, good empress!
Eros
Sir, sir!
Antony
35 Yes, my lord, yes. He at Philippi kept
His sword e'en like a dancer, while I struck
The lean and wrinkl'd Cassius, and 'twas I
That the mad Brutus ended. He alone
Dealt on lieutenantry, and no practice had
40 In the brave squares of war. Yet now—no matter.
Cleopatra
Ah, stand by.
Eros
The queen, my lord! The queen!
Iras
Go to him, madam; speak to him.
He is unqualited with very shame.
Cleopatra
45 Well then, sustain me. Oh!
Eros
Most noble sir, arise. The queen approaches.
Her head's declin'd, and death will seize her but
Your comfort makes the rescue.

31 *O fie*: Antony sighs.

35 *my lord*: Antony is so lost in his depression that he seems not to recognize Eros.
35–8 *He . . . ended*: Antony is remembering the battle of Philippi where he fought on the side of Octavius Caesar against Cassius and Brutus. Antony exaggerates his own personal achievements: both Cassius and Brutus committed suicide; see 'Events in history', p. vii.
35 *kept*: i.e. kept in the scabbard.
38–9 *He alone . . . lieutenantry*: relied entirely on what was done by his officers.
39 *practice*: practical experience.
40 *brave*: splendid.
   squares: matches, contests.
41 *by*: aside.
44 *unqualited*: beside himself, completely destroyed.
   very: absolute, utter.

49 *offended*: disgraced.

50 *unnoble swerving*: ignoble deviation;
Antony cannot respond to the address
by Eros, 'Most noble sir'.

52 *convey*: hide.

53 *what . . . behind*: to see everything I
have achieved.

54 *'Stroy'd*: destroyed.

57 *strings*: heart-strings.

60 *Thy beck*: a wave of your hand.

62 *young man*: i.e. Octavius Caesar.
treaties: entreaties, requests.

62–3 *dodge . . . lowness*: get involved in low
dodges and shifty dealings.

64 *play'd*: gambled.

67 *affection*: infatuation.

68 *on all cause*: whatever the reason.

69 *Fall . . . tear*: don't shed a single tear.
rates: is worth.

71 *Even this*: this alone.

72 *We*: The plural form indicates Antony's
reviving spirits.
schoolmaster: the master employed to
teach the children of Antony and
Cleopatra.
a: he.

Antony
I have offended reputation,
50 A most unnoble swerving.
Eros
                                    Sir, the queen!
Antony
O, whither hast thou led me, Egypt? See
How I convey my shame out of thine eyes
By looking back what I have left behind
'Stroy'd in dishonour.
Cleopatra
                                    O, my lord, my lord,
55 Forgive my fearful sails! I little thought
You would have follow'd.
Antony
                                    Egypt, thou knewst too well
My heart was to thy rudder tied by th' strings
And thou shouldst tow me after. O'er my spirit
Thy full supremacy thou knewst, and that
60 Thy beck might from the bidding of the gods
Command me.
Cleopatra
                                    Oh, my pardon!
Antony
                                    Now I must
To the young man send humble treaties; dodge
And palter in the shifts of lowness, who
With half the bulk o'th' world play'd as I pleas'd,
65 Making and marring fortunes. You did know
How much you were my conqueror, and that
My sword, made weak by my affection, would
Obey it on all cause.
Cleopatra
                                    Pardon, pardon!
Antony
Fall not a tear, I say; one of them rates
70 All that is won and lost. Give me a kiss. [*They kiss*]
Even this repays me.
We sent our schoolmaster. Is a come back?
Love, I am full of lead. Some wine
Within there and our viands! Fortune knows
75 We scorn her most when most she offers blows.
                                    [*Exeunt*

Act 3   Scene 12

The victorious Caesar, rejecting Antony's
humble plea to be allowed to live in Egypt
with Cleopatra, plans to set the two of them
against each other.

3 *argument*: sign, evidence.
  pluck'd: defeated.
4 *pinion*: feather.
5 *Which had*: who used to have.
6 *moons*: months.

6s.d. *Ambassador*: i.e. the schoolmaster.

8 *petty . . . ends*: insignificant for his
  purposes.

10 *To*: compared to.

12 *Requires*: requests.
13 *lessens*: reduces.

16 *confess*: acknowledge.

18 *circle of the Ptolemies*: crown of the
  dynasty of the Ptolemies.
19 *hazarded . . . grace*: forfeited (like the
  stake in a game of dice) to the disposal
  of your favour.

21 *Of . . . fail*: shall be given a hearing and
  be granted her requests.
  so: provided that.

24 *So . . . both*: deliver this message to
  them both.

Scene 12

> Caesar's *camp outside Alexandria*: enter
> Caesar, Agrippa, Dolabella, *and* Thidias
> *with others*

Caesar
Let him appear that's come from Antony.
Know you him?
Dolabella
                    Caesar, 'tis his schoolmaster;
An argument that he is pluck'd, when hither
He sends so poor a pinion of his wing,
5 Which had superfluous kings for messengers
Not many moons gone by.

> *Enter* Ambassador *from* Antony

Caesar
                    Approach, and speak.
Ambassador
Such as I am, I come from Antony.
I was of late as petty to his ends
As is the morn-dew on the myrtle leaf
10 To his grand sea.
Caesar
                    Be't so. Declare thine office.
Ambassador
Lord of his fortunes he salutes thee, and
Requires to live in Egypt; which not granted,
He lessens his requests and to thee sues
To let him breathe between the heavens and earth,
15 A private man in Athens. This for him.
Next, Cleopatra does confess thy greatness,
Submits her to thy might, and of thee craves
The circle of the Ptolemies for her heirs,
Now hazarded to thy grace.
Caesar
                    For Antony,
20 I have no ears to his request. The queen
Of audience nor desire shall fail, so she
From Egypt drive her all-disgraced friend
Or take his life there. This if she perform,
She shall not sue unheard. So to them both.

Ambassador
25 Fortune pursue thee!
　　Caesar
　　　　　　　　　　　　Bring him through the bands.
　　　　　　　　　　　[*Exit* Ambassador, *attended*
　　[*To* Thidias] To try thy eloquence now 'tis time.
　　　Dispatch.
　　From Antony win Cleopatra; promise,
　　And in our name, what she requires; add more,
　　From thine invention, offers. Women are not
30 In their best fortunes strong, but want will perjure
　　The ne'er-touch'd vestal. Try thy cunning, Thidias;
　　Make thine own edict for thy pains, which we
　　Will answer as a law.
　　　Thidias
　　　　　　　　　　Caesar, I go.
　　Caesar
　　Observe how Antony becomes his flaw,
35 And what thou think'st his very action speaks
　　In every power that moves.
　　　Thidias
　　　　　　　　　　　　Caesar, I shall.
　　　　　　　　　　　　　　　　[*Exeunt*

Marginal notes (left column):

25 *Bring . . . bands*: escort him through the lines of troops.

28 *in our name*: on my authority.

30 *In . . . fortunes*: in the most favourable circumstances.
30–1 *want . . . vestal*: destitution will force even the purest vestal virgin to break her vows.
32 *Make . . . pains*: name your own price for your efforts.
33 *answer as law*: settle up as though we had a contract.
34 *becomes his flaw*: comes to terms with his misfortune.
35–6 *what . . . moves*: how you interpret every move he makes.

Antony learns that Caesar has refused his request and he reacts with defiance, offering to encounter Caesar in single combat. He leaves the stage to write his challenge. Cleopatra receives Thidias and hears what Caesar is offering to her. She appears to look favourably on the messenger, and when Antony sees this he is outraged. He orders the punishment of Thidias and reviles Cleopatra most bitterly—but fresh courage revives with reconciliation. Enobarbus, however, has heard enough. He decides to leave Antony.

1 *Think*: despair, give in.
3 *will*: desire, sexual passion.
5 *face*: front.
　several ranges: different formations.
7 *affection*: lust.
8 *nick'd*: got the better.

Scene 13

　　Alexandria: enter Cleopatra, Enobarbus, Charmian, *and* Iras

Cleopatra
What shall we do, Enobarbus?
　　Enobarbus
　　　　　　　　　　　Think, and die.
　　Cleopatra
Is Antony or we in fault for this?
　　Enobarbus
Antony only, that would make his will
Lord of his reason. What though you fled
5 From that great face of war, whose several ranges
Frighted each other? Why should he follow?
The itch of his affection should not then
Have nick'd his captainship, at such a point,

10 *mered*: merèd; sole.
   question: cause of dispute.
11 *course*: chase after.

15 *have courtesy*: be treated with
   compassion.
   so: provided that.

20 *rose*: bloom.
21–2 *from . . . particular*: and because of
   this the world is expecting great things
   from him.
23 *ministers*: agents, subordinates.
24 *soon*: easily.
26 *gay caparisons*: splendid trappings.
27 *answer me declin'd*: encounter me now
   that I have been brought so low.
29 *high-battled*: commanding great armies.
30 *Unstate his happiness*: divest himself of
   his good fortune.
30–1 *be stag'd . . . sworder*: make an
   exhibition of himself fighting in single
   combat.
32 *parcel of*: of a piece with.
32–4 *things . . . alike*: external circumstances
   draw the inner man with them so that
   they all suffer together.

When half to half the world oppos'd, he being
10 The mered question. 'Twas a shame no less
Than was his loss, to course your flying flags
And leave his navy gazing.

Cleopatra
                              Prithee, peace.

Enter the Ambassador *with* Antony

Antony
Is that his answer?
Ambassador
Ay, my lord.
Antony
15 The queen shall then have courtesy, so she
Will yield us up.
Ambassador
                  He says so.
Antony
                              Let her know't.
To the boy Caesar send this grizzled head,
And he will fill thy wishes to the brim
With principalities.
Cleopatra
                     That head, my lord?
Antony
20 To him again! Tell him he wears the rose
Of youth upon him, from which the world should
   note
Something particular. His coin, ships, legions,
May be a coward's, whose ministers would prevail
Under the service of a child as soon
25 As i'th' command of Caesar. I dare him therefore
To lay his gay caparisons apart
And answer me declin'd, sword against sword,
Ourselves alone. I'll write it. Follow me.
                 [*Exeunt* Antony *and* Ambassador

Enobarbus
[*Aside*] Yes, like enough high-battled Caesar will
30 Unstate his happiness, and be stag'd to th' show
Against a sworder! I see men's judgements are
A parcel of their fortunes, and things outward
Do draw the inward quality after them
To suffer all alike. That he should dream,

35 *Knowing all measures*: with all his experience; 'measures' leads on to the images of 'full' and 'empty' in the next lines.

36 *Answer*: respond to.

40 *blown*: fallen.

42 'My honour and my self-interest begin to be at odds with each other.'

43-4 'Loyalty that stays faithful to fools makes the faith itself become foolish.'

46 *him*: i.e. Caesar.

47 *story*: history book, chronicle.

49 *apart*: in private.

50 *None*: i.e. there are none.

51 *haply*: perhaps.

53 *Or needs not us*: has no need of friends (i.e. his case is hopeless).

57 *in what . . . stand'st*: your situation.

58 *he is Caesar*: Thidias speaks ambiguously: by nature Caesar might be *either* magnanimous *or* tyrannical. *right royal*: a truly generous gesture.

---

35 Knowing all measures, the full Caesar will
Answer his emptiness! Caesar, thou hast subdu'd
His judgement too.

Enter a Servant

Servant
A messenger from Caesar.
Cleopatra
What, no more ceremony? See, my women,
40 Against the blown rose they may stop their nose
That kneel'd unto the buds. Admit him, sir.
[*Exit* Servant

Enobarbus
[*Aside*] Mine honesty and I begin to square.
The loyalty well held to fools does make
Our faith mere folly. Yet he that can endure
45 To follow with allegiance a fallen lord
Does conquer him that did his master conquer,
And earns a place i'th' story.

Enter Thidias

Cleopatra
Caesar's will?
Thidias
Hear it apart.
Cleopatra
50 None but friends. Say boldly.
Thidias
So haply they are friends to Antony.
Enobarbus
He needs as many, sir, as Caesar has,
Or needs not us. If Caesar please, our master
Will leap to be his friend. For us, you know,
55 Whose he is we are, and that is Caesar's.
Thidias
                                    So.
Thus then, thou most renown'd: Caesar entreats
Not to consider in what case thou stand'st
Further than he is Caesar.
Cleopatra
                        Go on; right royal.

Thidias
He knows that you embrace not Antony
60 As you did love, but as you fear'd him.
    Cleopatra
                           Oh!

Thidias
The scars upon your honour, therefore, he
Does pity as constrained blemishes,
Not as deserv'd.
    Cleopatra
                  He is a god and knows
What is most right. Mine honour was not yielded
65 But conquer'd merely.
    Enobarbus
[*Aside*] To be sure of that, I will ask Antony.
Sir, sir, thou art so leaky
That we must leave thee to thy sinking, for
Thy dearest quit thee.   [*Exit* Enobarbus
    Thidias
                  Shall I say to Caesar
70 What you require of him? For he partly begs
To be desir'd to give. It much would please him
That of his fortunes you should make a staff
To lean upon. But it would warm his spirits
To hear from me you had left Antony
75 And put yourself under his shroud,
The universal landlord.
    Cleopatra
                  What's your name?
    Thidias
My name is Thidias.
    Cleopatra
                Most kind messenger,
Say to great Caesar this in deputation:
I kiss his conqu'ring hand. Tell him I am prompt
80 To lay my crown at's feet, and there to kneel
Till from his all-obeying breath I hear
The doom of Egypt.
    Thidias
                'Tis your noblest course.
Wisdom and fortune combating together,
If that the former dare but what it can,

---

62 *constrained blemishes*: faults that have been forced upon you.

65 *merely*: utterly; Cleopatra also speaks ambiguously.

67 *leaky*: full of holes.

70 *require*: request.

75 *shroud*: protection.
76 *The universal landlord*: the lord of all the world.

78 *in deputation*: as my representative.

81 *all-obeying breath*: voice which is obeyed by everybody.
82 *The doom of Egypt*: his judgement and sentence on the queen of Egypt.

83–5 'Whenever wisdom and good fortune are fighting together, the wise man who stands firm will not be shaken by any change of fortune.'

85 No chance may shake it. Give me grace to lay
My duty on your hand.
Cleopatra
[*Offers him her hand*] Your Caesar's father oft,
When he hath mus'd of taking kingdoms in,
Bestow'd his lips on that unworthy place
90 As it rain'd kisses.

Enter Antony *and* Enobarbus

Antony
                    Favours? By Jove that thunders!
What art thou, fellow?
Thidias
                    One that but performs
The bidding of the fullest man and worthiest
To have command obey'd.
Enobarbus
[*Aside*]   You will be whipp'd.
Antony
[*Calls for* Servants] Approach there!—Ah, you
    kite!—Now, gods and devils,
95 Authority melts from me. Of late when I cried 'Ho!',
Like boys unto a muss, kings would start forth
And cry 'Your will?'

86   *duty*: respect.

88   *taking . . . in*: conquering kingdoms.

90   *As*: as if.
     Jove that thunders: Jupiter the god of
     thunder.

92   *fullest*: most fortunate, most successful;
     compare 'full' in line 35.

94   *kite*: scavenging bird of prey.

96   *boys . . . muss*: children running to pick
     up small objects thrown on the ground
     for them.
     start forth: spring to attention.

Enter Servants

                    Have you no ears? I am
Antony yet. Take hence the jack and whip him!

98   *jack*: knave, scoundrel.

Enobarbus

[*Aside*] 'Tis better playing with a lion's whelp

100 Than with an old one dying.

Antony

Moon and stars!

Whip him! Were't twenty of the greatest tributaries

That do acknowledge Caesar, should I find them

So saucy with the hand of she here—what's her name

Since she was Cleopatra? Whip him, fellows,

105 Till like a boy you see him cringe his face

And whine aloud for mercy. Take him hence!

Thidias

Mark Antony—

Antony

Tug him away! Being whipp'd,

Bring him again. The jack of Caesar's shall

Bear us an errand to him.

[*Exeunt* Servants *with* Thidias

110 You were half blasted ere I knew you. Ha?

Have I my pillow left unpress'd in Rome,

Forborne the getting of a lawful race,

And by a gem of women, to be abus'd

By one that looks on feeders?

Cleopatra

Good my lord—

Antony

115 You have been a boggler ever.

But when we in our viciousness grow hard—

Oh, misery on't!—the wise gods seel our eyes,

In our own filth drop our clear judgements, make us

Adore our errors, laugh at's while we strut

120 To our confusion.

101 *tributaries*: men who pay tribute.

103 *she*: this woman.

105 *cringe*: distort, screw up.

110 *blasted*: withered, blighted.

113 *abus'd*: deceived.
114 *looks on*: gives favours to.
feeders: parasites.

115 *boggler*: In falconry the term is applied to a hawk that does not select and follow a single quarry but turns to pursue first one and then another.
ever: always.
116–20 *But . . . confusion*: These lines echo words and ideas from the Bible— John 12:40, 'He hath blinded their eyes, and hardened their heart, that they should not see with their eyes, nor understand with their heart'; Psalms 2:4 'He that dwelleth in heaven shall laugh them to scorn' (see 'Commentary', p. xxxi).
116 *in our . . . hard*: become hardened to our own depravity.
117 *seel*: close up; a term in falconry for sewing up the eyes of a young hawk before it is trained to wear a hood.
120 *confusion*: ruin, damnation.

Cleopatra

　　　　　　Oh, is't come to this?

Antony

I found you as a morsel, cold upon
Dead Caesar's trencher—nay, you were a fragment
Of Gnaeus Pompey's, besides what hotter hours,
Unregister'd in vulgar fame, you have
125 Luxuriously pick'd out. For I am sure,
Though you can guess what temperance should be,
You know not what it is.

Cleopatra

　　　　　　　　Wherefore is this?

Antony

To let a fellow that will take rewards
And say 'God quit you!' be familiar with
130 My playfellow, your hand, this kingly seal
And plighter of high hearts! O that I were
Upon the hill of Basan, to outroar
The horned herd! For I have savage cause,
And to proclaim it civilly were like
135 A halter'd neck which does the hangman thank
For being yare about him.

Enter a Servant *with* Thidias

　　　　　　　　Is he whipp'd?

Servant

Soundly, my lord.

Antony

　　　　　Cried he? And begged 'a pardon?

Servant

He did ask favour.

Antony

[*To* Thidias] If that thy father live, let him repent
140 Thou wast not made his daughter; and be thou sorry
To follow Caesar in his triumph, since
Thou hast been whipp'd for following him.
　　Henceforth
The white hand of a lady fever thee;
Shake thou to look on't. Get thee back to Caesar;
145 Tell him thy entertainment. Look thou say
He makes me angry with him. For he seems
Proud and disdainful, harping on what I am,
Not what he knew I was. He makes me angry,

122–3 *Dead Caesar . . . Gnaeus Pompey*:
　　Cleopatra's lovers had included both
　　Julius Caesar and Gnaeus Pompey, son
　　of Pompey the Great.
122 *trencher*: wooden platter.
　　fragment: leftover scrap.
124 *Unregister'd . . . fame*: unknown to
　　common gossip.
125 *Luxuriously*: lasciviously.
　　pick'd out: indulged yourself in.
128 *rewards*: bribes, payments.
129 *God quit you*: may God reward you; a
　　form of thanks most often used by
　　inferiors.
130 *kingly seal*: royal signature (i.e. for
　　official documents).
131 *plighter . . . hearts*: that which has sealed
　　the pledges of noble lovers.
131–3 *O that . . . herd*: Antony visualizes
　　himself roaring like one of the bulls on
　　the high hill of Basan. Shakespeare
　　alludes to the Bible (Psalms 68:15 and
　　22:12), and to the popular Elizabethan
　　notion that horns would grow on the
　　head of a cuckold (= a man whose wife
　　is unfaithful to him).
134 *civilly*: in a civilized manner.
135 *A halter'd neck*: a man with a noose
　　round his neck.
136 *yare*: efficient.
137 *'a*: he.

141 *triumph*: triumphal procession.

143 *fever*: put you into a sweat.

145 *thy entertainment*: how you have been
　　treated.

150-1 *my good . . . orbs*: the planets that were my guiding stars have dropped out of their spheres. Antony alludes to a doctrine of Ptolemaic astronomy (see 2, 7, 14–15 note), once again using the language of the Bible. The author of Revelation describes how he 'saw a star fall from heaven unto the earth, and to him was given the key of the bottomless pit. And he opened the bottomless pit' (9:1–2).

154 *enfranch'd bondman*: emancipated slave.

156 *quit*: requite, repay.

158 *terrene moon*: earthly moon—i.e. Cleopatra (who was often associated with Isis, the Egyptian moon-goddess). *eclips'd*: An eclipse was thought to be a portent of imminent disaster.

159 *alone*: nothing but.
160 *stay his time*: wait until he is ready.
161 *mingle eyes*: exchange glances.
162 *ties his points*: fastens his clothes for him ('points' = laces with tags).
164–72 *From . . . prey*: Shakespeare again draws images from the Old Testament: after sending plagues of hail and flies, Jehovah declared that he would 'smite all the first-born in the land of Egypt' (Exodus 12:12).
166 *in my neck*: on my head. *determines*: melts, comes to an end.
167 *Caesarion*: Cleopatra's first child.
168 *memory . . . womb*: i.e. all my children.
169 *brave*: splendid.
170 *discandying . . . storm*: dissolving of his hailstorm.
172 *buried them*: i.e. by swarming down on them.
173 *sets down*: is encamped.
174 *fate*: destiny.
175 *held*: kept together.
176 *fleet*: are afloat. *most sea-like*: in good naval fashion.
177 Antony again finds his love with his courage, exchanging the formal *you* for the intimate *thou*.

And at this time most easy 'tis to do't,
150 When my good stars that were my former guides
Have empty left their orbs and shot their fires
Into th'abysm of hell. If he mislike
My speech and what is done, tell him he has
Hipparchus, my enfranch'd bondman, whom
155 He may at pleasure whip or hang or torture,
As he shall like to quit me. Urge it thou.
Hence with thy stripes! Be gone!
                                    [*Exit* Thidias *with* Servant

Cleopatra
                                    Have you done yet?

Antony
Alack, our terrene moon is now eclips'd
And it portends alone the fall of Antony.

Cleopatra
160 I must stay his time.

Antony
To flatter Caesar would you mingle eyes
With one that ties his points?

Cleopatra
                                    Not know me yet?

Antony
Cold-hearted toward me?

Cleopatra
                                    Ah, dear, if I be so,
From my cold heart let heaven engender hail
165 And poison it in the source, and the first stone
Drop in my neck; as it determines, so
Dissolve my life! The next Caesarion smite,
Till by degrees the memory of my womb,
Together with my brave Egyptians all,
170 By the discandying of this pelleted storm
Lie graveless, till the flies and gnats of Nile
Have buried them for prey!

Antony
                                    I am satisfied.
Caesar sets down in Alexandria, where
I will oppose his fate. Our force by land
175 Hath nobly held; our sever'd navy too
Have knit again, and fleet, threat'ning most sea-like.
Where hast thou been, my heart? Dost thou hear,
    lady?

179 *in blood*: full of vigour.
180 *chronicle*: place in history.

182 *brave*: magnificent.

183 *treble . . . breath'd*: have the strength,
    courage and breath of three men.
184 *maliciously*: furiously.
185 *nice and lucky*: prosperous and happy.
    ransom: redeem, purchase.
185-6 *ransom . . . jests*: buy their lives from
    me with nothing more than a joke.
188 *gaudy*: festive, revelling.

197 *sap*: life; Antony thinks of the sap rising
    in the springtime.
198-9 *contend . . . scythe*: destroy as many as
    the plague can kill.

200 *furious*: desperate in frenzy.

202 *estridge*: goshawk (a large short-winged
    hawk).
    still: all the time.
203-4 *A diminution . . . heart*: as Antony's
    reason gets weaker his courage grows
    stronger.

If from the field I shall return once more
To kiss these lips, I will appear in blood.
180 I and my sword will earn our chronicle.
There's hope in't yet.
    Cleopatra
That's my brave lord!
    Antony
I will be treble-sinew'd, hearted, breath'd,
And fight maliciously. For when mine hours
185 Were nice and lucky, men did ransom lives
Of me for jests. But now, I'll set my teeth
And send to darkness all that stop me. Come,
Let's have one other gaudy night. Call to me
All my sad captains. Fill our bowls once more.
190 Let's mock the midnight bell.
    Cleopatra
                                It is my birthday.
I had thought t'have held it poor, but since my lord
Is Antony again, I will be Cleopatra.
    Antony
We will yet do well.
    Cleopatra
[*To* Charmian *and* Iras] Call all his noble captains
    to my lord!
    Antony
195 Do so, we'll speak to them; and tonight I'll force
The wine peep through their scars. Come on, my
    queen,
There's sap in't yet! The next time I do fight
I'll make Death love me, for I will contend
Even with his pestilent scythe.
                                [*Exeunt all but* Enobarbus
    Enobarbus
200 Now he'll outstare the lightning. To be furious
Is to be frighted out of fear, and in that mood
The dove will peck the estridge; and I see still
A diminution in our captain's brain
Restores his heart. When valour preys on reason,
205 It eats the sword it fights with. I will seek
Some way to leave him.   [*Exit*

Act 4

Act 4   Scene 1

Caesar, angry but scornful, prepares to do
battle with Antony. He is confident of
success.

Scene 1

> *Outside Alexandria: enter* Caesar, Agrippa,
> *and* Maecenas, *with his army,* Caesar
> *reading a letter*

1 *as*: as though.

Caesar
He calls me boy, and chides as he had power
To beat me out of Egypt. My messenger
He hath whipp'd with rods; dares me to personal
   combat,
Caesar to Antony. Let the old ruffian know
5 I have many other ways to die; meantime
Laugh at his challenge.

Maecenas
         Caesar must think,
When one so great begins to rage, he's hunted

9 *falling*: exhaustion.
   breath: time to breathe.
10 *Make boot*: exploit, take advantage.

Even to falling. Give him no breath, but now
10 Make boot of his distraction. Never anger
Made good guard for itself.

11 *best heads*: chief officers.

Caesar
              Let our best heads
Know that tomorrow the last of many battles

13 *files*: ranks.
14 *but late*: just recently.
15 *fetch him in*: surround and capture him.
16 *store*: plenty.
17 *waste*: expense.

We mean to fight. Within our files there are,
Of those that serv'd Mark Antony but late,
15 Enough to fetch him in. See it done,
And feast the army. We have store to do't
And they have earn'd the waste. Poor Antony!
                           [Exeunt

Act 4   Scene 2

Antony also is preparing to fight, and he
looks to Enobarbus for support.

1 *fight*: i.e. in single combat.
  Domitius: Antony, for the first time,
  addresses Enobarbus by his first name.

5–6 *Or . . . Or*: either . . . or.

6–7 *bathe . . . live again*: i.e. cause such
  bloodshed that the glory will restore his
  honour.
  Woo't: wilt, are you going to.
8 *strike*: The verb is ambiguous: 'fight' *or*
  'surrender'.
  Take all: all or nothing; the call of a
  desperate gambler.

13 *fellows*: fellow servants.

14 *tricks*: wild ideas.

17 *clapp'd*: rolled.

Scene 2

> *Alexandria: enter* Antony, Cleopatra,
> Enobarbus, Charmian, Iras, Alexas *with*
> *others*

Antony
He will not fight with me, Domitius?
Enobarbus
                                        No.
Antony
Why should he not?
Enobarbus
He thinks, being twenty times of better fortune,
He is twenty men to one.
Antony
                        Tomorrow, soldier,
5 By sea and land I'll fight. Or I will live,
Or bathe my dying honour in the blood
Shall make it live again. Woo't thou fight well?
Enobarbus
I'll strike, and cry 'Take all!'
Antony
                            Well said! Come on!
Call forth my household servants.   [*Exit* Alexas
                            Let's tonight
10 Be bounteous at our meal.

> *Enter three or four* Servitors

                            Give me thy hand.
Thou hast been rightly honest; so hast thou,
Thou, and thou, and thou. You have serv'd me well
And kings have been your fellows.
Cleopatra
[*Aside to* Enobarbus]   What means this?
Enobarbus
[*Aside to* Cleopatra] 'Tis one of those odd tricks
    which sorrow shoots
15 Out of the mind.
Antony
                    And thou art honest too.
I wish I could be made so many men,
And all of you clapp'd up together in

An Antony, that I might do you service
So good as you have done.

All the Servants
                                    The gods forbid!

Antony
20 Well, my good fellows, wait on me tonight;
Scant not my cups, and make as much of me
As when mine empire was your fellow too
And suffer'd my command.

Cleopatra
[*Aside to* Enobarbus]   What does he mean?

Enobarbus
[*Aside to* Cleopatra] To make his followers weep.

Antony
                                    Tend me tonight.
25 May be it is the period of your duty.
Haply you shall not see me more, or if,
A mangled shadow. Perchance tomorrow
You'll serve another master. I look on you
As one that takes his leave. Mine honest friends,
30 I turn you not away, but, like a master
Married to your good service, stay till death.
Tend me tonight two hours—I ask no more—
And the gods yield you for't!

Enobarbus
                                    What mean you, sir,
To give them this discomfort? Look, they weep,
35 And I, an ass, am onion-eyed. For shame!
Transform us not to women!

Antony
                                    Ho, ho, ho!
Now the witch take me if I meant it thus!
Grace grow where those drops fall! My hearty
    friends,
You take me in too dolorous a sense,
40 For I spake to you for your comfort, did desire you
To burn this night with torches. Know, my hearts,
I hope well of tomorrow, and will lead you
Where rather I'll expect victorious life
Than death and honour. Let's to supper, come,
45 And drown consideration.
                                    [*Exeunt*

---

21 *Scant . . . cups*: keep my glasses filled.

23 *suffer'd*: submitted to.

25 *period*: end.
26 *Haply*: perhaps.
    if: if you do.
27 *mangled shadow*: disfigured ghost.

30 *turn . . . away*: am not dismissing you.

33 *yield*: reward.

35 *am onion-eyed*: i.e. my eyes are watering.

37 *the witch . . . me*: may I be bewitched.
38 *Grace*: the herb of grace, rue (which was
    associated with repentance and pity).
    hearty: good-hearted, loving.

40 *for your comfort*: to comfort you.

45 *consideration*: meditation, serious
    thought.

Act 4   Scene 3

It is the night before the battle, and the Soldiers on guard duty are nervous and apprehensive. They are perplexed by a mysterious noise (see 'Plutarch', p. 145).

os.d. *through one door*: The stage directions suggest that the guard is being changed.

2 *determine one way*: bring matters to an end one way or another.

5 *Belike*: probably.

10 *have . . . hope*: am fully confident.

11 *landmen*: army.
   stand up: be victorious.

Scene 3

Alexandria: enter through one door, First Soldier *and his* Company, *through the other door,* Second Soldier

First Soldier
Brother, good night. Tomorrow is the day.
    Second Soldier
It will determine one way. Fare you well.
Heard you of nothing strange about the streets?
    First Soldier
Nothing. What news?
    Second Soldier
5 Belike 'tis but a rumour. Good night to you.
    First Soldier
Well sir, good night.

      Other Soldiers *enter and join* Second Soldier

    Second Soldier
Soldiers, have careful watch.
    Third Soldier
And you. Good night, good night.

      They place themselves in every corner of the stage

    Second Soldier
Here we. And if tomorrow
10 Our navy thrive, I have an absolute hope
Our landmen will stand up.

12 *brave*: magnificent.
   full of purpose: most resolute.
12s.d. *hautboys*: oboes.

14 *List*: listen.

18 *signs*: augurs, promises.

21 *Hercules*: It was popularly believed that
   Antony was descended from Hercules,
   the classical superman and demi-god,
   whose qualities he seemed to share.

28 *so . . . quarter*: along our beat, so far as
   our watch extends.
29 *give off*: finish.

First Soldier
'Tis a brave army and full of purpose—

Music of the hautboys is under the stage

Second Soldier
Peace! What noise?
First Soldier
List, list!
Second Soldier
15 Hark!
First Soldier
Music i'th' air.
Third Soldier
Under the earth.
Fourth Soldier
It signs well, does it not?
Third Soldier
No.
First Soldier
20 Peace, I say! What should this mean?
Second Soldier
'Tis the god Hercules whom Antony lov'd
Now leaves him.
First Soldier
                Walk. Let's see if other watchmen
Do hear what we do.
Second Soldier
How now, masters?

Speak together

All
25 How now? How now? Do you hear this?
First Soldier
Ay. Is't not strange?
Third Soldier
Do you hear, masters? Do you hear?
First Soldier
Follow the noise so far as we have quarter.
Let's see how it will give off.
All
                Content. 'Tis strange.
                [*Exeunt*

Act 4   Scene 4

The night is over, and Antony is arming for
battle. Cleopatra gives her assistance.

1   *Eros*: The name of Antony's trusted
    friend and servant—also the Greek
    word for sexual love.

3   *thine iron*: i.e. that piece of armour you
    are holding for me; at line 10 Antony
    tells Eros to put on his own armour.
5   *brave*: defy.

7   *False . . . this*: Cleopatra has put
    something the wrong way, and Antony
    shows her how it should go.
8   *Sooth, la*: there now, yes indeed.

10 *Briefly*: in a moment.
13 *doff't*: take it off; Antony's language is
    now that of a courtly knight.
14 *squire*: In the English Middle Ages, this
    was a young man of noble birth who
    served some particular knight.
15 *tight*: skilled.
    Dispatch: hurry up.
16 *That*: if only.
    knew'st: could understand.
17 *occupation*: profession, trade.
18 *workman*: true craftsman.

Scene 4

> *Alexandria: enter* Antony *and* Cleopatra
> *with* Charmian *and others*

Antony
Eros! Mine armour, Eros!
   Cleopatra
               Sleep a little.
   Antony
No, my chuck. Eros! Come, mine armour, Eros!

> *Enter* Eros *with armour*

Come, good fellow, put thine iron on.
If fortune be not ours today, it is
5 Because we brave her. Come!
   Cleopatra
                   Nay, I'll help too.
What's this for?
   Antony
              Ah, let be, let be! Thou art
The armourer of my heart. False, false! This, this!
   Cleopatra
Sooth, la, I'll help. Thus it must be.
   Antony
                      Well, well!
We shall thrive now. Seest thou, my good fellow?
10 Go put on thy defences.
   Eros
                  Briefly, sir.
   Cleopatra
Is not this buckled well?
   Antony
              Rarely, rarely!
He that unbuckles this, till we do please
To doff't for our repose, shall hear a storm.
Thou fumblest, Eros, and my queen's a squire
15 More tight at this than thou. Dispatch. O love,
That thou couldst see my wars today and knew'st
The royal occupation, thou shouldst see
A workman in't.

> *Enter an armed* Soldier

19 *knows . . . charge*: has been given a warlike message to deliver.
20 *betime*: early.
22 *riveted trim*: armoured suiting; the various pieces of armour were fixed together with rivets.
23 *port*: gate.
   expect: await.
23s.d. *flourish*: sound a call to arms.
25 *'Tis well blown*: the morning is getting on; *or* that trumpet-call sounded fine.
27 *of note*: famous, outstanding.
28 *So . . . way*: Antony continues to assist Cleopatra in adjusting his armour.
   said: done.
29 *dame*: my lady.
31 *shameful check*: reproach as conduct unbecoming for a soldier.
   stand: insist.
32 *mechanic compliment*: formal leave-taking.
36 *That*: if only.

Good morrow to thee! Welcome!
Thou look'st like him that knows a warlike charge.
20 To business that we love we rise betime
And go to't with delight.
   Soldier
                              A thousand, sir,
Early though't be, have on their riveted trim
And at the port expect you.

Shout. Trumpets flourish

Enter Captains *and* Soldiers

   Captain
The morn is fair. Good morrow, General!
   All the Soldiers
25 Good morrow, General!
   Antony
                         'Tis well blown, lads!
This morning, like the spirit of a youth
That means to be of note, begins betimes.
[*To* Cleopatra] So, so. Come, give me that. This
   way. Well said.
Fare thee well, dame. Whate'er becomes of me,
30 This is a soldier's kiss. [*Kisses her*] Rebukable
And worthy shameful check it were, to stand
On more mechanic compliment. I'll leave thee
Now like a man of steel.—You that will fight,
Follow me close, I'll bring you to't. Adieu.
            [*Exeunt all but* Cleopatra *and* Charmian
   Charmian
35 Please you retire to your chamber?
   Cleopatra
                              Lead me.
He goes forth gallantly. That he and Caesar might
Determine this great war in single fight!
Then Antony—but now—. Well, on.
                                        [*Exeunt*

Scene 5

Alexandria. Trumpets sound. Enter Antony
and Eros. *A* Soldier *meets them*

Soldier
The gods make this a happy day to Antony!
    Antony
Would thou and those thy scars had once prevail'd
To make me fight at land!
    Soldier
                        Hadst thou done so,
The kings that have revolted and the soldier
5 That has this morning left thee would have still
Follow'd thy heels.
    Antony
                Who's gone this morning?
    Soldier
                           Who?
One ever near thee. Call for Enobarbus,
He shall not hear thee, or from Caesar's camp
Say 'I am none of thine.'
    Antony
                  What sayest thou?
    Soldier
                      Sir,
10 He is with Caesar.
    Eros
               Sir, his chests and treasure
He has not with him.
    Antony
             Is he gone?
    Soldier
                Most certain.
    Antony
Go, Eros, send his treasure after. Do it.
Detain no jot, I charge thee. Write to him—
I will subscribe—gentle adieus and greetings.
15 Say that I wish he never find more cause
To change a master. Oh, my fortunes have
Corrupted honest men! Dispatch.—Enobarbus!
                  [Exeunt

Caesar is preparing for victory—and
Enobarbus has joined his camp. But when he
learns of Antony's magnanimity Enobarbus is
overcome with remorse.

Scene 6

Caesar's *camp outside Alexandria. Flourish.*
Enter Agrippa, Caesar, *with* Enobarbus
and Dolabella

Caesar
Go forth, Agrippa, and begin the fight.
Our will is Antony be took alive.
Make it so known.
    Agrippa
Caesar, I shall.   [*Exit*
    Caesar
5 The time of universal peace is near.
Prove this a prosp'rous day, the three-nook'd world
Shall bear the olive freely.

Enter a Messenger

    Messenger
                      Antony
Is come into the field.
    Caesar
                  Go charge Agrippa
Plant those that have revolted in the van
10 That Antony may seem to spend his fury
Upon himself.   [*Exeunt all but* Enobarbus
    Enobarbus
Alexas did revolt and went to Jewry on
Affairs of Antony; there did dissuade
Great Herod to incline himself to Caesar
15 And leave his master Antony. For this pains
Caesar hath hang'd him. Canidius and the rest
That fell away have entertainment but
No honourable trust. I have done ill,
Of which I do accuse myself so sorely
20 That I will joy no more.

Enter a Soldier *of Caesar's*

    Soldier
Enobarbus, Antony
Hath after thee sent all thy treasure, with
His bounty overplus. The messenger
Came on my guard, and at thy tent is now
25 Unloading of his mules.

---

5 *time . . . peace*: That such a time would come was prophesied in the works of the Roman poet Virgil (*Eclogue* IV) and the Bible (Isaiah 2:4).
6 *Prove*: if this prove.
three-nook'd: divided into three parts—i.e. Asia, Africa, and Europe.
7 *bear*: bring forth.
olive: The olive tree was a symbol of peace and plenty.
8 *charge*: order.
9 *Plant*: position.
van: front line.
16–18 For the defection of Canidius see 3, 10, 33–5.
17 *fell away*: deserted.
entertainment: employment.
23 *bounty overplus*: generous gift in addition.
24 *on my guard*: whilst I was on guard.

Enobarbus
                  I give it you.
    Soldier
Mock not, Enobarbus.
I tell you true. Best you saf'd the bringer
Out of the host. I must attend mine office
Or would have done't myself. Your emperor

30 Continues still a Jove.   [*Exit*
    Enobarbus
I am alone the villain of the earth
And feel I am so most. O Antony,
Thou mine of bounty, how wouldst thou have paid
My better service, when my turpitude

35 Thou dost so crown with gold! This blows my heart.
If swift thought break it not, a swifter mean
Shall outstrike thought, but thought will do't, I feel.
I fight against thee? No, I will go seek
Some ditch wherein to die; the foul'st best fits

40 My latter part of life.
                                   [*Exit*

27 *saf'd*: gave safe conduct to.

28 *host*: troops.
    attend . . . office: return to my duties.

30 *a Jove*: to act like Jove in his generosity.

31 *alone*: the only, the worst.

32 *feel . . . most*: am more aware of it than anyone else.

33 *mine*: store.

35 *blows my heart*: makes my heart swell.

36 *thought*: despondency, melancholy.
    mean: means of killing myself.

Scene 7

The battlefield outside Alexandria. Alarum. Drums and Trumpets. Enter Agrippa *and others*

    Agrippa
Retire! We have engag'd ourselves too far.
Caesar himself has work, and our oppression
Exceeds what we expected.   [*Exeunt*

Alarums. Enter Antony, *and* Scarus *wounded*

    Scarus
O, my brave emperor, this is fought indeed!

5 Had we done so at first, we had droven them home
With clouts about their heads.
    Antony
                        Thou bleed'st apace.

Act 4   Scene 7

The land battle is engaged. Caesar is beaten back, and Antony emerges triumphant.

os.d. *Alarum*: a call to battle (on trumpets and drums).

2 *has work*: is having to work hard.
    our oppression: the pressure on us.

4 *is fought indeed*: was properly fought.

5 *had droven*: would have driven.

6 *clouts*: cloths, bandages.
    apace: heavily.

Scarus
I had a wound here that was like a T
But now 'tis made an H.

8 *an H*: Scarus puns on the sounds 'ache' and 'aitch'.

Sound retreat far off

Antony
                                    They do retire.

Scarus
9 *bench-holes*: bogs, latrines.
10 *scotches*: gashes.

We'll beat 'em into bench-holes. I have yet
10 Room for six scotches more.

Enter Eros

Eros
They're beaten, sir, and our advantage serves
For a fair victory.

Scarus

12 *score*: slash.
13 *take*: catch.
14 *runner*: runaway.

                        Let us score their backs
And snatch 'em up as we take hares—behind!
'Tis sport to maul a runner.

Antony
                                I will reward thee
15 *sprightly*: spirited, spirit-warming.
15 Once for thy sprightly comfort, and tenfold
For thy good valour. Come thee on!

Scarus
17 *halt after*: limp after you.
I'll halt after.

                                        [*Exeunt*

Act 4   Scene 8

The triumphant Antony returns to his lady.

2 *gests*: honourable deeds: Antony
   continues to use the language of
   chivalry.

5 *doughty-handed*: valiant in action.
6–7 *as . . . mine*: as though it were not a
   duty but as if every man had my cause
   at heart.
7 *shown all*: all shown yourselves.
   Hector: the warrior celebrated in the
   Trojan War.
8 *clip*: embrace, hug.
9 *feats*: exploits, achievements.
11 *whole*: better, healed again.

12 *fairy*: enchantress.
13 *day*: dayspring, light.

15 *proof of harness*: armour that has
   withstood the enemy.
16 *on . . . triumphing*: in triumph on my
   panting breast.

17 *virtue*: fortitude (Latin *virtus*).
18 *nightingale*: The English bird has a very
   beautiful evening song.

21 *nerves*: sinews.
22 *Get . . . youth*: win just as many goals as
   a young man.

Scene 8

> *Alexandria. Alarum. Enter* Antony *again in*
> *a march*; Scarus *with others*

Antony
We have beat him to his camp. Run one before
And let the queen know of our gests. [*Exit a* Soldier
                                  Tomorrow,
Before the sun shall see's, we'll spill the blood
That has today escap'd. I thank you all,
5 For doughty-handed are you, and have fought
Not as you serv'd the cause, but as't had been
Each man's like mine. You have shown all Hectors.
Enter the city; clip your wives, your friends;
Tell them your feats, whilst they with joyful tears
10 Wash the congealment from your wounds, and kiss
The honour'd gashes whole.

> *Enter* Cleopatra

[*To* Scarus]   Give me thy hand.
To this great fairy I'll commend thy acts,
Make her thanks bless thee. [*To* Cleopatra] O thou
    day o'th' world,
Chain mine arm'd neck! Leap thou, attire and all,
15 Through proof of harness to my heart, and there
Ride on the pants triumphing!

> *They embrace*

Cleopatra
                    Lord of lords!
O infinite virtue! Com'st thou smiling from
The world's great snare uncaught?
Antony
                    My nightingale,
We have beat them to their beds. What, girl!
    Though grey
20 Do something mingle with our younger brown, yet
    have we
A brain that nourishes our nerves and can
Get goal for goal of youth. Behold this man.
Commend unto his lips thy favouring hand.

> *She offers* Scarus *her hand*

25 *mankind*: (stressed on the first syllable)
    the human race.
26 *shape*: his image.

28 *carbuncled*: studded with precious stones.
29 *Phoebus' car*: the chariot of the sun god.

31 'Carry our shields, battered like the
    men who own them', *or*, 'Carry our
    battered shields, like the men who own
    them'.
    hack'd: battered.
    targets: shields.
    owe: own.
33 *camp*: accommodate.
34 *carouses*: toasts.
35 *royal peril*: the greatest danger.
37 *taborins*: small drums.

Kiss it, my warrior. He hath fought today
25 As if a god in hate of mankind had
Destroy'd in such a shape.
        Cleopatra
                        I'll give thee, friend,
An armour all of gold. It was a king's.
        Antony
He has deserv'd it, were it carbuncled
Like holy Phoebus' car. Give me thy hand.
30 Through Alexandria make a jolly march;
Bear our hack'd targets like the men that owe them.
Had our great palace the capacity
To camp this host, we all would sup together
And drink carouses to the next day's fate
35 Which promises royal peril. Trumpeters,
With brazen din blast you the city's ear;
Make mingle with our rattling taborins
That heaven and earth may strike their sounds
    together,
Applauding our approach.

Trumpets sound

[*Exeunt*

Act 4   Scene 9

Anxious sentries—this time guarding
Caesar's camp—wait for the next day's
battle. They overhear a solemn prayer, and
find that Enobarbus has died of grief.

2 *court of guard*: guardhouse.
3 *shiny*: bright with moonshine.
   embattle: prepare for battle; in Scene 8
   Antony said that they would fight
   'tomorrow', before dawn (4, 8, 2–4).
5 *day*: day of fighting.
   shrewd: tough, strenuous.

8 *close*: hidden.

10–11 *When . . . memory*: when other
   deserters are recorded, to their disgrace,
   in history books; 'record' is stressed on
   the second syllable.

15 *O sovereign . . . melancholy*: Enobarbus
   addresses the moon, whose influence
   was thought to produce mental
   disorders.
16 *disponge*: drop down as from a sponge.
17 *my will*: Enobarbus's will is to die.
20 *dried*: Every sigh of grief (it was
   thought) would use up a drop of
   blood—and consequently make the
   heart dry.
23 *in . . . particular*: as far as you can
   yourself.
24 *rank . . . register*: classify me in its
   records.
25 *master-leaver*: one who left his master.
   fugitive: deserter.

Scene 9

Caesar's *camp outside Alexandria*: *enter a*
Sentry *and his* Company of Watch.
Enobarbus *follows*

Sentry
If we be not reliev'd within this hour,
We must return to th' court of guard. The night
Is shiny, and they say we shall embattle
By th' second hour i'th' morn.
   First Watch
5 This last day was a shrewd one to's.
   Enobarbus
O bear me witness, night—
   Second Watch
What man is this?
   First Watch
Stand close and list him.

They stand aside

   Enobarbus
Be witness to me, O thou blessed moon,
10 When men revolted shall upon record
Bear hateful memory, poor Enobarbus did
Before thy face repent.
   Sentry
Enobarbus?
   Second Watch
Peace! Hark further.
   Enobarbus
15 O sovereign mistress of true melancholy,
The poisonous damp of night disponge upon me,
That life, a very rebel to my will,
May hang no longer on me. Throw my heart
Against the flint and harness of my fault,
20 Which, being dried with grief, will break to powder
And finish all foul thoughts. O Antony,
Nobler than my revolt is infamous
Forgive me in thine own particular,
But let the world rank me in register
25 A master-leaver and a fugitive.
O Antony! O Antony!

He sinks down

First Watch
Let's speak to him.
    Sentry
Let's hear him, for the things he speaks may concern
Caesar.
    Second Watch
30 Let's do so. But he sleeps.
    Sentry
Swoons rather, for so bad a prayer as his was never
yet for sleep.
    First Watch
Go we to him.
    Second Watch
Awake sir! Awake! Speak to us!
    First Watch
35 Hear you, sir?
    Sentry
The hand of death hath raught him. [*Drums afar off*]
                           Hark! The drums
Demurely wake the sleepers. Let us bear him
To th' court of guard. He is of note. Our hour
Is fully out.
    Second Watch
40 Come on, then. He may recover yet.
                        [*Exeunt with the body*

Scene 10

    The battlefield: enter Antony *and* Scarus
    with their army

    Antony
Their preparation is today by sea;
We please them not by land.
    Scarus
                For both, my lord.
    Antony
I would they'd fight i'th' fire or i'th' air;
We'd fight there too. But this it is: our foot
5 Upon the hills adjoining to the city
Shall stay with us—order for sea is given;
They have put forth the haven—
Where their appointment we may best discover
And look on their endeavour.
                      [*Exeunt*

---

31 *Swoons*: faints.
32 *for*: a preparation for.

36 *raught*: seized upon.

37 *Demurely*: solemnly.
38 *of note*: a man of importance.
   hour: shift.
39 *fully out*: completely finished.

Act 4   Scene 10

As the guards end their watch, the armies prepare to do battle. Antony sets out to survey Caesar's naval hostilities.

1 *Their preparation*: they are getting ready to fight.
2 *both*: i.e. to fight on land as well as on sea.
3 *I would . . . air*: I wish they could fight in the other two elements as well.
4 *foot*: infantry.
7 *They . . . haven*: our ships have left the harbour.
8 *appointment*: placement, position.
9 *endeavour*: efforts.

Act 4   Scene 11

Caesar plans his strategy.

1 'Unless we are attacked, we shall remain inactive on the land.'
2 *we shall*: i.e. remain inactive.
3 *Is forth*: has set out.
   vales: valleys.
4 *hold . . . advantage*: stay in the most favourable position.

Scene 11

The battlefield: enter Caesar *and his army*

Caesar
But being charg'd we will be still by land,
Which, as I take't, we shall, for his best force
Is forth to man his galleys. To the vales,
And hold our best advantage.

[*Exeunt*

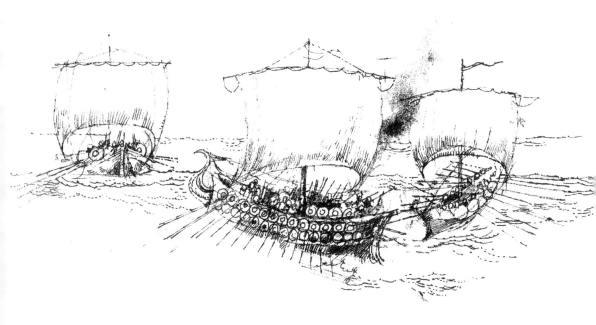

Act 4   Scene 12

Antony goes to view the battle and Scarus, alone on the stage, voices his unease about its outcome. Antony returns, infuriated: the Egyptian fleet has surrendered to Caesar, and he is convinced that Cleopatra has betrayed him. When she sees his rage, Cleopatra hurries to safety.

os.d. *Alarum . . . fight*: The trumpet-call announcing that the sea-battle is about to engage.
1 *join'd*: i.e. in battle.
3 *Straight*: immediately.

Scene 12

Alexandria. Alarum afar off, as at a sea fight. Enter Antony *and* Scarus

Antony
Yet they are not join'd. Where yond pine does stand
I shall discover all. I'll bring thee word
Straight how 'tis like to go.

[*Exit*

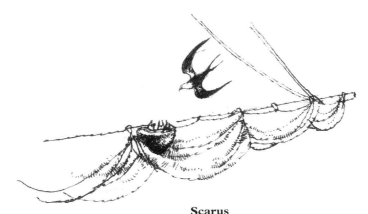

Scarus   Swallows have built
In Cleopatra's sails their nests. The augurs
5 Say they know not, they cannot tell; look grimly,
And dare not speak their knowledge. Antony
Is valiant and dejected, and by starts
His fretted fortunes give him hope and fear
Of what he has and has not.

Enter Antony

Antony   All is lost!
10 This foul Egyptian hath betrayed me.
My fleet hath yielded to the foe, and yonder
They cast their caps up and carouse together
Like friends long lost. Triple-turn'd whore! 'Tis thou
Hast sold me to this novice, and my heart
15 Makes only wars on thee. Bid them all fly!
For when I am reveng'd upon my charm,
I have done all. Bid them all fly! Be gone!
                                   [*Exit* Scarus
O sun, thy uprise shall I see no more.
Fortune and Antony part here; even here
20 Do we shake hands. All come to this! The hearts
That spaniel'd me at heels, to whom I gave
Their wishes, do discandy, melt their sweets
On blossoming Caesar, and this pine is bark'd
That overtopp'd them all. Betray'd I am.
25 O this false soul of Egypt! This grave charm
Whose eye beck'd forth my wars and call'd them
    home,

4 *sails*: ships.
  augurs: official soothsayers (who predicted the future by the interpretation of omens).
7 *by starts*: in turn.
8 *fretted*: chequered, varying.

10 *betrayed*: betrayèd.

13 *Triple-turn'd*: i.e. having turned from Julius Caesar to Gnaeus Pompey, from Pompey to Antony, and now (as he suspects) from Antony himself to Octavius Caesar.
14 *novice*: i.e. the young Caesar.
16 *charm*: enchantress (as at line 25).

20–1 *hearts . . . heels*: the loyalties of those men who followed me like spaniels.
22 *discandy*: dissolve, dribble away.
  sweets: affections.
23 *this pine*: i.e. Antony himself (compared to 'yond pine' (line 1) from which he observed the fighting).
  bark'd: stripped of its bark, dead.
25 *false*: treacherous, deceitful.
  grave charm: fatal witch.
26 *beck'd*: summoned.

27 *crownet*: coronet.
    chief end: main purpose.
28 *right gipsy*: typical Egyptian whore—see
    1, 1, 10.
    fast and loose: a game of deception;
    Antony refers to the trick in which a
    knot is tied and then released when the
    trickster pulls a string.
30 *Avaunt*: vanish, be off.
32 *give . . . deserving*: i.e. kill you.
33 *Caesar's triumph*: Antony envisages
    Caesar's triumphal procession through
    the streets of Rome, which would be
    spoiled without the captive person of
    Cleopatra.
34 *plebeians*: plébeians; common people.
35 *spot*: blemish, stain.
36 *monster*: Various creatures, unusual in
    shape, colour, or size, were exhibited at
    fairs or in travelling shows.
37 *poor'st diminutives*: the very lowest sorts
    of people.
    dolts: cretins, idiots.
39 *prepared*: prepared; grown and
    sharpened for the purpose.

Whose bosom was my crownet, my chief end,
Like a right gipsy hath at fast and loose
Beguil'd me to the very heart of loss.
30 What, Eros, Eros!

Enter Cleopatra

        Ah, thou spell! Avaunt!

Cleopatra
Why is my lord enrag'd against his love?
   Antony
Vanish, or I shall give thee thy deserving
And blemish Caesar's triumph. Let him take thee
And hoist thee up to the shouting plebeians!
35 Follow his chariot like the greatest spot
Of all thy sex; most monster-like be shown
For poor'st diminutives, for dolts, and let
Patient Octavia plough thy visage up
With her prepared nails!   [*Exit* Cleopatra

40 *If . . . live*: if you value your life.

                    'Tis well thou'rt gone
40 If it be well to live. But better 'twere
Thou fell'st into my fury, for one death
Might have prevented many. Eros, ho!

43-4 *shirt of Nessus*: Antony identifies
himself with Hercules ('Alcides') who
died in agony when he put on a shirt
soaked in the poisoned blood of the
centaur Nessus, which had been given
to him by his wife (who had intended a
love-token).

45 *Lichas*: the servant who had carried the
poisoned shirt to Hercules—and was
thrown into the sea by him.
horns o'th' moon: i.e. the tips of the
crescent moon.

46 *those . . . club*: hands like those that
grasped the club of Hercules.

47 *worthiest*: i.e. of death.

The shirt of Nessus is upon me. Teach me
Alcides, thou mine ancestor, thy rage;
45 Let me lodge Lichas on the horns o'th' moon,
And with those hands that grasp'd the heaviest club
Subdue my worthiest self. The witch shall die.
To the young Roman boy she hath sold me, and I fall
Under this plot. She dies for't. Eros, ho!

[*Exit*

Act 4   Scene 13

Cleopatra decides to retreat to her
monument, and sends Mardian to tell
Antony that she is dead.

2 *Telamon . . . shield*: Ajax, the son of
Telamon, killed himself in a furious
madness because he had not been
awarded the shield of Achilles after the
fall of Troy.
boar of Thessaly: a giant boar which
ravaged the countryside; it was killed by
Hercules.

3 *emboss'd*: foaming at the mouth with rage
and exhaustion.

5 *rive*: rend, tear.

6 *going off*: departing.

9 *word*: express.
piteously: so as to move pity.

10 *bring me*: bring me word.
monument: Cleopatra had already
prepared her own mausoleum—which
also served as a treasury.

Scene 13

Alexandria: enter Cleopatra, Charmian,
Iras, Mardian

Cleopatra
Help me, my women! Oh, he's more mad
Than Telamon for his shield; the boar of Thessaly
Was never so emboss'd.
Charmian
                                    To th' monument!
There lock yourself and send him word you are dead.
5 The soul and body rive not more in parting
Than greatness going off.
Cleopatra
                                    To th' monument!
Mardian, go tell him I have slain myself.
Say that the last I spoke was 'Antony',
And word it, prithee, piteously. Hence, Mardian,
10 And bring me how he takes my death. To th'
    monument!

[*Exeunt*

Act 4   Scene 14

Defeated in battle, and believing he has been
betrayed by Cleopatra, Antony decides that
this must be the end for him. Mardian brings
word of Cleopatra's death, and Antony asks
for assistance from Eros. He attempts
suicide, then hears that Cleopatra is not
dead.

2 *dragonish*: shaped like a dragon.

3 *vapour*: cloud, mist.

4 *pendent*: overhanging.

5 *forked*: forkèd; with twin peaks.

7 *mock*: deceive.

8 *black vesper's pageants*: the displays of
late evening.

9 *with a thought*: quick as a thought.

10 *The rack dislimns*: the cloud formation
disperses; behind this image is that of
the 'rack' as an instrument of torture
tearing limb from limb.

12 *knave*: lad, servant.

17 *whilst . . . mine*: i.e. before it was given
to Cleopatra.
annex'd: attached.

18 *more*: i.e. the hearts of Antony's
followers.

19 *Pack'd . . . Caesar*: shuffled the cards in
favour of Caesar.

20 *triumph*: trump card.

23 *sword*: soldiership, manhood.

Scene 14

Alexandria: enter Antony *and* Eros

Antony
Eros, thou yet behold'st me?
    Eros
                        Ay, noble lord.
    Antony
Sometime we see a cloud that's dragonish,
A vapour sometime like a bear or lion,
A tower'd citadel, a pendent rock,
5 A forked mountain, or blue promontory
With trees upon't that nod unto the world
And mock our eyes with air. Thou hast seen these
   signs?
They are black vesper's pageants.
    Eros
                        Ay, my lord.
    Antony
That which is now a horse, even with a thought
10 The rack dislimns and makes it indistinct
As water is in water.
    Eros
                  It does, my lord.
    Antony
My good knave Eros, now thy captain is
Even such a body. Here I am Antony,
Yet cannot hold this visible shape, my knave.
15 I made these wars for Egypt, and the queen—
Whose heart I thought I had, for she had mine,
Which, whilst it was mine, had annex'd unto't
A million more, now lost—she, Eros, has
Pack'd cards with Caesar, and false-play'd my glory
20 Unto an enemy's triumph.
Nay, weep not, gentle Eros. There is left us
Ourselves to end ourselves.

Enter Mardian

                    O thy vile lady!
She has robb'd me of my sword.
    Mardian
                   No, Antony,
My mistress lov'd thee and her fortunes mingled
25 With thine entirely.

Antony

Hence, saucy eunuch! Peace!
She hath betray'd me and shall die the death.

Mardian

Death of one person can be paid but once,
And that she has discharg'd. What thou wouldst do
Is done unto thy hand. The last she spake
30 Was 'Antony! Most noble Antony!'
Then, in the midst, a tearing groan did break
The name of Antony; it was divided
Between her heart and lips. She render'd life,
Thy name so buried in her.

Antony

Dead, then?

Mardian

Dead.

Antony

35 Unarm, Eros. The long day's task is done
And we must sleep. [*To* Mardian] That thou
    depart'st hence safe
Does pay thy labour richly. Go.   [*Exit* Mardian
Off! Pluck off!

Eros unarms him

The sevenfold shield of Ajax cannot keep
40 The battery from my heart. O, cleave, my sides!
Heart, once be stronger than thy continent;
Crack thy frail case! Apace, Eros, apace!
No more a soldier; bruised pieces go;
You have been nobly borne. From me awhile.
                    [*Exit* Eros
45 I will o'ertake thee, Cleopatra, and
Weep for my pardon. So it must be, for now
All length is torture; since the torch is out,
Lie down and stray no farther. Now all labour
Mars what it does—yea, very force entangles
50 Itself with strength. Seal then, and all is done.
Eros!—I come, my queen.—Eros!—Stay for me.
Where souls do couch on flowers we'll hand in hand
And with our sprightly port make the ghosts gaze.
Dido and her Aeneas shall want troops,
55 And all the haunt be ours. Come, Eros! Eros!

28 *discharg'd*: paid.
29 *done . . . hand*: already done for you.

33 *render'd*: surrendered, gave up.
34 *so buried*: i.e. because half the word was unspoken.

39 *sevenfold . . . Ajax*: The bronze shield of Ajax was backed with seven layers of bull's hide.
40 *battery*: bombardment.
   cleave: split apart.
41 *thy continent*: that which contains you.
42 *case*: casing, i.e. his body.
   Apace: quickly; Eros is taking off Antony's armour.
43 *bruised*: bruisèd; battered.
   pieces: pieces of armour.
44 *From me awhile*: leave me alone for a while.
47 *length*: length of life.
49–50 *very . . . strength*: the strength that struggles gets itself even more entangled.
50 *Seal*: finish.
52 *Where . . . hand*: we'll go hand in hand to the Elysian fields (= that part of the Underworld which, in classical mythology, was reserved for the ghosts of celebrated lovers).
53 *sprightly port*: lively conduct.
54 *Dido . . . Aeneas*: The queen of Carthage killed herself for love of the Trojan hero.
   want: lack.
55 *all . . . ours*: the entire resort—and the ghosts who frequent it—shall belong to us.

Enter Eros

Eros
What would my lord?
    Antony
                      Since Cleopatra died,
I have liv'd in such dishonour that the gods
Detest my baseness. I, that with my sword
Quarter'd the world and o'er green Neptune's back

60 With ships made cities, condemn myself to lack
The courage of a woman; less noble mind
Than she which, by her death, our Caesar tells
'I am conqueror of myself.' Thou art sworn, Eros,
That when the exigent should come—which now

65 Is come indeed—when I should see behind me
Th'inevitable prosecution of
Disgrace and horror, that on my command
Thou then wouldst kill me. Do't. The time is come
Thou strik'st not me; 'tis Caesar thou defeat'st.

70 Put colour in thy cheek.
    Eros
                      The gods withhold me!
Shall I do that which all the Parthian darts,
Though enemy, lost aim and could not?

    Antony
                            Eros,
Wouldst thou be window'd in great Rome and see
Thy master thus with pleach'd arms, bending down

75 His corrigible neck, his face subdued

59 *Quarter'd*: divided into quarters.
60 *cities*: Antony's large fleets looked like cities floating on the water.
    to lack: that I lack.

64 *exigent*: crunch, decisive moment.

66 *prosecution*: pursuing, overtaking.

70 *withhold*: forbid.

71 *darts*: arrows—see note to *3*, *1*, *1*.

73 *window'd*: looking from a window.
74 *pleach'd*: pinioned, trussed up. Antony's image of 'pleaching' refers to the process in which the branches of young trees are bent down and interlaced to form a hedge.
75 *corrigible*: submissive, subject to correction.

76 *penetrative*: wounding, piercing.
wheel'd seat: chariot.
77 *branded*: marked out.
78 *His . . . ensued*: the humiliation of the
man that followed.

84 *precedent*: previous; 'precedent' is
pronounced with long 'e' (as in
'precede') and with stress on the second
syllable.
85 *accidents unpurpos'd*: things that have
been done by chance and
unintentionally.
87 *Wherein . . . lies*: to which the whole
world pays homage.
88 *Lo thee*: there you are.

90 *why*: for which.

To penetrative shame, whilst the wheel'd seat
Of fortunate Caesar, drawn before him, branded
His baseness that ensued?

Eros
                                    I would not see't.

Antony
Come, then! For with a wound I must be cur'd.
80 Draw that thy honest sword which thou hast worn
Most useful for thy country.

Eros
                                O sir, pardon me!

Antony
When I did make thee free, swor'st thou not then
To do this when I bade thee? Do it at once,
Or thy precedent services are all
85 But accidents unpurpos'd. Draw, and come!

Eros
Turn from me then that noble countenance
Wherein the worship of the whole world lies.

Antony
[*Turns from him*] Lo thee!

Eros
My sword is drawn.

Antony
                         Then let it do at once
90 The thing why thou hast drawn it.

Eros
                                  My dear master,
My captain and my emperor, let me say,
Before I strike this bloody stroke, farewell.

Antony
'Tis said, man, and farewell.

Eros
Farewell, great chief. Shall I strike now?

Antony
                                  Now, Eros.

Eros
95 Why, there then! [*Kills himself*] Thus I do escape
    the sorrow
Of Antony's death.

Antony
                    Thrice nobler than myself!
Thou teachest me, O valiant Eros, what

99 *instruction*: example.
     got upon me: gained advantage over me.
100 *nobleness in record*: noble reputation in history.

I should and thou couldst not! My queen and Eros
Have by their brave instruction got upon me
100 A nobleness in record. But I will be
A bridegroom in my death and run into't
As to a lover's bed. Come then! And, Eros,
Thy master dies thy scholar. To do thus

Falls on his sword

I learn'd of thee. How? Not dead? Not dead?
105 The guard, ho! O, dispatch me.

Enter a Company of the Guard, *one of
them* Dercetus

First Guard
                                      What's the noise?
Antony
I have done my work ill, friends. O make an end
Of what I have begun.
Second Guard
                                  The star is fallen.

107 *The star*: i.e. the sun (that gave light to their world).

108 *period*: end.

First Guard
And time is at his period.
All the Guard
                                      Alas and woe!
Antony
Let him that loves me strike me dead.
First Guard
                                              Not I!
Second Guard
110 Nor I!
Third Guard
Nor any one!   [*Exeunt all the* Guard *but* Dercetus
Dercetus
Thy death and fortunes bid thy followers fly.
This sword but shown to Caesar with this tidings
Shall enter me with him.

113 *tidings*: news, information.
114 *enter . . . him*: get me into Caesar's good books.

Takes up Antony's sword

Enter Diomedes

Diomedes
115 Where's Antony?

Dercetus
There, Diomed, there!
Diomedes
Lives he? Wilt thou not answer, man?
　　　　　　　[*Exit* Dercetus *with the sword of* Antony

Antony
Art thou there, Diomed? Draw thy sword and give me
Suffing strokes for death.
Diomedes
　　　　　　　　　　Most absolute lord,
120 My mistress Cleopatra sent me to thee.
Antony
When did she send thee?
Diomedes
　　　　　　　　　　Now, my lord.
Antony
　　　　　　　　　　　　　Where is she?
Diomedes
Lock'd in her monument. She had a prophesying fear
Of what hath come to pass, for when she saw—
Which never shall be found—you did suspect
125 She had dispos'd with Caesar, and that your rage
Would not be purg'd, she sent you word she was dead,
But fearing since how it might work, hath sent
Me to proclaim the truth, and I am come,
I dread, too late.
Antony
130 Too late, good Diomed. Call my guard, I prithee.
Diomedes
What ho! The emperor's guard! The guard, what ho!
Come, your lord calls!

　　　　　Enter four or five of the Guard *of* Antony

Antony
Bear me, good friends, where Cleopatra bides.
'Tis the last service that I shall command you.
First Guard
135 Woe, woe are we, sir! You may not live to wear
All your true followers out.

24 *never . . . found*: will never happen.
25 *dispos'd*: come to an agreement, negotiated.
26 *purg'd*: remedied.
27 *since*: afterwards.
　　work: i.e. like a medicine.

35–6 *wear . . . out*: outlive all your true followers.

136 *heavy*: sorrowful.

137 *sharp*: cruel.
138 *To grace it*: by honouring it.
    Bid: if we bid.

Act 4   Scene 15

The dying Antony is brought to the
monument and Cleopatra, with her maids,
hauls him up. He dies in her arms and
Cleopatra, desolate without him, determines
her own course of action.

os.d. *aloft*: Cleopatra and her maids are
    positioned on the balcony—which
    formed an upper acting area in the early
    theatres (see 'Background', p. 165).

4 *we*: I; Cleopatra uses the 'royal plural'.

8 *o'th' other side*: Diomedes has entered at
    one of the stage doors, and Antony will
    be carried through the other one.

10–12 *O sun . . . world*: According to
    Ptolemaic astronomy, the sun—like all
    the other planets (see 2, 7, 14–15)—
    moved round the earth in its own
    crystalline sphere. If it burned the
    sphere it would fly off into outer space,
    leaving the world in total darkness
    ('Darkling').
12 *varying*: i.e. from daylight to darkness,
    and also, with the ebb and flow of the
    tide.

All the Guard

                                    Most heavy day!
  Antony
Nay, good my fellows, do not please sharp fate
To grace it with your sorrows. Bid that welcome
Which comes to punish us, and we punish it,
140 Seeming to bear it lightly. Take me up.
I have led you oft; carry me now, good friends,
And have my thanks for all.
                          [*Exeunt, bearing* Antony *and* Eros

Scene 15

        Cleopatra's *monument: enter* Cleopatra *and*
        her Maids *aloft, with* Charmian *and* Iras

  Cleopatra
O Charmian, I will never go from hence.
  Charmian
Be comforted, dear madam.
  Cleopatra
                          No, I will not.
All strange and terrible events are welcome,
But comforts we despise. Our size of sorrow,
5 Proportion'd to our cause, must be as great
As that which makes it.

        Enter Diomedes *below*

                          How now? Is he dead?
  Diomedes
His death's upon him, but not dead.
Look out o'th' other side your monument;
His guard have brought him thither.

        Enter below Antony *borne by the* Guard

  Cleopatra
10 O sun,
Burn the great sphere thou mov'st in! Darkling stand
The varying shore o'th' world! O Antony,
Antony, Antony! Help, Charmian! Help, Iras, help!
Help, friends below! Let's draw him hither.
  Antony
                                    Peace!

15–16 *Not . . . itself*: Antony (mistakenly) attributed this stoical attitude to Cleopatra (*4, 14, 61–3*).

15 Not Caesar's valour hath o'erthrown Antony,
But Antony's hath triumph'd on itself.
         Cleopatra
So it should be that none but Antony
Should conquer Antony, but woe 'tis so.
         Antony
I am dying, Egypt, dying. Only

20 *importune . . . awhile*: plead with death to hold back for a little time.

20 I here importune death awhile until
Of many thousand kisses the poor last
I lay upon thy lips.
         Cleopatra
                I dare not, dear.
Dear my lord, pardon. I dare not
Lest I be taken. Not th'imperious show

25 Of the full-fortun'd Caesar ever shall

26 *brooch'd*: adorned (as with a brooch).

Be brooch'd with me. If knife, drugs, serpents, have
Edge, sting or operation, I am safe.
Your wife Octavia, with her modest eyes

29 *still*: impassive.
   conclusion: judgement.
30 *Demuring*: looking smugly.

And still conclusion, shall acquire no honour
30 Demuring upon me. But come, come Antony—
Help me, my women—we must draw thee up.
Assist, good friends!

        They begin lifting

         Antony
                O quick, or I am gone!
         Cleopatra
Here's sport indeed! How heavy weighs my lord!
Our strength is all gone into heaviness;

34 *heaviness*: sorrow *and* weightiness.

35 That makes the weight. Had I great Juno's power,
The strong-wing'd Mercury should fetch thee up

36 *Mercury*: the winged messenger of the gods.

And set thee by Jove's side. Yet come a little;

38 *Wishers . . . fools*: mere wishing is just folly; the saying is proverbial.

Wishers were ever fools. O come, come, come,

      They heave Antony *aloft to* Cleopatra

39 *Die . . . lived*: i.e. don't die before you have lived.
40 *Quicken*: come to life.

And welcome, welcome! Die when thou hast lived;
40 Quicken with kissing. Had my lips that power,
Thus would I wear them out.

        Kisses him

        All the Guard
Ah, heavy sight!

45 *rail so high*: curse so vehemently.
46 *false huswife*: treacherous hussy.
   wheel: The goddess Fortune, often
   depicted as housewife with a spinning-
   wheel, turned the wheel of fate to
   determine the destinies of men.
47 *offence*: i.e. in defying her.

58–60 Antony has not surrendered to
   Caesar, his 'countryman', but
   honourably conquered himself.

61 *woo't*: wilt, will you.

66 *garland*: the crown of oak leaves
   awarded to a victorious Roman general.
67 *The soldier's . . . fallen*: The expression is
   capable of many interpretations, but no
   paraphrase: that which was once erect,
   and stood for all to measure themselves
   by, has now collapsed.
68 *odds*: distinctions.
70 *visiting*: changing.

Antony
I am dying, Egypt, dying.
Give me some wine and let me speak a little—
Cleopatra
45 No, let me speak, and let me rail so high
That the false huswife Fortune break her wheel,
Provok'd by my offence—
Antony
                              One word, sweet queen:
Of Caesar seek your honour with your safety. Oh!
Cleopatra
They do not go together.
Antony
                         Gentle, hear me.
50 None about Caesar trust but Proculeius.
Cleopatra
My resolution and my hands I'll trust;
None about Caesar.
Antony
The miserable change now at my end,
Lament nor sorrow at, but please your thoughts
55 In feeding them with those my former fortunes
Wherein I liv'd the greatest prince o'th' world,
The noblest; and do now not basely die,
Not cowardly put off my helmet to
My countryman; a Roman by a Roman
60 Valiantly vanquish'd. Now my spirit is going;
I can no more.
Cleopatra
                    Noblest of men, woo't die?
Hast thou no care of me? Shall I abide
In this dull world, which in thy absence is
No better than a sty? O see, my women,
65 The crown o'th' earth doth melt. My lord!

Antony dies

O wither'd is the garland of the war,
The soldier's pole is fallen; young boys and girls
Are level now with men; the odds is gone
And there is nothing left remarkable
70 Beneath the visiting moon.

She faints

Charmian
                O quietness, lady!
Iras
She's dead too, our sovereign.
Charmian
Lady!
Iras
Madam!
Charmian
O madam, madam, madam!
Iras
75 Royal Egypt! Empress!

      Cleopatra stirs

Charmian
Peace, peace, Iras.
Cleopatra
No more but e'en a woman, and commanded
By such poor passion as the maid that milks
And does the meanest chares. It were for me
80 To throw my sceptre at the injurious gods
To tell them that this world did equal theirs
Till they had stolen our jewel. All's but naught;
Patience is sottish, and impatience does
Become a dog that's mad. Then is it sin
85 To rush into the secret house of death
Ere death dare come to us? How do you, women?
What, what, good cheer! Why, how now, Charmian?
My noble girls! Ah, women, women! Look,
Our lamp is spent, it's out. Good sirs, take heart.
90 We'll bury him, and then what's brave, what's noble,
Let's do't after the high Roman fashion
And make death proud to take us. Come, away.
This case of that huge spirit now is cold.
Ah, women, women! Come, we have no friend
95 But resolution and the briefest end.
        [Exeunt, bearing off Antony's *body*

77 *No . . . woman*: I am now simply a woman (i.e. no longer 'Royal' and an 'Empress').
79 *chares*: chores.
   were: would be fitting.
82 *All's but naught*: there's nothing that matters.
83 *sottish*: stupid.
83–4 *does Become*: is only fit for.
87 *good cheer*: cheer up.
89 *sirs*: In Shakespeare's time this form of address could be used for women as well as men.
90 *what's . . . noble*: i.e. suicide; this is how Antony regarded the suicide of Eros and Cleopatra's supposed killing of herself.
95 *briefest*: swiftest.

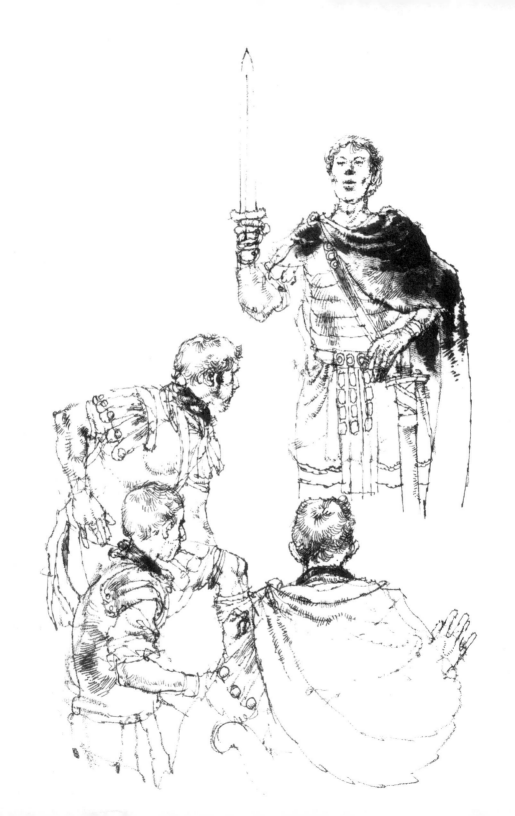

Act 5

Act 5   Scene 1

Caesar learns of Antony's death. Although he shows signs of grief, he quickly turns his attentions to the capture of Cleopatra and the prospect of his triumph in Rome. He sends words of comfort to Cleopatra—but they are not sincerely meant.

2 *frustrate*: ineffectual.
    mocks: makes ridiculous.

5 *thus*: i.e. with a naked and bloody sword.

9 *spend*: expend.

15 *crack*: explosion.
16 *lions*: Lions were seen in the streets of Rome when Julius Caesar was killed.
    civil: urban, city.
17 *their dens*: i.e. the lions' dens.

Scene 1

> Caesar's *camp outside Alexandria: enter* Caesar *with his Council of War:* Agrippa, Dolabella, Maecenas, Proculeius, Gallus

Caesar
Go to him, Dolabella, bid him yield.
Being so frustrate, tell him, he mocks
The pauses that he makes.
                      Dolabella
                              Caesar, I shall.   [*Exit*

> *Enter* Dercetus *with the sword of* Antony

Caesar
Wherefore is that? And what art thou that dar'st
5 Appear thus to us?
            Dercetus
                  I am call'd Dercetus.
Mark Antony I serv'd, who best was worthy
Best to be serv'd. Whilst he stood up and spoke
He was my master, and I wore my life
To spend upon his haters. If thou please
10 To take me to thee, as I was to him
I'll be to Caesar. If thou pleasest not,
I yield thee up my life.
                  Caesar
                              What is't thou say'st?
            Dercetus
I say, O Caesar, Antony is dead.
                  Caesar
The breaking of so great a thing should make
15 A greater crack. The round world
Should have shook lions into civil streets
And citizens to their dens. The death of Antony

19 *moiety*: half.

Is not a single doom; in the name lay
A moiety of the world.
                          Dercetus
                              He is dead, Caesar,
20 Not by a public minister of justice,

21 *hired*: hirèd.
    self: selfsame.

Nor by a hired knife, but that self hand
Which writ his honour in the acts it did
Hath, with the courage which the heart did lend it,
Splitted the heart. This is his sword;
25 I robbed his wound of it. Behold it stain'd
With his most noble blood.
                          Caesar
[*Points to the sword*]   Look you, sad friends.
The gods rebuke me, but it is tidings
To wash the eyes of kings.
                          Agrippa
                                      And strange it is
That nature must compel us to lament

30 *most . . . deeds*: those deeds we have most
    tried to accomplish.
    taints: blemishes.

30 Our most persisted deeds.
                          Maecenas
                                      His taints and honours

31 *Wag'd equal*: matched equally.

Wag'd equal with him.
                          Agrippa
                                      A rarer spirit never

32 *humanity*: a human being.
33 *touch'd*: moved.

Did steer humanity; but you gods will give us
Some faults to make us men. Caesar is touch'd.
                          Maecenas
When such a spacious mirror's set before him,

34 *mirror*: looking-glass *and also* model; it
    is 'spacious' because of the scope of
    Antony's achievements.

35 He needs must see himself.
                          Caesar
                                      O Antony,

36 *follow'd . . . this*: pursued you to this
    catastrophe.
    launch: lance.

I have follow'd thee to this; but we do launch
Diseases in our bodies. I must perforce
Have shown to thee such a declining day
Or look on thine. We could not stall together

39 *stall together*: share the same space,
    co-exist.

40 In the whole world. But yet let me lament
With tears as sovereign as the blood of hearts
That thou, my brother, my competitor

42 *competitor*: colleague, partner.
43 *top . . . design*: the most exalted
    enterprises.

In top of all design, my mate in empire,
Friend and companion in the front of war,

44 *in . . . war*: at the battle-front.

45 The arm of mine own body, and the heart

46 *his*: its.

Where mine his thoughts did kindle, that our stars,

47–8 *divide . . . to this*: separate us, who were so equally matched, to this extent—i.e. that Antony should be dead whilst Caesar is alive.
49 *meeter*: more appropriate.
50 'This man looks as though he has some important business.'

52 *yet*: at present (i.e. until Caesar declares his intentions).

55 *frame*: adjust.

57 *by some*: from representatives.

59 *lean*: incline himself.

65 *her life*: to have her alive.
66 *Would . . . triumph*: would make my triumph (= triumphal procession) remembered for ever.
67 *your speediest*: as quickly as you can.
68 *how . . . her*: what you find out about her.

74 *hardly*: reluctantly.

Unreconciliable, should divide
Our equalness to this. Hear me, good friends—

Enter an Egyptian

But I will tell you at some meeter season.
50 The business of this man looks out of him;
We'll hear him what he says. Whence are you?
        Egyptian
A poor Egyptian yet. The queen, my mistress,
Confin'd in all she has, her monument,
Of thy intents desires instruction,
55 That she preparedly may frame herself
To th' way she's forc'd to.
        Caesar
                        Bid her have good heart.
She soon shall know of us, by some of ours,
How honourable and how kindly we
Determine for her. For Caesar cannot lean
60 To be ungentle.
        Egyptian
                        So the gods preserve thee!   [*Exit*
        Caesar
Come hither, Proculeius. Go and say
We purpose her no shame. Give her what comforts
The quality of her passion shall require,
Lest, in her greatness, by some mortal stroke
65 She do defeat us. For her life in Rome
Would be eternal in our triumph. Go,
And with your speediest bring us what she says
And how you find of her.
        Proculeius
                        Caesar, I shall.
        Caesar
Gallus, go you along. [*Exeunt* Proculeius *and* Gallus
                        Where's Dolabella
70 To second Proculeius?
        All
                        Dolabella!
        Caesar
Let him alone, for I remember now
How he's employ'd. He shall in time be ready.
Go with me to my tent, where you shall see
How hardly I was drawn into this war,

75 *still*: constantly, always.

75 How calm and gentle I proceeded still
In all my writings. Go with me and see
What I can show in this.

[*Exeunt*

Act 5   Scene 2

Cleopatra, lamenting the death of Antony,
receives Proculeius, the emissary from Caesar,
who seems to offer some reassurance.
Cleopatra is wary, but acknowledges her
submission to Caesar. Suddenly the Roman
guards appear at the door, and she realizes
that there is only one way now for her to
escape. Dolabella takes over responsibility
from Proculeius, who returns to Caesar, and
Cleopatra confides in him her recollections
of Antony. She is then approached by Caesar
himself who, in veiled terms, offers conditions
for her surrender. Apparently acquiescing to
his demands, she makes an attempt to
deceive him over her treasure. This is easily
discovered—but it seems to win Caesar's
respect and to persuade him that she wants
to go on living. When Caesar has left the
stage, Cleopatra prepares for her final
appearance. Octavius Caesar returns, to view
the body and to pronounce the last words of
the play.

3 *knave*: servant, fool.
6 *shackles . . . change*: prevents any
   accidents from happening and guards
   against all change.
7 *palates*: tastes, relishes.
   dung: ordinary food, the products of the
   'dungy earth' which 'Feeds beast as well
   as man' (1, 1, 36).
10 *study on*: think seriously about.
14 *to be deceiv'd*: whether or not I am
   deceived.
15 *use*: need.
17 *keep decorum*: behave properly.

Scene 2

> Cleopatra's *monument: enter* Cleopatra,
> Charmian, *and* Iras

Cleopatra
My desolation does begin to make
A better life. 'Tis paltry to be Caesar.
Not being Fortune, he's but Fortune's knave,
A minister of her will. And it is great
5 To do that thing that ends all other deeds,
Which shackles accidents and bolts up change,
Which sleeps and never palates more the dung,
The beggar's nurse and Caesar's.

> *Enter* Proculeius

Proculeius
Caesar sends greeting to the queen of Egypt,
10 And bids thee study on what fair demands
Thou mean'st to have him grant thee.

Cleopatra
                                              What's thy name?

Proculeius
My name is Proculeius.

Cleopatra
                          Antony
Did tell me of you, bade me trust you, but
I do not greatly care to be deceiv'd
15 That have no use for trusting. If your master
Would have a queen his beggar, you must tell him
That majesty, to keep decorum, must
No less beg than a kingdom. If he please
To give me conquer'd Egypt for my son,
20 He gives me so much of mine own as I
Will kneel to him with thanks.

23 *Make . . . freely*: refer yourself
    completely and without hesitation.
24 *grace*: good will.

26 *sweet dependency*: meek submission.

27-8 *will . . . kneel'd to*: will beg to be
    shown how he can be of assistance
    when he is humbly asked for help.

29-30 *I am . . . got*: like a humble servant I
    pay homage to his good fortune, and I
    acknowledge the greatness he has
    achieved.
31 *doctrine of obedience*: what it is to be
    obedient.

35 *surpris'd*: apprehended, captured.

40 *Reliev'd*: rescued.
    of: from.

41 *languish*: suffering.

Proculeius
                                    Be of good cheer.
You're fallen into a princely hand; fear nothing.
Make your full reference freely to my lord,
Who is so full of grace that it flows over
25 On all that need. Let me report to him
Your sweet dependency, and you shall find
A conqueror that will pray in aid for kindness
Where he for grace is kneel'd to.
Cleopatra
                                         Pray you tell him
I am his fortune's vassal and I send him
30 The greatness he has got. I hourly learn
A doctrine of obedience, and would gladly
Look him i'th' face.
Proculeius
                            This I'll report, dear lady.
Have comfort, for I know your plight is pitied
Of him that caus'd it.

Enter Gallus *and* Roman Soldiers

35 [*To the* Soldiers] You see how easily she may be
        surprised.
Guard her till Caesar come.
Iras
                                    Royal queen!
Charmian
O Cleopatra, thou art taken, queen!
Cleopatra
Quick, quick, good hands.

Draws a dagger

Proculeius
                                Hold, worthy lady, hold!

Disarms her

Do not yourself such wrong, who are in this
40 Reliev'd, but not betray'd.
Cleopatra
                                    What, of death too,
That rids our dogs of languish?

Proculeius

Cleopatra,
Do not abuse my master's bounty by
Th'undoing of yourself. Let the world see
His nobleness well acted, which your death
45 Will never let come forth.

Cleopatra

Where art thou, Death?
Come hither, come! Come, come and take a queen
Worth many babes and beggars!

Proculeius

O temperance, lady!

Cleopatra

Sir, I will eat no meat; I'll not drink, sir;
If idle talk will once be necessary,
50 I'll not sleep neither. This mortal house I'll ruin,
Do Caesar what he can. Know, sir, that I
Will not wait pinion'd at your master's court,
Nor once be chastis'd with the sober eye
Of dull Octavia. Shall they hoist me up
55 And show me to the shouting varletry
Of censuring Rome? Rather a ditch in Egypt
Be gentle grave unto me! Rather on Nilus' mud
Lay me stark naked, and let the water-flies
Blow me into abhorring! Rather make
60 My country's high pyramides my gibbet
And hang me up in chains!

Proculeius

You do extend
These thoughts of horror further than you shall
Find cause in Caesar.

Enter Dolabella

Dolabella

Proculeius,
What thou hast done thy master Caesar knows,
65 And he hath sent for thee. For the queen,
I'll take her to my guard.

Proculeius

So, Dolabella
It shall content me best. Be gentle to her.

45 *let come forth*: allow it to show itself.

47 *babes and beggars*: i.e. those who are most frequently taken by Death.

49 *once*: for once.
necessary: i.e. to bring about her death.
50 *mortal house*: i.e. her body.

52 *pinion'd*: with arms bound.
53 *once*: ever.
chastis'd: chástis'd.

55 *varletry*: mob, common people.

59 *Blow me*: hatch out their eggs on me.
into abhorring: so that I become totally abhorrent.
60 *pyramides*: Cleopatra is referring to the obelisk mentioned in 2, 7, 18; the word is pronounced with four syllables.

[*To* Cleopatra] To Caesar I will speak what you
    shall please,
If you'll employ me to him.

Cleopatra
                                Say I would die.
                    [*Exit* Proculeius *with* Gallus *and* Soldiers

Dolabella

70 Most noble empress, you have heard of me?

Cleopatra

I cannot tell.

Dolabella
                        Assuredly you know me.

Cleopatra

No matter, sir, what I have heard or known.
You laugh when boys or women tell their dreams;
Is't not your trick?

Dolabella
                    I understand not, madam.

Cleopatra

75 I dreamt there was an emperor Antony.
O, such another sleep, that I might see
But such another man!

Dolabella
                            If it might please ye—

Cleopatra

His face was as the heavens, and therein stuck
A sun and moon which kept their course and lighted

80 The little O, the earth.

Dolabella
                        Most sovereign creature—

Cleopatra

His legs bestrid the ocean; his rear'd arm
Crested the world; his voice was propertied
As all the tuned spheres, and that to friends;
But when he meant to quail and shake the orb,

85 He was as rattling thunder. For his bounty,
There was no winter in't; an autumn it was
That grew the more by reaping. His delights
Were dolphin-like: they show'd his back above

74   *trick*: custom.
78–91 Cleopatra describes Antony with the
    hyperbole appropriate for a god.
81   *His legs . . . ocean*: Antony is compared
    to the Colossus of Rhodes, a giant
    statue of Apollo which was said to have
    stood astride the harbour of Rhodes.
    rear'd: upraised.
82   *Crested*: crowned, dominated.
    propertied: had the same qualities.
83   *tuned spheres*: Pythagoras taught that a
    perfect harmony was created by the
    notes of the planetary spheres revolving
    round the earth (see 2, 7, 14–15).
84   *quail*: quell, subdue.
85   *bounty*: generosity.
86   *an autumn*: i.e. a rich harvest.
87–9 *His delights . . . in*: his enjoyment of
    life was outstanding even among those
    who shared his pleasures—just as the
    dolphin's energy lifts it high above the
    water.

89–90 *In his . . . crownets*: kings and princes
    were his servants.
89 *livery*: uniform, the suit of clothes given
    by a master to his servants.
90 *crownets*: coronets.
91 *plates*: silver coins.

The element they lived in. In his livery
90 Walk'd crowns and crownets; realms and islands were
As plates dropp'd from his pocket.
    Dolabella
                                    Cleopatra—
    Cleopatra
Think you there was or might be such a man
As this I dreamt of?
    Dolabella
                        Gentle madam, no.
    Cleopatra
You lie up to the hearing of the gods!

95 *if . . . such*: if there should not be or
    have been such a man.
96 *It's . . . dreaming*: it would be too much
    to have dreamed.
96–7 *Nature . . . fancy*: Nature has not got
    enough material to compete with the
    imagination in creating such marvellous
    beings.
97–8 *t'imagine . . . fancy*: to conceive of this
    Antony would be to create a natural
    masterpiece far surpassing any fantasy.
    According to Enobarbus (2, 2, 209–10),
    Cleopatra was herself such a masterpiece
    of nature, excelling the creation of any
    artist's imagination.
99 *shadows*: fantasies, insubstantial
    creations of the imagination.
101 *As answering . . . weight*: appropriately
    for its magnitude.
101–4 *Would . . . root*: may I never achieve
    my aim if I do not feel, by reflecting
    your grief, a sorrow that strikes to the
    bottom of my heart.

95 But if there be nor ever were one such,
It's past the size of dreaming. Nature wants stuff
To vie strange forms with fancy; yet t'imagine
An Antony were nature's piece 'gainst fancy,
Condemning shadows quite.
    Dolabella
                                Hear me, good madam.
100 Your loss is as yourself, great, and you bear it
As answering to the weight. Would I might never
O'ertake pursu'd success, but I do feel,
By the rebound of yours, a grief that smites
My very heart at root.
    Cleopatra
                        I thank you, sir.
105 Know you what Caesar means to do with me?
    Dolabella
I am loath to tell you what I would you knew.
    Cleopatra
Nay, pray you, sir.
    Dolabella
                        Though he be honourable—
    Cleopatra
He'll lead me, then, in triumph.
    Dolabella
Madam, he will. I know't.

            Flourish. Enter Proculeius, Caesar, Gallus,
            Maecenas *and others of his train*

        All
110 Make way there! Caesar!

Caesar
Which is the queen of Egypt?
 Dolabella
It is the emperor, madam.

Cleopatra kneels

 Caesar
Arise! You shall not kneel.
I pray you rise. Rise, Egypt.
 Cleopatra
                                  Sir, the gods
115 Will have it thus. My master and my lord
I must obey.

She stands

 Caesar
                    Take to you no hard thoughts.
The record of what injuries you did us,
Though written in our flesh, we shall remember
As things but done by chance.
 Cleopatra
                                    Sole sir o'th' world,
120 I cannot project mine own cause so well
To make it clear, but do confess I have
Been laden with like frailties which before
Have often sham'd our sex.
 Caesar
                              Cleopatra, know
We will extenuate rather than enforce.
125 If you apply yourself to our intents,
Which towards you are most gentle, you shall find
A benefit in this change; but if you seek
To lay on me a cruelty by taking
Antony's course, you shall bereave yourself
130 Of my good purposes, and put your children
To that destruction which I'll guard them from
If thereon you rely. I'll take my leave.
 Cleopatra
And may through all the world! 'Tis yours, and we,
Your scutcheons and your signs of conquest, shall
135 Hang in what place you please. Here, my good lord.

Hands him a paper

119 *sir o'th'world*: master of the world.
120 *project*: próject; present, set out.
121 *clear*: innocent.
122 *like*: the same.

124 *extenuate*: excuse.
      enforce: insist on.
125 *apply*: conform, adapt.

128 *lay . . . cruelty*: force me to be cruel.
129 *Antony's course*: i.e. of killing yourself.
      bereave: deny.

134 *scutcheons*: i.e. trophies of war; the
      'scutcheons' (= armorial shields) of the
      vanquished were carried in procession,
      or hung up in triumph, by their
      conquerors.

136 *all for*: everything relating to.

137 *brief*: summary, inventory.

139 *Not . . . admitted*: not including the very small things.

Caesar
You shall advise me in all for Cleopatra.
Cleopatra
This is the brief of money, plate and jewels
I am possess'd of. 'Tis exactly valued,
Not petty things admitted. Where's Seleucus?

Enter Seleucus

Seleucus
140 Here, madam.
Cleopatra
This is my treasurer. Let him speak, my lord,
Upon his peril, that I have reserv'd
To myself nothing. Speak the truth, Seleucus.
Seleucus
Madam,

145 *seel*: stitch up (like the eyes of a young hawk; the term is from falconry—see 3, 13, 117).

145 I had rather seel my lips than to my peril
Speak that which is not.
Cleopatra
                  What have I kept back?
Seleucus
Enough to purchase what you have made known.
Caesar
Nay, blush not, Cleopatra. I approve
Your wisdom in the deed.
Cleopatra
              See, Caesar! O behold

150 *How . . . follow'd*: what happens to those in high positions.
Mine . . . yours: my followers will now become your followers.

154 *hir'd*: bought, paid for.

150 How pomp is follow'd! Mine will now be yours
And, should we shift estates, yours would be mine.
The ingratitude of this Seleucus does
Even make me wild. O slave, of no more trust
Than love that's hir'd! What, go'st thou back? Thou shalt
155 Go back, I warrant thee! But I'll catch thine eyes
Though they had wings! Slave! Soulless villain! Dog!
O rarely base!

157 *rarely*: exceptionally.

Caesar
            Good queen, let us entreat you.
Cleopatra
O Caesar, what a wounding shame is this,
That—thou vouchsafing here to visit me,

159 *thou*: Cleopatra, trying to ingratiate herself with Caesar, switches to the informal pronoun.
vouchsafing: condescending.

160 Doing the honour of thy lordliness

162–3 *Parcel . . . envy*: make up the sum
  total of my shame by the addition of his
  malice.
164 *lady*: feminine.
165 *Immoment toys*: trifling knick-knacks.
166 *modern*: ordinary.

168 *Livia*: the wife of Octavius Caesar.
169 *unfolded*: exposed.
170 *With*: by.
  bred: brought up, trained.

172 *cinders*: dying embers.
173 *chance*: fortune.
  Wert thou a man: Seleucus may have
  been a eunuch (and the dramatic role
  doubled with that of Mardian).
174 *Forbear*: withdraw.

175 *misthought*: misjudged.

177 *answer . . . name*: are held to be
  responsible for everything (good or bad)
  done in our name by other people.

182 *make prize*: haggle, quibble.

184 *Make . . . prisons*: don't imagine you
  will be a prisoner.

To one so meek—that mine own servant should
Parcel the sum of my disgraces by
Addition of his envy! Say, good Caesar,
That I some lady trifles have reserv'd,
165 Immoment toys, things of such dignity
As we greet modern friends withal; and say
Some nobler token I have kept apart
For Livia and Octavia, to induce
Their mediation, must I be unfolded
170 With one that I have bred? The gods! It smites me
Beneath the fall I have. [*To Seleucus*] Prithee go
    hence,
Or I shall show the cinders of my spirits
Through th'ashes of my chance. Wert thou a man,
Thou wouldst have mercy on me.
    Caesar
                Forbear, Seleucus
                [*Exit* Seleucus
    Cleopatra
175 Be it known that we, the greatest, are misthought
For things that others do, and when we fall,
We answer others' merits in our name,
Are therefore to be pitied.
    Caesar
                Cleopatra,
Not what you have reserv'd nor what acknowledg'd
180 Put we i'th' roll of conquest. Still be't yours;
Bestow it at your pleasure, and believe
Caesar's no merchant to make prize with you
Of things that merchants sold. Therefore be cheer'd;
Make not your thoughts your prisons. No, dear
    queen,
185 For we intend so to dispose you as
Yourself shall give us counsel. Feed and sleep.
Our care and pity is so much upon you
That we remain your friend; and so, adieu.
    Cleopatra
My master and my lord!
    Caesar
                Not so. Adieu.

    Flourish.   [*Exeunt* Caesar *and his train*

190 *He words me*: these are just words he's
    giving me.
191 *Be . . . myself*: do that which is
    honourable for me (i.e. commit suicide).

193 *Hie thee again*: hurry back.

195 *put . . . haste*: do it quickly.

198 *makes . . . obey*: obeys religiously.

208 *Mechanic slaves*: common artisans.
209 *rules*: carpenters' rulers.

Cleopatra
190 He words me, girls, he words me, that I should not
    Be noble to myself. But hark thee, Charmian.

Whispers to Charmian

Charmian
Finish, good lady. The bright day is done
And we are for the dark.
Cleopatra
                                    Hie thee again.
I have spoke already and it is provided.
195 Go put it to the haste.
Charmian
                        Madam, I will.

Enter Dolabella

Dolabella
Where's the queen?
Charmian
                        Behold, sir.   [*Exit*
Cleopatra
                                Dolabella!
Dolabella
Madam, as thereto sworn by your command,
Which my love makes religion to obey,
I tell you this: Caesar through Syria
200 Intends his journey, and within three days
You with your children will he send before.
Make your best use of this. I have perform'd
Your pleasure and my promise.
Cleopatra
                                Dolabella,
I shall remain your debtor.
Dolabella
                            I, your servant.
205 Adieu, good queen. I must attend on Caesar.
Cleopatra
Farewell and thanks.   [*Exit* Dolabella
                    Now, Iras, what think'st thou?
Thou an Egyptian puppet shall be shown
In Rome as well as I. Mechanic slaves
With greasy aprons, rules and hammers shall
210 Uplift us to the view. In their thick breaths,

211 *Rank . . . diet*: stinking of their coarse
  food.

212 *drink . . . vapour*: inhale their foul breath.

213 *Saucy*: insolent, lecherous.
  lictors: Roman officials who carried out
  the sentences imposed by magistrates;
  Shakespeare thinks of them as
  Elizabethan beadles, charged to keep the
  streets clear of prostitutes ('strumpets').

214 *scald rhymers*: wretched song-writers.

215 *Ballad us*: Ballads written on topical
  subjects were sold, like newspapers, on
  the London streets.
  quick: quick-witted, clever.
  comedians: players, actors.

216 *Extemporally . . . us*: will present
  improvisations on stage.

219 *boy my greatness*: reduce my greatness to
  what his shrill voice can mimic.

Rank of gross diet, shall we be enclouded
And forc'd to drink their vapour.

Iras
                                    The gods forbid!

Cleopatra
Nay, 'tis most certain, Iras. Saucy lictors
Will catch at us like strumpets, and scald rhymers

215 Ballad us out o'tune. The quick comedians
Extemporally will stage us and present
Our Alexandrian revels; Antony
Shall be brought drunken forth; and I shall see
Some squeaking Cleopatra boy my greatness

220 I'th' posture of a whore.

Iras
                                    O the good gods!

Cleopatra
Nay, that's certain.

Iras
I'll never see't, for I am sure my nails
Are stronger than mine eyes!

Cleopatra
                                        Why, that's the way
To fool their preparation and to conquer
225 Their most absurd intents.

Enter Charmian

                                        Now, Charmian!
Show me, my women, like a queen. Go fetch
My best attires. I am again for Cydnus
To meet Mark Antony. Sirrah Iras, go.
Now, noble Charmian, we'll dispatch indeed,
230 And when thou hast done this chare, I'll give thee
    leave
To play till doomsday. Bring our crown and all.
                                        [*Exit* Iras

A noise within

Wherefore's this noise?

Enter a Guardsman

Guardsman
                                        Here is a rural fellow
That will not be denied your highness' presence.
He brings you figs.
                    Cleopatra
235 Let him come in.   [*Exit* Guardsman
                                What poor an instrument
May do a noble deed! He brings me liberty.
My resolution's plac'd, and I have nothing
Of woman in me. Now from head to foot
I am marble-constant. Now the fleeting moon
240 No planet is of mine.

Enter Guardsman *and* Clown *with a basket*

Guardsman
                                This is the man.
                    Cleopatra
Avoid, and leave him.   [*Exit* Guardsman
Hast thou the pretty worm of Nilus there
That kills and pains not?
                    Clown
Truly, I have him; but I would not be the party that
245 should desire you to touch him, for his biting is

224 *preparation*: scheming.

226 *Show*: present, display.
227 *Cydnus*: i.e. the place where she first encountered Antony (see *2, 2, 196*); Cleopatra prepares for a grand reunion.
228 *Sirrah*: Like 'sir', this form of address could be used to address women as well as men.
229 *dispatch*: get things over and done with.
230 *chare*: chore.
231 *play*: take a holiday, rest.

235 *What*: how.

237 *plac'd*: fixed.

239 *fleeting*: changing.
240 *No . . . mine*: Cleopatra rejects her usual association with Isis, the Egyptian moon-goddess.
240s.d. *Clown*: The word was often used to describe a countryman—and it was also an indication that the theatrical role would be taken by the dramatic company's comic actor.
241 *Avoid*: go away.
242 *worm*: snake.

246 *immortal*: The Clown seems to mistake the word 'mortal' (= deadly).

immortal. Those that do die of it do seldom or never recover.

Cleopatra
Remember'st thou any that have died on't?

Clown
Very many; men and women too. I heard of one of
250 them no longer than yesterday—a very honest

251 *lie*: tell lies, *and*, lie with men.
252 *honesty*: respectability.

woman, but something given to lie, as a woman should not do but in the way of honesty—how she died of the biting of it, what pain she felt. Truly, she makes a very good report o'th' worm; but he that
255 will believe all that they say shall never be saved by

256 *they*: i.e. women.
falliable: The Clown's mistake for 'infallible'.

half that they do. But this is most falliable, the worm's an odd worm.

Cleopatra
Get thee hence. Farewell.

Clown
I wish you all joy of the worm.

Sets down his basket

Cleopatra
260 Farewell.

Clown
You must think this, look you, that the worm will do
262 *do his kind*: act according to his nature, only do what is natural.

his kind.

Cleopatra
Ay, ay. Farewell.

Clown
Look you, the worm is not to be trusted but in the
265 keeping of wise people; for, indeed, there is no goodness in the worm.

Cleopatra
Take thou no care; it shall be heeded.

Clown
Very good. Give it nothing, I pray you, for it is not worth the feeding.

Cleopatra
270 Will it eat me?

Clown
You must not think I am so simple but I know the devil himself will not eat a woman. I know that a

273 *dress*: prepare (as for cooking).
274 *whoreson*: pestilent.

woman is a dish for the gods if the devil dress her not. But truly, these same whoreson devils do the

275 gods great harm in their women, for in every ten that
they make, the devils mar five.
Cleopatra
Well, get thee gone. Farewell.
Clown
Yes, forsooth. I wish you joy o'th'worm.   [*Exit*

Enter Iras *with a robe, crown, and other
jewels*

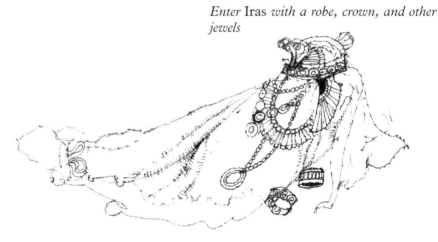

Cleopatra
Give me my robe. Put on my crown. I have
280 Immortal longings in me. Now no more
The juice of Egypt's grape shall moist this lip.

The women dress her

282 *Yare*: smartly.

Yare, yare, good Iras! Quick! Methinks I hear
Antony call. I see him rouse himself
To praise my noble act. I hear him mock
285 The luck of Caesar, which the gods give men

286 *To excuse . . . wrath*: to justify the anger
which they show later (in bringing men
low again).
287 *title*: right, claim.
288 *fire and air*: Cleopatra rejects the baser
elements (earth and water) of which the
human body is composed.

To excuse their after wrath. Husband, I come!
Now to that name my courage prove my title!
I am fire and air; my other elements
I give to baser life. So, have you done?
290 Come, then, and take the last warmth of my lips.
Farewell, kind Charmian. Iras, long farewell.

Kisses them. Iras *falls and dies*

292 *aspic*: asp, venom.

Have I the aspic in my lips? Dost fall?
If thou and nature can so gently part,

The stroke of death is as a lover's pinch
295 Which hurts and is desir'd. Dost thou lie still?
If thus thou vanishest, thou tell'st the world
It is not worth leave-taking.
            Charmian
Dissolve, thick cloud, and rain, that I may say
The gods themselves do weep!
            Cleopatra
                                    This proves me base.

299 *This . . . base*: The death of Iras puts Cleopatra to shame—just as that of Eros shamed Antony (*4, 14, 96*).

300 *curled*: curlèd. Antony had been 'barbered ten times o'er' for his first meeting with Cleopatra.

302 *mortal*: deadly.

303–4 *knot . . . Of life*: subtle connection of body and soul; 'intrinsicate' fuses the senses of 'intricate' and 'intrinsic'.

300 If she first meet the curled Antony,
He'll make demand of her, and spend that kiss
Which is my heaven to have. [*To the asp; applying it
    to her breast*] Come, thou mortal wretch,
With thy sharp teeth this knot intrinsicate
Of life at once untie. Poor venomous fool,
305 Be angry and dispatch. O, couldst thou speak,
That I might hear thee call great Caesar ass
Unpolicied!
            Charmian
                        O eastern star!
            Cleopatra
                                        Peace, peace!
Dost thou not see my baby at my breast
That sucks the nurse asleep?
            Charmian
                                        O break! O break!
            Cleopatra
310 As sweet as balm, as soft as air, as gentle—
O Antony!—Nay, I will take thee too.

307 *Unpolicied*: politically out-manoeuvred.
eastern star: Venus, the morning star, is visible in the east before sunrise.

                    Applies another asp to her arm

312 *What*: why.

What should I stay—

                    Dies

            Charmian
In this vile world? So fare thee well.
Now boast thee, Death, in thy possession lies
315 A lass unparallel'd. Downy windows, close,
And golden Phoebus, never be beheld
Of eyes again so royal! Your crown's awry;
I'll mend it, and then play.

315 *windows*: i.e. eyelids.

318 *play*: rest—compare lines 230–1.

318s.d. *rustling*: clattering.

                    Enter the Guard, *rustling in*

First Guard
Where's the queen?
Charmian
                              Speak softly. Wake her not.
First Guard
320 Caesar hath sent—
Charmian
                              Too slow a messenger.

Applies an asp

321 *apace*: swiftly.

O come apace! Dispatch! I partly feel thee.
First Guard
Approach ho! All's not well. Caesar's beguil'd.
Second Guard
There's Dolabella sent from Caesar. Call him.
                              [*Exit a* Guardsman
First Guard
What work is here, Charmian? Is this well done?
Charmian
325 It is well done, and fitting for a princess
Descended of so many royal kings.
Ah, soldier!

Charmian *dies*

Enter Dolabella

Dolabella
How goes it here?
Second Guard
                              All dead.
Dolabella

328 *thoughts*: suspicions.
329 *Touch their effects*: meet with their
      realization.

                              Caesar, thy thoughts
Touch their effects in this. Thyself art coming
330 To see perform'd the dreaded act which thou
So sought'st to hinder.

Enter Caesar *and all his train, marching*

All but Caesar
A way there! A way for Caesar!
Dolabella

333 *augurer*: prophet.

O sir, you are too sure an augurer:
That you did fear is done.

Caesar

334 *Bravest*: most magnificent.

335 *levell'd*: guessed.

Bravest at the last,
335 She levell'd at our purposes and, being royal,
Took her own way. The manner of their deaths?
I do not see them bleed.

Dolabella

Who was last with them?

First Guard

A simple countryman that brought her figs.
This was his basket.

Caesar

Poison'd, then.

First Guard

O Caesar,

340 *but*: just.

340 This Charmian liv'd but now, she stood and spake.
I found her trimming up the diadem
On her dead mistress. Tremblingly she stood,
And on the sudden dropp'd.

Caesar

O noble weakness!
If they had swallow'd poison, 'twould appear

345 *like sleep*: as though she were asleep.

345 By external swelling; but she looks like sleep,
As she would catch another Antony

347 *her . . . grace*: the powerful snare of her fascination.

In her strong toil of grace.

Dolabella

Here on her breast

348 *vent*: discharge, issue.
blown: deposited, left on the skin.

There is a vent of blood, and something blown;
The like is on her arm.

First Guard

350 This is an aspic's trail, and these fig leaves
Have slime upon them such as th'aspic leaves
Upon the caves of Nile.

Caesar

Most probable
That so she died, for her physician tells me
She hath pursu'd conclusions infinite

354 *conclusions infinite*: innumerable experiments; see 'Plutarch', p. 145.

355 Of easy ways to die. Take up her bed,
And bear her women from the monument.
She shall be buried by her Antony.

358 *clip*: embrace, enfold.

No grave upon the earth shall clip in it

359 *High events*: tragic catastrophes.

A pair so famous. High events as these

360 *Strike*: distress.
    make: cause.
360–1 *their story . . . his glory*: the pity
    aroused for Antony and Cleopatra in
    their tragic downfall is no less than the
    glory won by him (i.e. Caesar himself)
    who caused this catastrophe.
365 *solemnity*: ceremony.

360 Strike those that make them, and their story is
    No less in pity than his glory which
    Brought them to be lamented. Our army shall
    In solemn show attend this funeral,
    And then to Rome. Come, Dolabella, see
365 High order in this great solemnity.
        [*Exeunt omnes, the* Soldiers *bearing the dead bodies*

Plutarch

'The Life of Marcus Antonius'

Parallel Lives of the Greeks and Romans translated by
Sir Thomas North (1579, 3rd edition 1603)

Act 1, Scene 4, lines 57–69: Antony the survivor

[At Modena] It was a wonderful example to the soldiers, to see
Antonius, that was brought up in all fineness and superfluity, so
easily to drink puddle water, and to eat wild fruits and roots; and
moreover it is reported, that even as they passed the Alps, they did
eat the barks of trees, and such beasts, as never man tasted of their
flesh before.

Act 2, Scene 2, lines 190–1: Alexandrian entertainment

. . . I have heard my grandfather Lampryas report that one Philotas
a physician, born in the city of Amphissa, told him that he was at
that present time in Alexandria and studied physic; and that,
having acquaintance with one of Antonius' cooks, he took him to
Antonius' house (being a young man desirous to see things), to
show him the wonderful sumptuous charge and preparation of only
one supper. When he was in the kitchen and saw a world of
diversities of meats, and amongst others, eight wild boars roasted
whole, he began to wonder at it and said:
  'Sure you have a great number of guests to supper.'
The cook fell a-laughing, and answered him:
  'No,' quoth he, 'not many guests, nor above twelve in all: but
yet all that is boiled or roasted must be served in whole, or else it
would be marred straight. For Antonius peradventure will sup
presently; or it may be a pretty while hence; or likely enough he will
defer it longer, for that he hath drunk well today or else had some
other great matters in hand; and therefore we do not dress one
supper only, but many suppers, because we are uncertain of the
hour he will sup in.'

Act 2, Scene 2, lines 201–28: Cleopatra at Cydnus

Therefore when she was sent unto by divers letters, both from
Antonius himself and also from his friends, she made so light of it
and mocked Antonius so much that she disdained to set forward
otherwise but to take her barge in the river of Cydnus, the poop
whereof was gold, the sail of purple, and the oars of silver, which
kept stroke in rowing after the sound of the music of flutes,
howboys, citherns, viols, and such other instruments as they played
upon in the barge. And now for the person of herself: she was laid
under a pavilion of cloth of gold of tissue, apparelled and attired
like the goddess Venus commonly drawn in picture; and hard by
her, on either hand of her, pretty fair boys apparelled as painters do
set forth god Cupid, with little fans in their hands, with the which
they fanned wind upon her. Her ladies and gentlewomen also, the
fairest of them were apparelled like the nymphs Nereides (which
are the mermaids of the waters) and like the Graces, some steering
the helm, others tending the tackle and ropes of the barge, out of
which there came a wonderful passing sweet savour of perfumes,
that perfumed the wharf's side, pestered with innumerable
multitudes of people. Some of them followed the barge all along
the river's side; others also ran out of the city to see her coming in;
so that in the end there ran such multitudes of people one after
another to see her that Antonius was left post-alone in the market-
place in his imperial seat to give audience. And there went a
rumour in the people's mouths that the goddess Venus was come
to play with the god Bacchus, for the general good of all Asia.

Act 2, Scene 5, lines 15–18: Fishing with Cleopatra

But to reckon up all the foolish sports they made, revelling in this
sort, it were too fond of a part of me: and therefore I will only tell
you one among the rest. On a time he went to angle for fish; and
when he could take none he was angry as could be, because
Cleopatra stood by. Wherefore he secretly commanded the
fisherman that when he cast in his line, they should straight dive
under the water and put a fish on his hook which they had taken
before; and so snatched up his angling rod and brought up fish
twice or thrice. Cleopatra found it straight; yet she seemed not to
see it, but wondered at his excellent fishing. But when she was
alone by herself among her own people, she told them how it was
and bade them the next morning to be on the water to see the
fishing. A number of people came to the haven and got into the

fisher boats to see the fishing. Antonius then threw in his line; and Cleopatra straight commanded one of her men to dive under water before Antonius' men and to put some old salt fish upon his bait, like unto those that are brought out of the country of Pont. When he had hung the fish on his hook, Antonius, thinking he had taken a fish indeed, snatched up his line presently. Then they all fell a-laughing.

Act 2, Scene 6, lines 68–70: A secret assignation

Caesar . . . secretly sent for Cleopatra which was in the country to come to him. She, only taking Apollodorus Sicilian of all her friends, took a little boat . . . and came and landed hard by the foot of the castle. Then having no other means to come into the court, without being known, she laid herself down upon a mattress . . . which Apollodorus her friend tied and bound together like a bundle with a great leather thong . . . and brought her thus hampered in this fardel unto Caesar.

Act 4, Scene 3: Antony's god deserts him

Furthermore, the self same night within little of midnight, when all the city was quiet, full of fear and sorrow, thinking what would be the issue and end of this war, it is said that suddenly they heard a marvellous sweet harmony of sundry sorts of instruments of music, with the cry of a multitude of people, as they had been dancing and had sung as they use in Bacchus' feasts, with movings and turnings after the manners of the Satyrs. And it seemed that this dance went through the city unto the gate that opened to the enemies, and that all the troop that made this noise they heard went out of the city at that gate. Now such as in reason sought the depth of the interpretation of this wonder thought that it was the god unto whom Antonius bare singular devotion to counterfeit and resemble him, that did forsake them.

Act 5, Scene 2: Cleopatra's experiments

Cleopatra in the meantime was very careful in gathering all sorts of poisons together, to destroy men. Now, to make proof of those poisons which made men die with least pain, she tried it upon condemned men in prison. For, when she saw the poisons that were sudden and vehement and brought speedy death with grievous torments, and, in contrary manner, that such as were more mild and gentle had not that quick speed and force to make one die suddenly, she afterwards went about to prove the stinging of snakes and adders, and made some to be applied to men in her sight, some in one sort and some in another. So, when she had daily made divers and sundry proofs, she found none of them all she had proved so fit as the biting of an aspic, the which causeth only a heaviness of the head, without swounding or complaining, and bringeth a great desire also to sleep, with a little sweat in the face, and so by little and little taketh away the senses and vital powers, no living creature perceiving that the patients feel any pain. For they are so sorry when anybody awaketh them and taketh them up, as those that being taken out of a sound sleep are very heavy and desirous to sleep.

Enobarbus: a twentieth-century view

D. J. Enright: Roman Reasons

No wide-eyed innocent, he
Had heard tell of villainy,
Had noticed
That one's loot was one's pay.
Yet he could say
—Seeking no comfort in numbers,
In mutuality's immunity—
'I am alone the villain of the earth'.

Finding good reasons,
(Reasons are good),
Finding reasons
For the serial assassinations,
For the quotidian killings
(One's pay was one's loot),
The convenient weddings,
And the other treasons.
But not for what he had done.

Despite the logic, the prior logic,
The good, the worthy reasons,
Ratified by that old manual,
Those *Hints for Roman Soldiers*,
Those counsels scratched in red—

The reasons, the decent reasons,
Each day stronger,
For his leaving their service
—An ageing general, all heart and no brain,
An ageing native woman, all wrinkles and wiles—
Who couldn't be served any longer.

And yet, when it was done,
Expeditiously and quietly done—
An emperor, a Jove, a breaker of hearts,
A queen, a Venus, a breaker of hearts.
Larger than life—unfair, unfair!
From time to time men die, it would seem,
For love, and the crocodiles eat them.

Healthy, cheerful, realistic. Yet
Somehow unable to excuse himself.
Those *Hints* less lucid than he'd thought,
And logic a botched breastplate.
Alone the villain of the earth. Alone.
So, heart failure in a ditch,
Expeditiously and quietly done.
Unnoticed by *Les Nouvelles d'Egypte*
Or the Roman *Gazette*,
Their columns packed with acts and scenes,

Enobarbus, wine-bearded captain
You are the hero of my play!

What the Critics have said

John Dryden
'I doubt not but the same motive has prevailed with all of us in this attempt; I mean the excellency of the moral. For the chief persons represented were famous patterns of unlawful love; and their end accordingly was unfortunate.'

from the Preface to *All for Love* (1678)

Samuel Johnson
'The events, of which the principle are described according to the history, are produced without any art of connection or care of disposition.'

from *Shakespeare's Works* (1765)

Augustus William Schlegel
'Although the mutual passion of herself [Cleopatra] and Antony is without moral dignity, it still excites our sympathy as an insurmountable fascination:—they seem formed for each other, and Cleopatra is as remarkable for her seductive charms as Antony for the splendour of his deeds. As they die for each other, we forgive them for having lived for each other. The open and lavish character of Antony is admirably contrasted with the heartless littleness of Octavius Caesar, whom Shakespeare seems to have completely seen through without allowing himself to be led astray by the fortune and the fame of Augustus.'

from *Lectures on Dramatic Literature* (1809–11)

William Hazlitt
'The play is full of that pervading comprehensive power by which the poet could always make himself master of time and circumstances. It presents a fine picture of Roman pride and Eastern magnificence: and in the struggle between the two, the empire of the world seems suspended, "like the swan's down feather,

> That stands upon the swell at the full of tide,
> And neither way inclines."

The characters breathe, move and live. Shakespeare does not stand reasoning on what his characters would do or say, but at once *becomes* them, and speaks and acts for them. He does not present us with groups of stage-puppets or poetical machines making set speeches on human life, and acting from a calculation of problematical motives, but he brings living men and women on the scene, who speak and act from real feelings.'

from *The Characters of Shakespeare's Plays* (1817)

Mrs Jameson

'Great crimes, springing from high passions, grafted on high qualities, are the legitimate source of tragic poetry. But to make the extreme of littleness produce an effect like grandeur—to make the excess of frailty produce an effect like power—to heap up together all that is most unsubstantial, frivolous, vain, contemptible, and variable, till the worthlessness be lost in the magnitude, and a sense of the sublime spring from the very elements of littleness—to do this belonged only to Shakespeare, that worker of miracles.'

from *Characteristics of Women* (1833)

Charles Bathurst

'[*Antony and Cleopatra*] is carelessly written, with no attempt at dignity, considering what great personages are introduced, but with a great deal of nature, spirit, and knowledge of character, in very many parts, and with several most beautiful passages of poetry and imagination; as, for instance, the dream of Cleopatra.'

from *Remarks on . . . Shakespeare's Versification* (1857)

Edward Dowden

'The transition from the *Julius Caesar* of Shakespeare to his *Antony and Cleopatra* produces in us the change of pulse and temper experienced in passing from a gallery of antique sculpture to a room splendid with the colours of Titian and Paul Veronese. In the characters of the *Julius Caesar* there is a severity of outline; they impose themselves with strict authority upon the imagination subordinated to the great spirit of Caesar, the conspirators appear as figures of life-size, but they impress us as no larger than life. The demand which they make is exact; such and such tribute must be rendered by the soul to each. The characters of the *Antony and Cleopatra* insinuate themselves through the senses, trouble the blood, ensnare the imagination, invade our whole being like colour or like music. The figures dilate to proportions greater than human, and are seen through a golden haze of sensuous splendour.'

from *Shakespeare: A Critical Study of his Mind and Art* (1875)

Georg Brandes

'But the greatness of the world-historic drama proceeds from the genius with which he has entwined the private relations of the two lovers with the course of history and the fate of empires. Just as Antony's ruin results from his connection with Cleopatra, so does the fall of the Roman republic result from the contract of the simple hardihood of the West with the luxury of the East. Antony is Rome. Cleopatra is the Orient. When he perishes, a prey to the voluptuousness of the East, it seems as though Roman greatness and the Roman republic expired with him.'

from *William Shakespeare* (Copenhagen, 1896)

Classwork and Examinations

The plays of Shakespeare are studied all over the world, and this classroom edition is being used in many different countries. Teaching methods vary from school to school and there are many different ways of examining a student's work. Some teachers and examiners expect detailed knowledge of Shakespeare's text; others ask for imaginative involvement with his characters and their situations; and there are some teachers who want their students, by means of 'workshop' activities, to share in the theatrical experience of directing and performing a play. Most people use a variety of methods. This section of the book offers a few suggestions for approaches to *Antony and Cleopatra* which could be used in schools and colleges to help with students' understanding and *enjoyment* of the play.

> A Discussion
> B Character Study
> C Activities
> D Context Questions
> E Comprehension Questions
> F Essays
> G Projects

A   Discussion

Talking about the play—about the issues it raises and the characters who are involved—is one of the most rewarding and pleasurable ways of studying Shakespeare. It makes sense to discuss each scene as it is read, sharing impressions—and perhaps correcting misapprehensions. It can be useful to compare aspects of this play with other fictions—plays, novels, films—or with modern life. A large class can divide into small groups, each with a leader, who can discuss different aspects of a single topic and then report back to the main assembly.

Suggestions

A1 What do you expect? Shakespeare's first audiences would have been familiar with the story of the play and the names of its characters, but what do *you* know about the Roman Empire, the Caesars, Antony and Cleopatra? *Before* embarking on a study of the play, discuss your own preconceptions and expectations.

A2 How to describe them? Mythologies provide standards of comparison—'plated Mars', Hercules, Venus and Isis. The Elizabethans shared the common currency of the Greeks and Romans for such comparisons, but nowadays we no longer have access to it. What standards for comparisons can our multi-cultural society supply instead?

A3 'Nay, but this dotage of our general's . . . ' Philo feels himself to have been betrayed by the man who was his hero and whom he worshipped as a god. Can you suggest parallel situations and modern equivalents? Does an idol have responsibilities to his/her followers? Should we admit different moral standards for them?

A4 'Let Rome in Tiber melt' (*1*, 1, 34): Antony is prepared to sacrifice his career for the sake of his life with Cleopatra. Would you do the same? Is personal happiness—'home life'—more important to you than professional/financial success?

A5 The opening of the play gives, unusually, little guidance for the direction of the audience's emotions. What were your first impressions on reading *Act 1*, Scene 1? And Scene 2?

A6 Antony and Cleopatra hardly ever speak in soliloquy: we rarely know their minds. Must great men/women be always isolated?

A7 'Will Caesar weep?' (*3*, 2, 51): Agrippa and Enobarbus both seem to deplore the open expression of masculine emotions. Would you respect a man who sheds tears in public?

A8 Are there limits to loyalty? Discuss the ideas of Enobarbus:

> The loyalty well held to fools does make
> Our faith mere folly. Yet he that can endure
> To follow with allegiance a fallen lord
> Does conquer him that did his master conquer,
> And earns a place i'th' story. (*3*, 13, 43–7)

B Character Study

Shakespeare is famous for his creation of characters who seem like real people. We can judge their actions and we can try to comprehend their thoughts and feelings—just as we criticize and try to understand the people we know. As the play progresses, we learn to like or dislike, love or hate, them—just as though they lived in *our* world.

Characters can be studied *from the outside*, by observing what they do and listening sensitively to what they say. This is the scholar's method: the scholar—or any reader—has access to the entire play, and can see the function of every character within the whole scheme of that play.

Another approach works *from the inside*, taking a single character and looking at the action and the other characters from his/her point of view. This is the way an actor prepares for performance, creating a personality who can have only a partial notion of what is going on, and it asks for a student's inventive imagination and creative writing.

The two methods—both useful in different ways—are really complementary to each other, and for both of them it can be very helpful to re-frame the character's speeches *in your own words*, using the vocabulary and idiom of everyday parlance.

Suggestions

a) from 'outside' the character

B1 Philo introduces Antony with the promise that we shall see

The triple pillar of the world transform'd
Into a strumpet's fool.   (I, I, 12–13)

Explain how this judgement might be arrived at. Do you accept the verdict?

B2 'Our reactions to the protagonists alter with every new scene of *Antony and Cleopatra*.' Discuss this statement with reference to *either* Antony *or* Cleopatra.

B3 'Shakespeare demonstrates Cleopatra's "infinite variety", certainly, but the character shows no real development.' Is this true?

B4 Can you think of either Antony or Cleopatra as truly tragic figures?

B5 'It is impossible to *like* him, but it must be admitted that Octavius Caesar is in a very difficult situation. Be fair to the man.' Try to give an impartial assessment of the 'Sole sir o'th' world' (5, 2, 119).

B6 Is Lepidus no more than a foil to the other triumvirs and a laughing-stock for their servants?

B7 'your old smock brings forth a new petticoat' (*1*, 2, 171–2). Give an account of *either* Fulvia, the 'old smock', *or* Octavia, Antony's 'new petticoat'.

B8 'Although he presents a serious threat to the triumvirs, Pompey appears as a rather confused pirate who is really a good chap at heart.' Is this your impression?

B9 According to D. J. Enright (see p. 147), the death of Enobarbus was

> Unnoticed by *Les Nouvelles d'Egypte*
> Or the Roman *Gazette*

In the style of newspapers with which you are familiar, or which you consider to be appropriate, write the obituary notices for Enobarbus.

B10 'Leaders get the followers they deserve.' Give an account of the characters and functions of two or three of the supporters (excluding Enobarbus) of Antony, Cleopatra, Caesar, and Pompey.

> b) from 'inside' the character.

B11 Demetrius is told to 'Look . . . Take but good note . . . you shall see . . . ' What does he see and how does he describe it in letters to Rome addressed to

> a) Octavius Caesar
> b) the Roman news agency
> c) his wife and family?

B12   Who's born that day
>   When I forget to send to Antony
>   Shall die a beggar.   (*1*, 5, 66–8)

Create this correspondence, remembering that Cleopatra was famous for her wit and learning.

B13 'The barge she sat in . . . ' (2, 2, 200–27). This is a man's description of Cleopatra—but how do the women see her? Write these accounts:

> a) Charmian's feature article for *Woman's Own*
> b) the letter from Iras to her boyfriend
> c) the diary of a citizen in Cydnus.

B14 Lepidus writes his own personal record of the encounter between Octavius Caesar and Antony.

B15 Octavia confides (in a diary or letters to her best friend) her feelings about her marriage to Antony and the political situation in which she has become involved.

B16 Pompey puts his demands and grievances on paper.

B17 An unusual commission for a schoolmaster, who

> was of late as petty to his ends
> As is the morn-dew on the myrtle leaf
> To his grand sea.   (3, 12, 8–10)

Antony's ambassador meditates (possibly in verse) on his new task and its implications.

B18 Thidias writes a letter of complaint about the treatment he has received in Alexandria.

B19 A soldier tells his story: the events of the night described (in official report or private correspondence) by one of the guards

> i) in Antony's camp (*Act 4*, Scene 3)
> ii) in Caesar's camp (*Act 4*, Scene 9)

B20 Go with me to my tent, where you shall see
> How hardly I was drawn into this war,
> How calm and gentle I proceeded still
> In all my writings.   (5, 1, 73–6)

Write Caesar's account of his dealings with Cleopatra and his discovery of her death.

C Activities

These can involve two or more students, preferably working *away from* the desk or study-table. They can help students to develop a sense of drama and the dramatic aspects of Shakespeare's play—which was written to be *performed*, not read!

C1 Act the play—or at least part of it!

C2 Madam, methinks if you did love him dearly,
> You do not hold the method to enforce
> The like from him.   (1, 3, 7–9)

Devise a scene in which Charmian and Iras gossip about Cleopatra and her conquests.

C3   World leaders unite to combat terrorist aggression! Nowadays the conflict between Caesar, Antony, and Pompey would be given full media coverage, with considerable debate about the principles and personalities involved and much speculation about the likely outcome. Transpose one or more of the events of *Act 2* into the twentieth century and supply this cover, using the techniques of television, radio, newspapers. Investigate the background. (Why do 'flush youth revolt' (*1*, 4, 53)? Ask their parents.) Get as many interviews as you can—from the fishermen who can't put out to sea (*1*, 4, 54); from on-the-spot observers and the political commentators at the summit meeting; from the palace spokesman (?Agrippa) about the marriage; and don't forget the Soothsayer.

C4   A sister I bequeath you, whom no brother
    Did ever love so dearly.   (*2*, 2, 157–8)

Devise a scene in which Caesar (perhaps supported by Agrippa) explains the situation to Octavia.

C5   The battle of Actium: another opportunity for news coverage! The press agencies send out the war correspondents (including a woman journalist to report on Cleopatra's role). Debate the role of women in war (remember Enobarbus, 'If we should serve with horse and mares together, The horse were merely lost', *3*, 7, 7–8). Military professionals discuss tactics; naval experts compare Antony's fighting ships with Caesar's fleet; on-the-spot observers give blow-by-blow accounts of the battle. Interviews with anyone who will offer an opinion.

    a) from the Alexandrian side
    b) from the Roman side.

C6   'Friends, be gone': after the battle of Actium, Antony urges his followers to take care for themselves—

                    Pray you, look not sad
    Nor make replies of loathness; take the hint
    Which my despair proclaims. Let that be left
    Which leaves itself. To the sea-side straightway.
                             (*3*, 11, 17–20)

Invent a scene and conversation for this small band of Antony's followers as they trudge to the shore.

C7   Charmian

To th' monument!
There lock yourself and send him word you are dead.

(4, 13, 3–4)

Devise a scene in which Charmian and Iras discuss this suggestion
and its catastrophic result.

C8 Media coverage for the death of Cleopatra with (e.g.)
flashbacks to her life; reminiscences by former friends and
servants; description (by one of Caesar's guards) of the scene in the
monument; interview with countryman (who wishes to remain
anonymous) about his meeting with the queen; official obituary by
Octavius Caesar.

D   Context Questions

In written examinations, these questions present you with short
passages from the play and ask you to explain them. They are
intended to test your knowledge of the play and your
understanding of its words. Usually you have to make a choice of
passages: there may be five on the paper, and you are asked to
choose three. Be very sure that you know exactly how many
passages you must choose. Study the ones offered to you, and
select those you feel most certain of. Make your answers accurate
and concise—don't waste time writing more than the examiner is
asking for.

D1 Why, this it is to have a name in great men's fellowship. I had
as lief have a reed that will do me no service as a partisan I
could not heave.

(i) Who is being referred to, and who are the 'great men'?
(ii) What is the status of the speaker of these words, and on
what occasion are they spoken?
(iii) What event has taken place?

D2 I do not much dislike the matter but
The manner of his speech; for't cannot be
We shall remain in friendship, our conditions
So differing in their acts.

(i) Who is the speaker, and to whom is he speaking?
(ii) Whose 'speech' is referred to?
(iii) Do they 'remain in friendship'?

D3 There's a great spirit gone! Thus did I desire it.
      What our contempts doth often hurl from us
      We wish it ours again.

    (i)   Who was the 'great spirit', and what has happened?
   (ii) Who is the speaker, and what is his relationship with the 'spirit'?
  (iii) With whom does the speaker next have this relationship?

D4 Most worthy sir, you therein throw away
      The absolute soldiership you have by land;
      Distract your army, which doth most consist
      Of war-mark'd footmen, leave unexecuted
      Your own renowned knowledge.

    (i)   Who is speaking, and to whom?
   (ii) What does the 'worthy sir' want to do?
  (iii) Is the speaker's argument successful?
  (iv) What happens next?

E   Comprehension Questions

These also present passages from the play and ask questions about them; again you often have a choice of passages. But the extracts are much longer than those presented as context questions. A detailed knowledge of the language of the play is required here, and you must be able to express unusual or archaic phrases in your own words; you may also be asked to comment critically on the dramatic techniques of the passage and the poetic effectiveness of Shakespeare's language.

E1   **Pompey**
                        I shall do well.
The people love me, and the sea is mine;
My powers are crescent, and my auguring hope
Says it will come to th' full. Mark Antony
In Egypt sits at dinner, and will make   5
No wars without doors; Caesar gets money where
He loses hearts; Lepidus flatters both,
Of both is flatter'd; but he neither loves,
Nor either cares for him.
       Menas
                    Caesar and Lepidus
Are in the field. A mighty strength they carry.   10

Pompey

Where have you this? 'Tis false.

Menas

From Silvius, sir.

Pompey

He dreams. I know they are in Rome together,
Looking for Antony. But all the charms of love,
Salt Cleopatra, soften thy wan'd lip!
Let witchcraft join with beauty, lust with both;   15
Tie up the libertine in a field of feasts;
Keep his brain fuming. Epicurean cooks
Sharpen with cloyless sauce his appetite
That sleep and feeding may prorogue his honour
Even till a Lethe'd dullness—

Enter Varrius

How now, Varrius?   20

Varrius

This is most certain that I shall deliver:
Mark Antony is every hour in Rome
Expected. Since he went from Egypt 'tis
A space for farther travel.

(i)   What is meant by '*field*' (line 10); '*Salt*' (line 14); '*wan'd*'
       (line 14); '*A space*' (line 24)?
(ii) Express in your own words the full sense of 'My powers
       . . . to the full' (lines 3–4); 'Epicurean . . . dullness' (lines
       17–20).
(iii) What do you find particularly striking in the imagery of
       this passage?
(iv) Comment on the dramatic ironies in this scene.

E2   *Enter* Antony *and* Eros

Antony

Eros, thou yet behold'st me?

Eros

Ay, noble lord.

Antony

Sometime we see a cloud that's dragonish,
A vapour sometime like a bear or lion,
A tower'd citadel, a pendent rock,
A forked mountain, or blue promontory   5
With trees upon't that nod unto the world

And mock our eyes with air. Thou hast seen these signs?
They are black vesper's pageants.
    Eros
                        Ay, my lord.
    Antony
That which is now a horse, even with a thought
The rack dislimns and makes it indistinct   10
As water is in water.
    Eros
                It does, my lord.
    Antony
My good knave Eros, now thy captain is
Even such a body. Here I am Antony,
Yet cannot hold this visible shape, my knave.
I made these wars for Egypt, and the queen—   15
Whose heart I thought I had, for she had mine,
Which, whilst it was mine, had annex'd unto't
A million more, now lost—she, Eros, has
Pack'd cards with Caesar, and false-play'd my glory
Unto an enemy's triumph.   20
Nay, weep not, gentle Eros. There is left us
Ourselves to end ourselves.

(i) Comment on the imagery of lines 10–11 ('The rack . . . in water'); lines 19–20 ('Pack'd . . . triumph').
(ii) Explain the meaning of '*vesper*' (line 8); '*pageants*' (line 8); '*now*' (line 9).
(iii) Discuss the part played by Eros in this passage.

F   Essays

These will usually give you a specific topic to discuss, or perhaps a question that must be answered, in writing, *with a reasoned argument*. They *never* want you to tell the story of the play—so don't! Your examiner—or teacher—has read the play, and does not need to be reminded of it. Relevant quotations will always help you to make your points more strongly.

F1   Do you agree with Dr Johnson that 'The events . . . are produced without any art of connection or care of disposition'?

F2   Enobarbus speaks of Cleopatra's 'infinite variety': show how this is illustrated in the play.

F3   Discuss the functions of comedy in *Antony and Cleopatra*.

F4 'The open and lavish character of Antony is admirably contrasted with the heartless littleness of Octavius Caesar, whom Shakespeare seems to have completely seen through without allowing himself to be led astray by the fortune and fame of Augustus' (Schlegel). Demonstrate the evidence for this judgement. Do you have any reservations?

F5 Grand spectacular or intimate theatre? How would you stage *Antony and Cleopatra*?

F6 'I'th' East my pleasure lies' (2, 3, 39). Show how Shakespeare creates and contrasts the worlds of East and West, Alexandria and Rome.

F7 'Antony is never seen to *earn* his status of tragic hero.' Is this true and, if so, does it matter?

F8 How important in this play is the element of the supernatural?

G Projects

In some schools, students are required to do more 'free-ranging' work, which takes them outside the text—but which should always be relevant to the play. Such Projects may demand skills other than reading and writing: design and artwork, for instance, may be involved. Sometimes a 'portfolio' of work is assembled over a considerable period of time; and this can be offered to the examiner for assessment.

The availability of resources will, obviously, do much to determine the nature of the Projects; but this is something that only the local teachers will understand. However, there is always help to be found in libraries, museums, and art galleries.

Suggested Subjects

G1 Great actors and actresses in *Antony and Cleopatra*.
G2 The gods and goddesses of Greece, Rome, and Egypt.
G3 Costumes and scenery for *Antony and Cleopatra*.
G4 The Roman Empire.
G5 Octavius Caesar.
G6 The conquests of Cleopatra.

Background

England c. 1605

When Shakespeare was writing *Antony and Cleopatra*, many people still believed that the sun went round the earth. They were taught that this was a divinely ordered scheme of things, and that—in England—God had instituted a Church and ordained a Monarchy for the right government of the land and the populace.

'The past is a foreign country; they do things differently there.'

L. P. Hartley

Government

For most of Shakespeare's life, the reigning monarch of England was Queen Elizabeth I: when she died, she was succeeded by King James I. He was also king of Scotland (James VI), and the two kingdoms were united in 1603 by his accession to the English throne. With his counsellors and ministers, James governed the nation (population less than six million) from London, although fewer than half a million people inhabited the capital city. In the rest of the country, law and order were maintained by the land-owners and enforced by their deputies. The average man had no vote, and his wife had no rights at all.

Religion

At this time, England was a Christian country. All children were baptized, soon after they were born, into the Church of England; they were taught the essentials of the Christian faith, and instructed in their duty to God and to humankind. Marriages were performed, and funerals conducted, only by the licensed clergy and in accordance with the Church's rites and ceremonies. Attendance at divine service was compulsory; absences (without good—medical—reason) could be punished by fines. By such means, the authorities were able to keep some check on the populace—recording births, marriages, and deaths; being alert to any religious nonconformity, which could be politically dangerous; and ensuring a minimum of orthodox instruction through the official 'Homilies' which were regularly preached from the pulpits of all parish churches throughout the realm.

Following Henry VIII's break away from the Church of Rome, all people in England were able to hear the church services *in their own language*. The Book of Common Prayer was used in every church, and an English translation of the Bible was read aloud in public. The Christian religion had never been so well taught before!

Education

School education reinforced the Church's teaching. From the age of four, boys might attend the 'petty school' (French *'petite école'*) to learn the rudiments of reading and writing along with a few prayers; some schools also included work with numbers. At the age of seven, the boy was ready for the grammar school (if his father was willing and able to pay the fees).

Here, a thorough grounding in Latin grammar was followed by translation work and the study of Roman authors, paying attention as much to style as to matter. The arts of fine writing were thus inculcated from early youth. A very few students proceeded to university; these were either clever scholarship boys, or else the sons of noblemen. Girls stayed at home, and acquired domestic and social skills—cooking, sewing, perhaps even music. The lucky ones might learn to read and write.

Language

At the start of the sixteenth century the English had a very poor opinion of their own language: there was little serious writing in English, and hardly any literature. Latin was the language of international scholarship, and Englishmen admired the eloquence of the Romans. They made many translations, and in this way they extended the resources of their own language, increasing its vocabulary and stretching its grammatical structures. French, Italian, and Spanish works were also translated and, for the first time, there were English versions of the Bible. By the end of the century, English was a language to be proud of: it was rich in synonyms, capable of infinite variety and subtlety, and ready for all kinds of word-play—especially the *puns*, for which Elizabethan English is renowned.

Drama

The great art-form of the Elizabethan and Jacobean age was its drama. The Elizabethans inherited a tradition of play-acting from the Middle Ages, and they reinforced this by reading and translating the Roman playwrights. At the beginning of the sixteenth century plays were performed by groups of actors, all-male companies (boys acted the female roles) who travelled from town to town, setting up their stages in open places (such as inn-yards) or, with the permission of the owner, in the hall of some noble house. The touring companies continued in the provinces into the seventeenth century; but in London, in 1576, a new building was erected for the performance of plays. This was the Theatre, the first purpose-built playhouse in England. Other playhouses followed, (including the Globe, where most of Shakespeare's plays were performed), and the English drama reached new heights of eloquence.

There were those who disapproved, of course. The theatres, which brought large crowds together, could encourage the spread of disease—and dangerous ideas. During the summer, when the plague was at its worst, the playhouses were closed. A constant censorship was imposed, more or less severe at different times. The Puritan faction tried to close down the theatres, but—partly because there was royal favour for the drama, and partly because the buildings were outside the city limits—they did not succeed until 1642.

Theatre

From contemporary comments and sketches—most particularly a drawing by a Dutch visitor, Johannes de Witt—it is possible to form some idea of the typical Elizabethan playhouse for which most of Shakespeare's plays were written. Hexagonal in shape, it had three roofed galleries encircling an open courtyard. The plain, high stage projected into the yard, where it was surrounded by the audience of standing 'groundlings'. At the back were two doors for the actors' entrances and exits; and above these doors was a balcony—useful for a musicians' gallery or for the acting of scenes '*above*'. Over the stage was a thatched roof, supported on two pillars, forming a canopy—which seems to have been painted with the sun, moon, and stars for the 'heavens'.

Underneath was space (concealed by curtaining) which could be used by characters ascending and descending through a trap-door in the stage. Costumes and properties were kept backstage, in the 'tiring house'. The actors dressed lavishly, often wearing the secondhand clothes bestowed by rich patrons. Stage properties were important for defining a location, but the dramatist's own words were needed to explain the time of day, since all performances took place in the early afternoon.

Further Reading

Antony and Cleopatra has inspired some excellent critical writing in books and essays which interpret and re-interpret the play for successive generations of readers and audiences. Two 'Casebook' collections are especially informative:

Brown, John Russell (ed.), *Shakespeare: 'Antony and Cleopatra'*, (Casebook Series, London, 1968).
Drakakis, John, *'Antony and Cleopatra'*, (New Casebooks, 1994).

Recommended individual studies are:

Adelman, Janet, *The Common Liar: An Essay on 'Antony and Cleopatra'*, (London, 1973).
Bethell, S. L., *Shakespeare and The Popular Dramatic Tradition*, (London, 1944).
Danby, John F., *Poets on Fortune's Hill*, (London, 1952).
Granville-Barker, Harley, *Prefaces to Shakespeare*, 2nd series, (London, 1930).
Honigmann, E. A. J., *Shakespeare, Seven Tragedies: The Dramatist's Manipulation of Response*, (London, 1976).
Jones, Emrys, *Scenic form in Shakespeare*, (Oxford, 1971).
Knight, G. Wilson, *The Imperial Theme: Further Interpretations of Shakespeare's Tragedies Including the Roman Plays*, (London, 1954).
Knights, L. C., *Some Shakespearean Themes*, (London, 1959).
Leggatt, Alexander, *Shakespeare's Political Drama: The History Plays and the Roman Plays*, (London, 1989).
Miola, Robert S., *Shakespeare's Rome*, (Cambridge, 1983).
Muir, Kenneth, *'Antony and Cleopatra': A Critical Study*, (Harmondsworth, 1988).
Traversi, Derek, *Shakespeare: The Roman Plays*, (London 1963).

All the source material for *Antony and Cleopatra* is printed in:

Bullough, Geoffrey (ed.), *Narrative and Dramatic Sources of Shakespeare*, 8 vols (1957–75), vol. 5 (London, 1964).

Additional background reading is provided by:

Blake, N. F., *Shakespeare's Language: an Introduction*, (London, 1983).
Muir, K., and Schoenbaum, S., *A New Companion to Shakespeare Studies*, (Cambridge, 1971).
Schoenbaum, S., *William Shakespeare: A Documentary Life*, (Oxford, 1975).
Thomson, Peter, *Shakespeare's Theatre*, (London, 1983).

William Shakespeare, 1564–1616

Elizabeth I was Queen of England when Shakespeare was born in 1564. He was the son of a tradesman who made and sold gloves in the small town of Stratford-upon-Avon, and he was educated at the grammar school in that town. Shakespeare did not go to university when he left school, but worked, perhaps, in his father's business. When he was eighteen he married Anne Hathaway, who became the mother of his daughter, Susanna, in 1583, and of twins in 1585.

There is nothing exciting, or even unusual, in this story; and from 1585 until 1592 there are no documents that can tell us anything at all about Shakespeare. But we have learned that in 1592 he was known in London, and that he had become both an actor and a playwright.

We do not know when Shakespeare wrote his first play, and indeed we are not sure of the order in which he wrote his works. If you look on page 171 at the list of his writings and their approximate dates, you will see how he started by writing plays on subjects taken from the history of England. No doubt this was partly because he was always an intensely patriotic man—but he was also a very shrewd business-man. He could see that the theatre audiences enjoyed being shown their own history, and it was certain that he would make a profit from this kind of drama.

The plays in the next group are mainly comedies, with romantic love-stories of young people who fall in love with one another, and at the end of the play marry and live happily ever after.

At the end of the sixteenth century the happiness disappears, and Shakespeare's plays become melancholy, bitter, and tragic. This change may have been caused by some sadness in the writer's life (one of his twins died in 1596). Shakespeare, however, was not the only writer whose works at this time were very serious. The whole of England was facing a crisis. Queen Elizabeth I was growing old. She was greatly loved, and the people were sad to think she must soon die; they were also afraid, for the queen had never married, and so there was no child to succeed her.

When James I came to the throne in 1603, Shakespeare continued to write serious drama—the great tragedies and the plays based on Roman history (such as *Julius Caesar*) for which he is most famous. Finally, before he retired from the theatre, he wrote another set of comedies. These all have the same theme: they tell of happiness which is lost, and then found again.

Shakespeare returned from London to Stratford, his home town. He was rich and successful, and he owned one of the biggest houses in the town. He died in 1616.

Shakespeare also wrote two long poems, and a collection of sonnets. The sonnets describe two love-affairs, but we do not know who the lovers were. Although there are many public documents concerned with his career as a writer and a business-man, Shakespeare has hidden his personal life from us. A nineteenth-century poet, Matthew Arnold, addressed Shakespeare in a poem, and wrote 'We ask and ask—Thou smilest, and art still'.

There is not even a trustworthy portrait of the world's greatest dramatist.

Approximate order of composition of Shakespeare's works

Period	Comedies	History plays	Tragedies	Poems
I 1594	Comedy of Errors Taming of the Shrew Two Gentlemen of Verona Love's Labour's Lost	Henry VI, part 1 Henry VI, part 2 Henry VI, part 3 Richard III King John	Titus Andronicus	Venus and Adonis Rape of Lucrece
II 1599	Midsummer Night's Dream Merchant of Venice Merry Wives of Windsor Much Ado About Nothing As You Like It	Richard II Henry IV, part 1 Henry IV, part 2 Henry V	Romeo and Juliet	Sonnets
III 1608	Twelfth Night Troilus and Cressida Measure for Measure All's Well That Ends Well		Julius Caesar Hamlet Othello Timon of Athens King Lear Macbeth Antony and Cleopatra Coriolanus	
IV 1613	Pericles Cymbeline The Winter's Tale The Tempest	Henry VIII		